## THE NEW COMMONSENSE GUIDE TO MUTUAL FUNDS
### by Mary Rowland

### Selected by Money Book Club

#### Praise for the earlier edition:

"Ms. Rowland offers a section on the nuts and bolts of fund investing for the true neophyte, **PLUS AN EXCELLENT SECTION ON MEASURING AN INVESTOR'S TOLERANCE FOR RISK** . . . you will most assuredly refer to it again and again."

STANLEY W. ANGRIST
*The Wall Street Journal*

"**THE ORGANIZATION OF THIS BOOK IS ABSOLUTELY BRILLIANT AND INTUITIVE.** . . . an investor can use this vest-pocket-size book **AS A READY REFERENCE** . . . Her advice is **AUTHORITATIVE, SPICED WITH REFERENCES TO THE MOST PIPED-IN PROS** in the mutual funds universe."

MICHAEL PELLECCHIA
*BookPage*

"We've found **A WINNER** . . . **A CONCISE READ THAT EXPLAINS TERMS, TESTS YOUR TOLERANCE FOR RISK AND GIVES PLENTY OF DOs AND DON'Ts FOR INVESTING IN MUTUAL FUNDS.** . . . What's fun about this book is that you really don't have to read it from cover to cover. You can flip through it, see a topic you like, and learn something."

SUSAN TOMPOR
*The Detroit News*

"Rowland's book **STANDS OUT FOR ITS SERIES OF SHORT, FORCEFUL 'DO' AND 'DON'T' ESSAYS** . . . Good advice, clearly presented."

*U.S. News & World Report*

"It's **AN OUTSTANDING RESOURCE: CONCISE, COMPLETE, INFORMATIVE, AND STRAIGHTFORWARD.** The writing is crisp, elegant, and in as plain an English as you can hope for when talking about mutual funds . . ."

> CHARLES JAFFE
> *The Boston Globe*

"**DOESN'T ADD TO THE MUTUAL FUND CLUTTER BUT HELPS CLEAR IT AWAY** . . . Rowland is a rare breed among financial journalists, one that puts her own money where her mouth is and does so above board, so you know **YOU CAN TRUST WHAT SHE WRITES.**"

> HUMBERTO CRUZ
> *Fort Lauderdale Sun-Sentinel*

"At a time when intelligent investment strategies are ever more complex, **IT'S REFRESHING TO SEE A BOOK THAT CUTS THROUGH THE CLUTTER** and actually **PROVIDES A RATIONAL PROCESS FOR IMPROVING INVESTMENT RESULTS.**"

> JON FOSSEL, CHAIRMAN
> OppenheimerFunds, Inc.

"Mary Rowland is **RIGHT ON TARGET WITH THIS HIGHLY ACCESSIBLE BOOK** on the essentials of mutual fund investing. I love the DOs and DON'Ts format, which **MAKES IT EASY TO UNDERSTAND, AND PROFIT FROM, MUTUAL FUNDS.**"

> SHELDON JACOBS, PRESIDENT
> *The No-Load Fund Investor*

# The NEW Commonsense GUIDE To MUTUAL FUNDS

BLOOMBERG PERSONAL BOOKSHELF

Mary Rowland

# The NEW Commonsense GUIDE To MUTUAL FUNDS

BLOOMBERG PRESS

PRINCETON

First paperback edition published 1998
1 3 5 7 9 10 8 6 4 2

Rowland, Mary.
    The new commonsense guide to mutual funds / Mary Rowland
        p.   cm. – (Bloomberg personal bookshelf)
    Rev. ed. of: A commonsense guide to mutual funds.
    1st ed. 1996.
    Includes index.
    ISBN 1-57660-063-7
    1. Mutual funds–United States–Handbooks, manuals, etc.
  I. Rowland, Mary. Commonsense guide to mutual funds.
  II. Title.  III. Title: Mutual funds
  HG4930.R68     1998
  332. 63'27- -dc21               98-36088
                                     CIP

Acquired and edited by Christine Miles
**Book design by Don Morris Design**

*To Krista and Thomas*

# INTRODUCTION

ANOTHER BOOK ON MUTUAL funds? Funds promised to simplify investing for Americans, yet they grow ever more complex. Nearly 600 new funds were introduced in 1997, bringing the total to over 9,000 funds! Certainly there's no shortage of information available about mutual funds. Yet surveys continue to show that even though more than 63 million Americans own them, most investors don't understand what they have.

Nearly everyone needs to know the basics about mutual funds. You might need to know how to choose investments for a 401(k) plan, how to invest money from an insurance or divorce settlement, or how to get started as an investor. But you probably don't want to plow through a mutual fund textbook. And you don't need to. You need a concise guide to mutual fund investing.

I started to research mutual funds a decade ago to write a mutual fund primer. As a result of that book, a column I write for *Bloomberg Personal Finance,* and one that I wrote for *The New York Times* every Sunday for six years, I have received hundreds of letters from readers asking for investing advice. I now write an investing column on-line for *Microsoft Investor* where I have a chance to "talk" with investors on the Web every day. What I've learned is that people don't want generic information. They want advice; they want to know which funds to buy and which funds to avoid.

That's why **PART 1** of this book provides **DOs** and **DON'Ts**. One could quibble that the device is too simplistic. Or too opinionated. But the letters and newsgroup queries I get hammer home the point that investors want those things.

If you have some experience in mutual funds,

dip right into the **DOs** and **DON'Ts**. Start anywhere. Read anything that catches your eye. For example:

**DON'T** jump in just before a fund closes to new investors.

**DO** manage your own cash.

**DON'T** buy bond funds.

**DO** take a skeptical attitude toward mutual fund ratings.

**DON'T** neglect the buying opportunity in new funds.

If you are a beginner and need to start with the basics, read **PART 2: BUILDING BLOCKS** and **PART 3: RISK AND ASSET ALLOCATION** before you start the **DOs** and **DON'Ts**. **PART 4: COMMONSENSE STRATEGIES** describes investment strategies— some basic ones for beginners and some more advanced strategies for veterans, including a look at how some of my favorite investors buy funds. And **PART 5: RESOURCES** provides additional information, including some tips on how to get help with investing.

The result is a guide that takes a strong, authoritative view. It is based on my 25 years of reporting and writing about business and personal finance, as well as the fresh research I did on mutual funds for this book. I learned a good deal while writing it, including some things that helped me become a better investor.

I hope you will learn something about yourself and what kind of investor you are, as well as how to set goals and develop strategies for investing in mutual funds. They are still the best investment vehicle available. Yet in the 10 years I've been writing about them, they have not become more consumer friendly. More has definitely not meant better. Household-name funds are probably not the ones you want, either. Today it is more difficult than ever to separate the wheat from the chaff. But what you get out of mutual funds can mean the difference between creating the life you want and just scraping by.

Your goal as an investor should be to build a portfolio of mutual funds that will help accomplish your goals. Obviously, if you don't own any mutual funds at all, and don't have any stock market investments, you haven't built much of a portfolio yet. And you may have trouble accomplishing your financial goals. If that's the case, you should get started, and this book will tell you how.

But what if you already own a bunch of mutual funds? You still may not be building a portfolio that will work for you. An investment portfolio should be more than just a list of the mutual funds that you own. Some thought should be given to how these investments fit together.

Unfortunately, many people don't spend much time on that part of it. They buy funds haphazardly, based on tips from friends or recommendations from brokers. If they get a year-end bonus, they buy a fund. If it's April 15 and IRA time, they buy another fund. They read that a hot fund is about to close to new investors and they jump in with their money before the deadline. What they end up with is a grab bag of funds. How that grab bag will perform is anybody's guess. But *my* guess is the results will be disappointing.

As you read this book, I hope you will think, too, about where you should go for help with your mutual fund investing. Not so long ago, I thought investing should be a do-it-yourself project. Everyone *can* learn enough about investing to master the basics and select some good mutual funds. If you are reading this book, there is no question that you can do that. There probably is some question, though, about whether you want to spend the required time and an even bigger question about whether you can wring the emotion out of your decision making when you are dealing with your own money.

So I no longer believe that the decision rests on whether you can do the job yourself. You can. But will you do a good job? Will you enjoy it? You probably hire people to do lots of different kinds of jobs for you either because they will do a better job than you could do or because you don't have time. Financial planning is certainly a logical task to farm out if it doesn't appeal to you.

There is another factor at work here, too. A decade ago, good financial planners were hard to find. There weren't many of them and there wasn't a well-established network. That has changed remarkably. Today financial planning is a well-respected profession that attracts top minds. There is a solid network of perhaps 200 top financial planners with several hundred more waiting in the wings and honing their abilities. These planners meet regularly to talk about all aspects of planning and investing and to sharpen their skills. Thousands of Americans are much happier and in much better financial shape because they've used their services. So finding a good planner today is not like looking for a needle in a haystack.

Whether you use a planner or do it yourself, you need basic information about investing. I hope you will find what you need here. When you get to the Resources section at the back of the book, you should have a better idea of what kind of help you need: the additional resources to find your own funds or the best route to the most qualified planners.

Successful investing does not require a planner. But it does require a plan. Don't buy another fund until you have developed one. This book will help you do that. If you're just starting from scratch, you are in an ideal situation to plan your investments and choose your funds carefully. If you already own a grab bag of too many overlapping funds, don't despair. This book will help you take a look at what's in your collection with an eye toward restructuring and building a portfolio that will work for you.

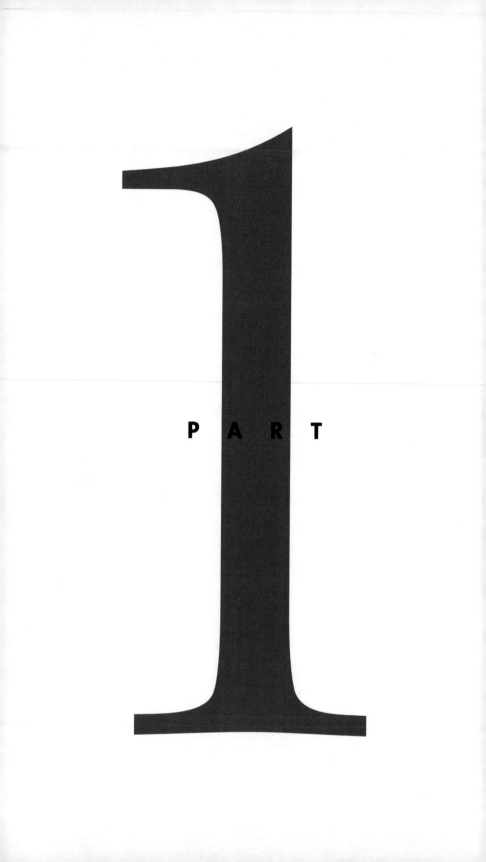

PART

1

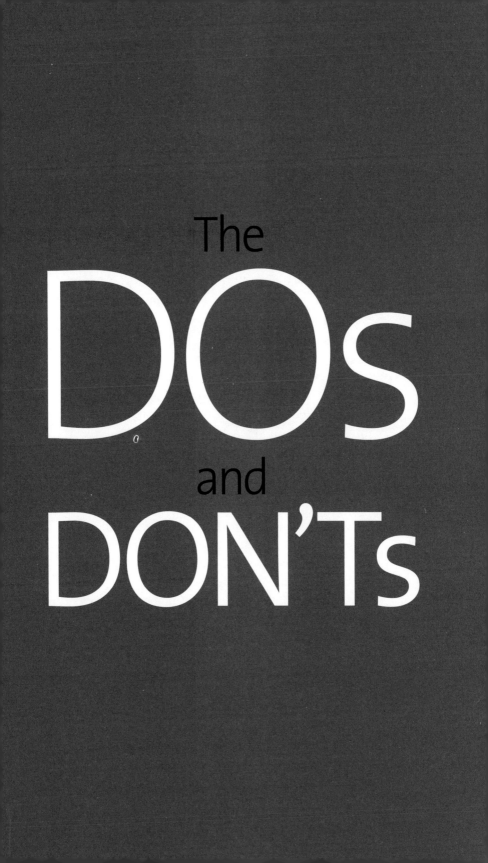

The

# DOs
and
# DON'Ts

# DO invest chiefly in the stock market.

Stocks provide the best performance over time. Period. Everyone has heard the statistics by now. So why doesn't everyone plow all their money into stocks? Because of the stock market's volatility in the short term. Stocks do not beat bonds and money market funds every year. Investors who need some money over the short term for retirement income, college tuition, or a down payment on a house should not have all their money in stocks. But long-term investors should put the bulk of their assets in a variety of stock funds, including international funds, and some more-conservative choices like equity-income funds.

Before you put your money in stocks, though, prepare for a bumpy ride, including some years when you would have been better off with your money under the mattress. For example, in 1994, money market investments beat both stocks and bonds. Sometimes the stock market has a bad run for several years in a row. Or it might be up 25 percent one year and down 5 percent the next. That's what investors call volatility, which means moving quickly and unpredictably.

Still, the course of the market is ever upward. Consider the movement of the Dow Jones Average of 30 industrial companies, which is often used as a measure of the market. While it is the Dow index that is widely quoted on the evening news, it is the Standard & Poor's index of 500 stocks (S&P 500)—a measure of the broader market—that we use when we look back to see how stocks did in a particular year.

Some professionals argue that you would do best to be out of stocks when they dive and in the stock market when they're soaring. That may be true, but no one has consistently predicted those swings. Those investors who try to guess when stocks will do well and when they will do poorly lose out. When you consider the path of the Dow, you can see there are periods when it languishes. It took 13 years—from 1972 to 1985—for it to climb just 500 points, from 1,000 to 1,500. But there are times when it soars, often unexpectedly, as in late 1990 and early 1991, when it rebounded following fears about war in the Middle East.

Consider this: The Dow finished 1993—a respectable year when the S&P 500 gained 10 percent—at just over 3,700. The following year was pretty unremarkable, with the S&P 500 returning just 1.31 percent and the Dow making little progress. Many discouraged investors contemplated getting out of stocks by the end of 1994. In 1995, the market exploded, gaining 37.5 percent on the broad market, as measured by the S&P. In early 1996, the Dow passed three 100-point marks in only six sessions to reach 5,600, adding another 22-plus points for the year. And although 1997 provided a bumpier ride—complete with a short minicrash in October—it too provided solid, double-digit returns. The Dow added 24.88 percent and the S&P 33.35 percent for the year.

That is not to suggest the market has nowhere to go but up. The point is, rather, that the moves are not predictable. Those who were sitting on the sidelines in 1995, 1996, and 1997, arguing that the market was overpriced, were the losers.

Investing in stocks—and in stock mutual funds—does require research. But it is not akin to gambling, as some fearful investors claim. Among the thousands of mutual funds available, there are dozens of fine performers with strong, consistent records of 10 years or more. They make a good starting point.

Finally, here are the numbers: From 1960 to 1997, the compound annual return on stocks was 11.59 percent; on bonds, 7.31 percent; on Treasury bills, 6.05 percent (stocks measured by the S&P 500 Index, bonds by long-term governments, and T-bills of 30-day maturity). Inflation during the period averaged 4.58 percent.

# DON'T buy bond funds.

Sure it's a broad-brush generalization. Obviously there are some circumstances in which a bond fund will do. I'm going to list some good options here. But most investors buying bond funds could do better elsewhere. Even those looking for income can find alternatives.

Bonds hold less return potential than stocks—a good two percentage points less on average, according to Sanford C. Bernstein & Co., a Wall Street research house. But when you put a bond in a bond fund, you run into some additional problems.

Bond funds carry high expenses. In 1997, the average municipal bond fund sported expenses of 1.01 percent; the average corporate bond fund .91 percent; the average government bond fund 1.08 percent; the average international bond fund 1.40 percent; and the average emerging market bond fund 1.78 percent, according to Martha Conlon at Morningstar Mutual Funds, the Chicago mutual funds rating company.

A study by New York bond dealers Gabriele, Hueglin & Cashman comparing yields (the coupon rate of interest divided by the purchase price) on individual bonds, unit investment trusts, and bond mutual funds found that bond funds consistently underperformed the other two, sometimes by more than 2 percent a year, as they did in 1980 and 1981. The funds' fees depressed their yields year after year, making them "less attractive the longer they are held," according to the study.

Bond funds are inconsistent performers, making it impossible to select one winner from a bad batch, according to a study by Lewis J. Altfest, a financial planner and professor at Pace University in New York City. "There are no Peter Lynches in the bond market," Altfest says. "There are no bond funds that consistently outperform the average." Altfest found that other mutual funds showed some consistency in performance, but bond funds did not. "One bond fund manager was just as good as another. And no one could outperform the indexes," Altfest says.

Few funds offer unique strategies. "The thing that gives a mutual fund its franchise—the quality of management—plays a smaller role in bond funds," says Morningstar chief executive Don Phillips. "The best bond fund manager might turn in 11 percent and the worst 9 percent." In contrast, stock fund performance might range from +95 percent to –40 percent.

Bond funds don't allow you to target your own goals or employ your own strategies. If you buy a bond fund because you think bonds are a good value now compared with stocks, or because you think interest rates will fall and bond prices will rise, the bond manager can defeat you by moving into shorter-term bonds.

What should you do? Investors looking for income might try some funds with a mix of high-dividend stocks, preferred stocks, utilities, and, sometimes, REITs, which invest in real estate. Candidates: Berwyn Income, Hotchkis & Wiley Balanced, Vanguard STAR, Vanguard/Wellesley Income. Keep in mind that the recent records of these funds will probably not impress you given that the stock market blew balanced and income funds out of the water in the mid to late 1990s.

A couple of additional thoughts: If you have a high risk tolerance, you might consider emerging markets bonds. Or take a look at what some financial advisers do to reap income from a stock portfolio (see page 48).

Finally, two acceptable bond funds: First, Spectrum Income, which T. Rowe Price bills as "the only bond fund you need," because it is diversified into eight other bond funds—including treasuries, corporates, junk, emerging markets, and one equity fund. Second, a short-maturity (under five years) fund like Vanguard Short-Term Bond.

## DO build your portfolio with at least three "core" mutual funds.

The core should represent at least 50 percent of your holdings. Once you've established it, you can build around it. But don't get carried away—just a few funds will do. Consider three areas: stocks with a large market capitalization, small-company stocks, and international stocks.

Large-cap U.S. funds should represent 25 to 50 percent of a long-term portfolio. If you have already started a portfolio with a balanced fund like Vanguard/Wellington, it can serve as a large-cap core holding. If not, an obvious choice is the Vanguard Index 500. Other possibilities: Dodge & Cox Stock, Harbor Capital Appreciation, or Vanguard/Windsor II. A newer possibility is a trust, with the nickname of "spider," that holds the shares of stock and trades on the stock exchange. *(See page 62 for details.)*

Small-cap funds should represent 12 to 25 percent of a long-term portfolio. Picking a good fund in this category is one of the toughest exercises for an investor because few funds are solid long-term performers. When a fund establishes a great track record, assets explode and the manager often can't find enough good small companies to buy.

That leaves you with two possible solutions. The first is to pick an index fund like Vanguard Index Extended Market, which invests in the Wilshire 4500, representing all the stocks that are traded on exchanges minus the Standard & Poor's 500, or the Vanguard Index Small-Cap Stock fund, which follows the Russell 2000. Index funds do not attempt to select the best of the small companies. So they will not do as well as a good small-cap manager, but they will beat a bad small-cap manager. Although the academics argue that the small-cap market is less efficient and that indexing is less appealing here, the alternatives are not very appealing either. For many investors, this is the best choice.

Another possibility is to get in on the ground floor with a good small-cap fund. For example, when Harris Associates, the savvy value management shop in Chicago, added Oakmark Small Cap to its stable of funds in 1995, experienced investors jumped in and rode the fund for a couple of stunning years of performance. Of course, this strategy is hardly foolproof when you consider that many promising small-cap managers like Garrett Van Wagoner, a manager with a red-hot three-year record at Govett Smaller Companies fund, turn in disappointing results when they open their own funds. (Van Wagoner Emerging Growth lost 20 percent in 1997, its second full year.) But it still pays to look for these funds.

International-stock funds should represent 12 to 25 percent of a long-term portfolio. Look for a pure international play that includes investment in Japan. You should understand the distinction between these funds and global funds, which invest all over the world, including the United States. Because you are picking your own U.S. funds, you want an international fund that excludes the United States.

There are many international funds with good, solid long-term records, including Harbor International, Hotchkis & Wiley International, T. Rowe Price International Stock, Scudder International, Templeton Foreign, and Vanguard International Growth. Oakmark International, a newer fund with a great record, albeit only five years long, is also worth a look.

Once you've selected your core funds, sit tight. These are long-term, buy-and-hold investments. You should not sell them unless there is a substantial change in the fund *(see selling dos and don'ts on page 180)*. As your portfolio grows, you can add specialty funds around them.

# DON'T buy alphabet soup funds (B shares, C shares, M shares, Y shares).

The simpler the better is the rule. If you must buy a load fund, or one that charges a commission, get one with a front-end load and no 12b-1 fee. You're better off with a straightforward, up-front haircut on your investment than little trims over the years.

When you buy a fund from a broker, you pay a sales charge or commission, supposedly for the advice he offers. These commissions have been around as long as mutual funds. But in 1980, the Securities and Exchange Commission (SEC) wrote Rule 12b-1, authorizing fund companies to add a new annual charge for marketing and distribution, which might include advertising costs or an annual payout to the broker who sold you the fund. This fee, like the fund's other expenses, is deducted each and every year from the fund's assets.

In the mid 1980s, as investors began to resist paying commissions to buy funds, two big fund groups devised a way to hide them. They paid brokers out of their own pockets and recovered the money a little at a time with the annual 12b-1 fee they charged. Just to make sure that you didn't bail out of the fund before you'd ponied up all of the money, they tacked on a surrender fee that declined over six or seven years.

Most broker-sold fund groups followed this trend, creating two classes of mutual fund shares. The A shares carried the traditional sales commission that investors paid up front. The B shares substituted an annual 12b-1 fee and a surrender fee for the up-front load.

In July 1992, the National Association of Securities Dealers capped the 12b-1 at .75 percent to recover the sales commission and another .25 percent as a broker's service fee. But fund companies continued to add new share classes, devising a mutual fund "hub" with various "spokes" or funds with different price structures but the same underlying assets. Performance, of course, varies, depending on how much each of the "spokes" costs. The fund company doesn't expect consumers to notice that. Clearly you should be focusing on what you pay to buy the assets.

But the cost is only half the story. Studies show that these fees can force portfolio managers to take on more risk. A 1995 bond fund study by Morningstar Mutual Funds found that portfolio managers saddled with the high annual expenses of B shares took on additional investment risk in an effort to match the performance of funds with lower expenses.

Morningstar broke the bond fund universe into two camps: those with 12b-1 fees and those without. The first group had an average expense ratio of 1.10 percent; the second, .64 percent. Some quick math shows that if the managers all held the same bonds, the funds with B shares would return .46 percent less. But there was almost no difference between the returns, as the chart below shows.

The managers of funds with B shares took on much more risk—measured by a higher standard deviation—in order to compete with managers who enjoyed low expenses. In 1994, when the bond market went in the tank, that risk boomeranged. Bond funds with no B expenses lost 3.78 percent. Those with B fees dropped 5.27 percent. And those with B fees of .75 percent or more lost 6.4 percent.

| RETURN ON BOND FUNDS | | |
| --- | --- | --- |
| ANNUALIZED RETURN | B SHARES | W/O 12B-I FEES |
| 3-year | 5.22% | 5.45% |
| 5-year | 7.43% | 7.50% |
| 10-year | 8.54% | 8.54% |

## DO start with just one fund if that's all you can afford.

A portfolio or group of three or more funds is ideal. But starting with just one fund is much better than keeping your money in the bank. Don't be intimidated by the suggestion that you must be an investment pro with lots of money to invest.

◆ Think of your single fund as the core of what will someday be a group of funds.

◆ Buy a fund that's a proven winner. Don't experiment.

◆ If you can't come up with the minimum initial deposit, find a fund that will waive the minimum if you make regular, systematic deposits from your paycheck or bank account.

◆ Plan to buy and hold. You should think of investing as a long-term program.

Here are some funds for a "starter kit":

**Balanced Funds** These funds invest in both the stock and bond markets. Some require the manager to hold a mix of, say, 60 percent stocks and 40 percent bonds. Others give their managers more leeway. But all balanced funds invest in both markets, which makes their returns less volatile. It also keeps these returns somewhat lower than a pure stock fund's.

An excellent choice is the Vanguard/Wellington fund. This veteran, set up in July 1929, returned an average of 8.3 percent a year from inception through the end of 1997. That compares with an average annual return of 10.08 percent for the Standard & Poor's 500 Stock Index and 5.15 percent for bonds. So the fund has done just what it set out to do: provide balance.

Another solid performer is Dodge & Cox Balanced. This fund group uses a team approach to managing, providing consistent returns on low cost. You needn't worry about the manager leaving because each member of the team understands the entire portfolio.

**Index Funds** Index funds contain a mix of securities that mimics a market index such as the Standard & Poor's 500. Because such a fund holds securities in the same relative weightings as the index and trades infrequently, expenses are low. In a good index fund, returns parallel the market. Index funds work well for beginners because there is no portfolio manager to monitor.

The best index fund, hands down, is the Vanguard Index 500 Trust, set up in 1976. The good news starts with low expenses: The fund charges about 20 basis points—or $\frac{2}{10}$ of a percentage point—in expenses, compared with 1.4 percent for the average stock fund. Although the fund is huge—over $50 billion in assets—size is not a problem. The money simply goes into the stocks that make up the index. Thanks to its efficiencies and low costs, this fund has done an excellent job of following the market.

**Equity-Income Funds** These are among the most conservative of stock fund offerings. Good choices include Fidelity Equity-Income II, Hotchkis & Wiley Equity-Income, T. Rowe Price Equity-Income, and Vanguard Equity-Income.

Finally, here is an unusual choice: SoGen International is a global asset allocation fund that provides exposure to all types of assets all over the world in a single fund. As a category, asset allocation funds are not good performers. This fund, under Jean-Marie Eveillard's management, is an exception to the rule and well worth considering as the basis of a one-fund portfolio.

Remember, though, that you look for something different in a single fund than in a group of funds that make up a portfolio. When you begin to add funds, you'll need to take extra care to avoid overlap because your single fund probably covers a lot of bases.

# DON'T follow the crowd.

By the crowd, I mean the financial press. Mutual fund news is big business for newspapers and magazines. When you stop by a newsstand, you're likely to see a dozen magazines with mutual fund cover stories. That's because a mutual fund cover is a must for newsstand sales. The same pressure is on for newspaper business sections to write about mutual funds.

The result is predictable. What all publications give us now is "the hot funds." By that I mean the funds with the leading performance for the past six to 12 months. The leading performer is invariably a volatile fund. It can land as easily on the bottom of the heap as the top.

I've gotten plenty of assignments that amounted to following the crowd. For example, in the fourth quarter of 1994, *The New York Times* asked me to write a profile of James Crabbe, manager of Crabbe Huson Special Fund. At the time, Crabbe seemed to have the Midas touch. He beat the market by 25 points in 1992 and 1993.

And 1994 was going well for him, too. In a basically flat market, Crabbe had managed an 11 percent gain. But just as Crabbe was being profiled in the press as the man with the golden touch, his run was over, at least for the time.

To his credit, Crabbe told me that his fund's best moments would come in bear markets and that he would underperform in bull markets. Still, I wonder how many readers rushed out to buy his fund just in time for the 1995 bull market. Crabbe is a value investor who looks for stocks that are beaten down and undervalued. He believed tech stocks were overpriced in 1995, and he sold them short, betting that they would come down. Instead, they led the market up and in 1995, he trailed the market by 25 points.

I've followed the crowd myself. At the end of 1995, when I was doing research to find out which fund managers had bought the year's winners in the small-cap area for an article in *Bloomberg Personal Finance,* Garrett Van Wagoner at Govett Smaller Companies headed the list. Van Wagoner had established a spectacular record at Govett, with average annual returns of over 50 percent for 1993, 1994, and 1995. When I called him to find out how he did it, he told me he planned to start his own fund, Van Wagoner Emerging Growth, at the beginning of 1996.

Van Wagoner seemed credible. And the 50 percent returns seemed irresistible. I bought the fund, only to watch it turn in disappointing results that year. In 1997, the fund's results were dismal, like those of most small-cap funds that focus on the technology sector. The point is, I didn't follow my own advice and I didn't really understand what Van Wagoner was doing to achieve his returns.

So I know from experience that it's understandable to want to get in on the performance of the hot funds. But too often investors—like me—get in just in time for the cool-down. By the time you read about a fund in a personal finance magazine, it's usually too late to jump on the bandwagon. Remember, too, that a fund that provides a much higher return than the market delivers a much higher risk, too.

Many of these spectacular gainers invest in one segment of the market or a particular industry. You never know what will turn that sector around. Others have a particular investing style that does well in certain market environments and poorly in others. Van Wagoner and Crabbe probably fall in both those groups. When the market shines on their investing style, they, too, will have another day in the sun. But the lesson here is don't follow the crowd into hot funds. Buy basic funds that represent the major asset categories. Then stick with your investment plan.

## DO take a skeptical attitude toward mutual fund ratings.

Investors are often told to consider only those funds that have received a four-star or five-star rating from Morningstar Mutual Funds—funds such as Baron Asset, Fidelity Low-Priced Stock, Mutual Discovery, and Vanguard Specialized Health. The problem is this: the rationale behind the star ratings relies almost entirely on recent past performance. For example, Fidelity Select Biotechnology had no stars at its trough and five stars at its peak.

The ratings were never intended to be predictive, says Don Phillips, CEO of Morningstar. "We're the first to concede the limitations of the star ratings," Phillips says. "We label it as a historical profile. It's 100 percent accurate in measuring past performance." In the case of Fidelity Select Biotechnology, it makes perfect sense that when the fund was new, it had no track record and no stars. When the fund established a great track record, it got five stars.

Phillips compares the star system to baseball batting averages; on opening day, everyone starts with zero. "If you have a player who goes four for four on opening day, he starts the day with an average of zero and ends the day with a 1.000," Phillips says. "When it's zero, you know he's not going to go the whole season without getting a hit. At the end of opening day, you don't expect him to bat 1.000 all year."

The ratings can be useful to investors who use them as one piece of information. But they are not a security blanket, as investors in PBHG Growth learned. At the beginning of 1996, that fund enjoyed a five-star rating as well as a stunning 10-year record. But PBHG underperformed the market by 13 points in 1996 and finished 1997 with a loss of 3.4 percent against a 33 percent gain for the S&P 500. It lost one of its stars in January 1997, becoming a four-star fund.

Those who had taken the time to read the analysis, though, would have known that PBHG's momentum style of investing—or buying stocks on rising earnings and price movement—was volatile and that the fund could lose big as well as win big.

Clearly you should dig deeper than a glance at the star ratings before you buy a fund.

Here are some tips for evaluating a fund:

♦ **Check the fund's history.** The ratings are most helpful for diversified funds—like Dodge & Cox Stock or Clipper—with a long history under the same manager.

♦ **Disregard ratings for sector funds like Fidelity Select Regional Banks.** Here the ratings depict the recent popularity of that sector as much as the manager's ability. If the sector has been hot in the recent past, it may be set for a cool-down.

♦ **Be careful of ratings for aggressive growth funds like the Kaufmann Fund and Rydex Nova, which can be volatile performers.** Look at the annual returns for each year over the past decade to see if you can handle the potential losses.

♦ **Check to see how long the fund has been rated and its average score.** For example, Sequoia has an average rating of 4.9 stars over 12 years. Those shareholders who got in before this fund closed in 1982 are lucky indeed.

♦ **Read the Morningstar analysis carefully.** You will learn, for example, that the two managers of the Kaufmann Fund "short" stock, or borrow stock and sell it, believing that the price will go down so that they can buy the stock at a lower price and repay the loan, making a profit. This is a high-risk strategy.

♦ **Look to see if the fund has grown dramatically in size.** For example, assets in PBHG Growth exploded when the company removed the fund's load in 1993. Rapidly growing assets can make it difficult for managers to hold to their strategy.

# DON'T pay attention to what a fund calls itself.

What's in a fund name? Is Fidelity Balanced a balanced fund? How about Fidelity Growth & Income? Investing in different types of funds with different objectives is an important investment goal. But selecting a fund based on its name is a big mistake.

There are two problems with using names for guidance. First, some fund companies attempt to maneuver their funds into a category in which they will achieve better performance than the rest of the group. For example, I might name my aggressive growth fund Rowland Growth & Income. If my aggressive strategy works, I should outperform the more conservative growth-and-income funds. But the name conceals the risks I'm taking—and you're taking them along with me.

Other misleading names are the product of the funds' marketing departments. If you wanted to sell a fund, would you call it XYZ High Risk? Probably not. XYZ Conservative Growth has a much better ring, doesn't it? Solid, yet on the prowl for growth. But the name is designed to soothe and woo investors rather than give them information about the fund's objective.

If you were thumbing through the mutual fund tables looking for a large-cap growth fund, you might think that Fidelity Blue Chip Growth would be just the ticket. Well, yes and no. Fidelity, the supreme marketer in this business, has a habit of giving funds catchy names and then allowing portfolio managers to do just about whatever they want with them, often with good—albeit unpredictable—results.

When Michael Gordon managed the fund from 1993 to 1996, he got rid of all the blue-chip stocks and loaded up on small- and medium-size stocks. That wasn't surprising to those who knew that Gordon started his career as an analyst of initial public offerings (IPOs), or private companies that are being offered to the market for the first time. Gordon also stocked up on foreign securities. So the "blue chips" of the fund's name were nowhere to be found. Then in April 1996, when John McDowell took over the fund, he brought with him a large-cap growth approach, creating a portfolio of big, well-known companies. So within a decade, this fund was really three different funds.

Just to be fair to Fidelity, which has been beaten up consistently during the mid to late '90s, that company is addressing many of these issues—specifically fund objective and fund size.

Diversifying your portfolio requires that you have a clear idea of the role each fund plays. You cannot get that from its name. Fortunately for investors, though, Morningstar introduced new categories in November 1996 that make this task much easier. Rather than organizing funds by "aggressive growth," "growth and income," and the other vague categories, Morningstar regrouped funds according to their management style.

The new categories are based on both the size of the companies the fund manager buys and whether he employs a growth strategy, a value strategy, or a blend of the two. Morningstar also adds "specialty," "convertible," and "domestic hybrid" to the U.S. equity fund groups. International equities are grouped by the region of the world the fund invests in.

These new categories are one of the most investor-friendly developments in the fund marketplace over the past several years. By looking at the style—and its consistency—you can begin to set up a portfolio. If we look at Fidelity Blue Chip, by the way, we see that from 1990 to 1992, it was a large-cap growth fund. Then it moved to mid-cap blend, then mid-cap growth, and finally large-cap blend. That information is far more helpful than the fund's name.

# DO use index funds.

OK, it's not glamorous to be average. But only about one-quarter of portfolio managers beat the market in a given year. And they're not always the same ones. The argument for matching the market is compelling, even if it is not exciting. Most managers fail to beat the market because the costs of trading, administration, and other fees eat into returns. Expenses for the average managed stock fund total 1.4 percent a year. An index fund minimizes trading, eliminates management fees, and reduces other costs of doing business by simply putting together a basket of the same stocks that make up the overall market index. The investor who buys an index fund duplicates the market's performance at a low cost.

Institutional investors, such as pension funds, pour billions into low-cost index funds. But retail customers came around to them slowly. John C. Bogle, chairman of the Vanguard Group, introduced the first index fund for individuals in 1976. That fund, the Vanguard Index 500, duplicates the performance of the Standard & Poor's 500 Index *(see graph)*. When Vanguard opened the fund, the expense ratio was 45 basis points, or less than one-half of 1 percent of assets under management. By 1998, expenses had dropped to just 20 basis points. The Vanguard Index 500 tracks the S&P, just slightly underperforming due to the fund's expenses.

Investors were slow to embrace index funds. But money poured into the Vanguard fund during the mid to late 1990s when the large-cap stocks that make up the index led the market's bull run. By 1998, the Vanguard 500 was the second-largest fund, with more than $50 billion in assets. So persuasive was the case for indexing by then that Morningstar's Don Phillips claimed that responding to the challenge of indexing was the biggest issue facing the fund industry.

Be wary of index funds that add some fancy twist that detracts from performance and hikes expenses, though. Some of them even carry loads. Vanguard, too, expanded on the idea, adding funds that follow other indexes. For example, the Vanguard Index Total Stock Market attempts to replicate the performance of the Wilshire 5000. The Vanguard Index Extended Market buys stocks in the Wilshire 4500, which is the Wilshire 5000 minus the S&P 500, and the Vanguard Index Small-Cap Stock fund seeks to replicate returns of the Russell 2000. Vanguard also offers overseas index funds.

Small-cap and overseas markets are less efficient than the large-cap arena of the S&P 500. A good manager can add value by stock picking. But if you are an investor who does not want to monitor investments, this is a perfectly fine way to set up an all-stock portfolio:

**50%** Vanguard Index 500 Trust

**25%** Vanguard Index Extended Market

**25%** split between Vanguard International
         Equity Index European and Vanguard
         International Equity Index Pacific

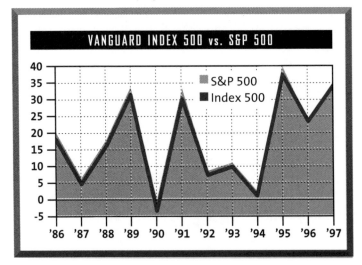

# DON'T try to time the market.

The market goes up and down in sudden spurts. But the long-term direction is up. You can stay invested and ride along the upward (sometimes rocky) path, or you can stay on the sidelines and lose out on much of the long-term return.

Stocks often lose out to bonds or money market instruments in the short term. Consider the year-by-year comparison from 1965 to 1997 in the chart at right.

As you can see, the market's pattern is unpredictable. Forecasters talk about interest rates, employment, corporate profiles, and confidence in the economy as predictors of where the market will go. But the truth is, no one knows.

Market timers use various types of technical analysis to examine trends and look for patterns in the market. For example, many consider the movement of small investors into the market to be a signal that it's time to get out. But as you know if you read *The Wall Street Journal* or other business publications, these timers are often predicting doomsday while the market marches merrily ahead.

Just when things seem gloomiest—as they did in 1973 and 1974—the market takes off. And sometimes, when market timers are predicting a correction, it seems like the good times roll on forever—or almost—as they did during the 1980s.

At the end of 1994, when stocks finished the year with a gain of just over 1 percent, financial advisers said they fielded dozens of calls from clients asking if they should get out of stocks. Then, in 1995, the market exploded in one of its most spectacular rallies in history, up 37.5 percent for the year, followed by nearly 23 percent in 1996, and 33 percent in 1997. "I'd love to be chatting with the market timers now," said Deena Katz, a financial planner in Coral Gables, Florida.

## RETURNS ON STOCKS AND BONDS

| YEAR | STOCKS | BONDS | T-BILLS |
|------|--------|-------|---------|
| 1965 | 12.5 | 1.0 | 3.9 |
| 1966 | −10.1 | 4.7 | 4.8 |
| 1967 | 24.0 | 1.0 | 4.2 |
| 1968 | 11.1 | 4.5 | 5.2 |
| 1969 | −8.5 | −0.7 | 6.6 |
| 1970 | 4.0 | 16.9 | 6.5 |
| 1971 | 14.3 | 8.7 | 4.4 |
| 1972 | 19.0 | 5.2 | 3.8 |
| 1973 | −14.7 | 4.6 | 6.9 |
| 1974 | −26.5 | 5.7 | 8.0 |
| 1975 | 37.2 | 7.8 | 5.8 |
| 1976 | 23.8 | 12.9 | 5.1 |
| 1977 | −7.2 | 1.4 | 5.1 |
| 1978 | 6.6 | 3.5 | 7.2 |
| 1979 | 18.4 | 4.1 | 10.4 |
| 1980 | 32.4 | 3.9 | 11.2 |
| 1981 | −4.9 | 9.5 | 14.7 |
| 1982 | 21.4 | 29.1 | 10.5 |
| 1983 | 22.5 | 7.4 | 8.8 |
| 1984 | 6.3 | 14.0 | 9.8 |
| 1985 | 32.2 | 20.3 | 7.7 |
| 1986 | 18.5 | 15.1 | 6.2 |
| 1987 | 5.2 | 2.9 | 5.5 |
| 1988 | 16.8 | 6.1 | 6.3 |
| 1989 | 31.5 | 13.3 | 8.4 |
| 1990 | −3.2 | 9.7 | 7.8 |
| 1991 | 30.5 | 15.5 | 5.6 |
| 1992 | 7.7 | 7.2 | 3.5 |
| 1993 | 10.0 | 11.2 | 2.9 |
| 1994 | 1.3 | −3.5 | 3.9 |
| 1995 | 37.5 | 30.0 | 3.8 |
| 1996 | 22.95 | -.59 | 5.26 |
| 1997 | 33.35 | 12.00 | 5.31 |

# DO invest in different asset classes.

A study by Brinson, Hood and Beebower, published in the *Financial Analysts Journal* in July/August 1986, found that 93.6 percent of investment return was determined by asset allocation—selecting the right mix of asset classes, such as international stocks, small-company stocks, large-company stocks. Only the paltry remainder is determined by the actual securities you select.

Not surprisingly, then, asset allocation became the 1990s' buzzword in investing. But what does it really mean? Simply that you should include a broad range of funds or individual securities in your portfolio.

Many investors consider just three asset classes: stocks, bonds, and cash. That's too narrow. You should invest in different types of stock funds, including those that invest for value, those that invest for growth, those that buy small companies, those that buy large companies, and those that invest overseas.

Here are some asset classes, all of which are represented by mutual funds:

**Cash Equivalents**
- money market funds and Treasury bills

**Bonds**
- short-term bonds (3- to 5-year maturities)
- intermediate-term bonds (5- to 10-year maturities)

**U.S. Small-Company Stocks**
- growth
- value
- micro (invest in tiny companies)

**U.S. Large-Company Stocks**
- core, like the S&P 500 Stock Index
- growth
- value
- yield, such as an equity income fund

**International**
- developed countries
- emerging markets

**Hedges**
- natural resources funds
- real estate funds
- energy funds
- real asset funds
- market neutral funds

**Specialty**
- sector funds

For most investors, stocks should represent the bulk of their portfolio. How much? Many money managers invest 100 percent of their personal portfolios in stocks. But some studies show there is little to be gained with the final 15 percent. In other words, a long-term portfolio that is 85 percent stocks and 15 percent short-term bonds or cash might be ideal for growth in that it provides stock market returns with a small cushion against stock market volatility.

The 85 percent that is in stocks should be spread across the stock groups listed above. Some investors neglect to put money into large, established U.S. companies because they believe that the real growth will come from small, undiscovered companies or from those companies just getting established in developing countries. That's a mistake.

A final note for insiders only: An article called "The Asset Allocation Hoax," by William W. Jahnke—published in the February 1997 issue of the *Journal of Financial Planning*—set the investment world abuzz. Jahnke claimed that the Brinson study was flawed and that asset allocation explained only 14.6 percent of portfolio returns. When the dust settled, most professionals agreed that 93.6 percent seemed artificially high; and 14.6 percent was too low. But certainly asset allocation is important.

# DON'T buy asset allocation funds for your portfolio.

You need asset allocation, right? Then why not get someone to do it for you? Because it has turned into yet another gimmick. Like so many investment ideas, asset allocation started with a valuable concept that worked for investors in the institutional world. But then it dribbled out as a marketing idea in the retail market.

When the stock market crashed in October 1987, mutual fund marketers frantically searched for a way to keep investors from heading for the exits. This was their thinking: Investors are afraid of the stock market. Why not promote funds that "allocate" their assets among a variety of types of securities, cushioning them from big swings in any single market?

One of the most pretentious of the early offerings was the National Securities Strategic Allocation Fund. Four times a year, a group of money managers from around the world met in a town house on Manhattan's Upper East Side to discuss the international economy and decide how to allocate the assets in the fund.

"This particular fund," said Andre Sharon, the fund's "allocator," at a meeting in March 1988, "represents the ideal way of managing money by looking at the whole world as your potential oyster, folding in and out of different sectors when you feel the relative real rates of return will favor one sector over another."

I went to one of these meetings and watched the five market specialists plus Sharon sip coffee and orange juice and munch on croissants while they discussed the pros and cons of, say, precious metals versus foreign stocks. Not surprisingly, each specialist liked the outlook for his own sector. I left feeling I wouldn't want my money drifting around the world based on the whims of this group. Not only does this mumbo jumbo result in high expenses, but all that asset shifting makes the fund a market timer and, eventually, a failure.

In the first quarter of 1988, the fund gained 2.47 percent versus 6.6 percent for the S&P. It no longer exists.

Asset allocation funds have these problems:

◆ **They cannot really be categorized.** One fund might be all in cash; another might invest its money in other mutual funds. That means you don't know what you're getting. It's difficult to compare returns of apples and oranges.

◆ **Performance is poor.** In 1994, a disastrous year in the stock and bond markets, the average asset allocation fund did worse than both market averages, with a loss of 3.05 percent, according to Morningstar Mutual Funds. That compared with a gain of 1.32 percent for the S&P 500, a loss of 2.66 for the Wilshire 5000 Index, and a loss of 2.92 for the Lehman Brothers Aggregate Bond Index.

◆ **A soothing name can hide a lot of sins.** Consider Fidelity Asset Manager, one of the fastest-growing funds in history, out of the gate in 1988 and up to $12 billion in assets at the end of 1994. As it turned out, the fund was allocating its assets to very aggressive investments in '94, with 8 percent in derivatives tied to foreign interest rates and commodities, and nearly half in foreign securities, including 17 percent in Mexico when the peso crashed. The fund lost 6.6 percent for the year.

So you need to learn to allocate your own assets. It needn't be complicated. You could use a group of three index funds to provide adequate diversification *(see page 28)*. Or you could buy a mutual fund that diversifies its assets into other mutual funds, providing you with an instantly diversified portfolio for the price of one investment *(see page 128)*. If you do that, though, stick with Vanguard STAR fund or the T. Rowe Price Spectrum funds, which do not add a layer of fees.

Remember to look for simplicity and to avoid the high-priced gimmicks.

# DO manage your own cash.

In early 1998, *The Wall Street Journal* reported that Foster Friess had sold virtually all of the technology stocks in his popular Brandywine Fund and moved two-thirds of the fund's $9.5 billion into cash. I'll bet many of the shareholders of Brandywine Fund thought they were paying Friess to buy stocks, not to time the market.

Friess is not alone. As the number of mutual funds available climbs toward 10,000, finding a great fund manager is akin to finding a needle in a haystack. One screen you should use is to avoid stock funds with large holdings (more than 10 percent of assets) in cash. Some managers move into cash when they believe the markets are heading down. You should look for a manager who stays invested. You are paying a manager to invest for you, not to sit on the sidelines and charge you big bucks for doing nothing. Or to frenetically move money among cash, stocks, bonds, and so forth. Investment pros are no better at timing the market than you are. Frequent trading also runs up transaction costs and generates taxes.

A large cash position does not always mean the manager is timing the market. It is possible that a manager has accumulated a lot of cash because the fund suddenly became very popular, and he cannot find enough good investments for the inflows. In that case, perhaps he should consider closing the fund. Either way, it is not a good time for you to invest in that fund.

A 1995 Morningstar study found that funds with large cash positions underperformed funds with small cash positions. The study compared funds that stayed fully invested with those that sometimes used a cash cushion and those that timed the market by moving large amounts of assets into and out of cash.

The results were clear-cut: the two extremes did the worst. The funds that never had money in cash had an average annual return of 8.26 percent over a five-year period. Those that timed the market by moving 50 percent or more of assets into cash did somewhat worse, with 8.25 percent annual return over five years. The most reliable performers were those that altered their cash positions by less than 15 percent, which is the group you should be looking at. Average annual returns here were 9.04 percent over five years. Equally significant, even the worst performers in this group showed positive returns.

The best performers were those that sometimes raised cash—15 to 25 percent of the fund—with an average annual return of 9.58 percent over five years. The problem with this group, though, is that it also included a number of losers. "Although funds using flexible approaches to cash had the best overall total returns, it is clear that this investment style still supplies plenty of rope for funds to hang themselves with," wrote Jeff Kelley, a Morningstar analyst.

Further, the more cash funds used, the greater the disparity in their performance. Many of the worst performers in the group that used more than 35 percent cash had negative returns. "The wider a fund's cash range, the greater the amount of disappointment it can deliver," Kelley explained.

To find out how a fund uses cash, read the reports the fund sends. Managers may say that they are "defensive," because they think the market is too high and are selling securities and raising cash. You could also call the company and ask if the fund always stays fully invested. Or check the Morningstar analysis. Consider Crabbe Huson Equity, a fund that trounced the competition in 1991, '92 and '93. By 1995, comanagers Dick Huson and Jahn Maack had grown cautious and resisted investing the incoming cash stream. Cash ranged between 20 percent and 35 percent of assets, according to Morningstar. Of course, the market soared, and the fund did not fully share in those gains.

# DON'T buy and sell with your emotions.

People often write to me for investing advice. Most of them have made the same mistake: investing on impulse. Some of them choose a fund because it's a household name. Some buy one when they read that it is about to close or because it was the No. 1 performer over the past year. Some lose money and vow never to invest again. For all of them, the solution I offer is the same: choose an investment dispassionately and then stick with it. Discipline—not picking the best performer—is the key to investment success.

Rocky markets with lots of economic uncertainty can shake even the most disciplined investors. If you know that you will be tested by such periods, you can resolve not to make the mistake of jumping ship. If you're a new investor, it may be difficult for you to imagine market dips and swoons. You've heard about them. But they seem to be ancient history. Indeed, looking back on the investment markets in the spring of 1998, the only recent flaw in the U.S. market is the 500-plus point drop in the Dow in October 1997. And that was recovered in the blink of an eye.

But it hasn't always been like that. And there will be plenty of times when it won't be like that again. If you invested in emerging markets in recent years, you experienced a real rout in the fourth quarter of 1997 that continued into the third quarter of 1998 with little relief. Tech investors have had some rocky times, too.

But for the domestic large-company stock market, we need to go back to the period of July 1990 through March 1991 to find a real rough spot. These nine months were a time of great investor fears fed by recession, massive layoffs, the Persian Gulf war, and uncertainty in the insurance industry because of the failure of Executive Life, a major insurer.

The benefits-consulting firm of Foster Higgins in Princeton, New Jersey, did a survey of 50 employers in March 1991, asking them if employees had responded to these troubling events by altering the investments in their 401(k) plans. They had. Most of them fled to safety, moving out of the stock market and into "safe" investments like a money market fund. As it happens, though, investors who moved out of equities did so at the stock market trough in August 1990. The market rebounded quickly, showing one of its strongest rallies in the fall of 1990 and winter of 1991.

"The majority of transfers were out of stocks and into fixed-income funds," said Richard J. Knapp, who was then a principal at Foster Higgins. "People are shifting their money in the wrong direction. They are buying high and selling low."

The year 1994 was another testing ground for investors. Bonds turned in one of their worst years in history, and stocks, as measured by the S&P 500 Stock Index, gained a measly 1.32 percent. But investors who got discouraged and pulled out of the markets missed the spectacular rally of 1995.

Successful investing is just the opposite of buying and selling on whim. Never buy on the spur of the moment. Never buy the hot fund. Never sell because the market drops. Instead:

◆ **Compile a list of funds—and stocks if you like—that interest you.** Gather information about each one. Call the companies and ask questions.

◆ **Invest with a plan in mind.** Five years should be your minimum time horizon; 10 years is better.

◆ **Decide before you invest what conditions would prompt a sale.** For example, the portfolio manager leaves, the fund requests changes in investment strategy, it grows too large, or it consistently lags behind its peers (other funds with the same investment objectives). Otherwise, sit tight.

# DO look under the hood.

Make sure any funds you are considering (and the ones you already own) follow their investment objectives. If you take the trouble to select a fund that will use a value approach to picking small-company stocks, you want to be certain that that is what the manager does.

Many funds drift from their stated objectives to wherever the best current returns are. Over the past couple of years, fund companies have requested changes in investment policy to give managers broad powers to go wherever they think they can make some money. This is usually bad news for investors. You may believe you have carefully diversified your portfolio only to find that funds of every stripe have selected the same high-flying company or sector. Only when the hot stock or industry runs into trouble do you discover that you were overexposed.

To avoid that, you need to get an idea of how your fund portfolio is invested. Some of this information is in the fund's regular reports. But fund companies are required to report their entire portfolio only twice a year. And then they have two months from the closing of the period to get the report out. That means the information you get may be eight months old.

For more current information, you can call the fund company. Or you can use the Internet, starting with the fund company's Web site. Cebra Graves, editor of morningstar.net, Morningstar's on-line publication, particularly likes Fidelity's Web site (www.fidelity. com) because that company releases the top 10 holdings as well as the sector weightings and any major changes in the portfolio each quarter.

Vanguard Group (www.vanguard.com) goes one better by listing the top 10 holdings every month, according to John Woerth, a Vanguard spokesman.

T. Rowe Price & Associates (www.troweprice.com) lists the top 10 holdings two weeks following the end of each quarter and will provide the 25 largest holdings on request, according to Steve Norwitz, a T. Rowe spokesman.

Most other fund companies provide similar information. Charles Schwab Online (www.schwab.com) provides information about Schwab's own funds as well as OneSource (no transaction fee) funds and fund tools. A few funds offer daily disclosures: (www.munder.net) and (www.mosaicfunds.com).

You'll need some tools as well. One good option is the "X-ray" function on morningstar.net. X-ray breaks down a portfolio's asset allocation into stocks, bonds, and cash. This is important stuff for mutual fund investors. Perhaps you don't need to know every single security in your fund's portfolio. But there are key questions you should be able to answer about your fund: How consistent is the manager in his approach? How concentrated is the fund? What are the sector weightings—both industry and regional?

Morningstar's premium service, introduced on-line in May 1998, allows investors to break out the top 25 names in a fund portfolio and look at year-to-date returns for each stock. "All the ticker symbols are links to the companies," Graves says. "So you should go beyond looking at the portfolio and look at these companies."

It will also show the portfolio's exposure to different regions—like Asia and Europe—and to different industry sectors, such as technology or financials. The service costs $9.95 per month—or $99 a year.

Of course, you don't want to second-guess the portfolio manager or begin trading in and out of mutual funds because you don't like the stocks your fund is buying. But getting a handle on what's under the hood helps you become a better investor and put together a more successful portfolio.

# DON'T buy (or sell) a fund based on recent performance alone.

Personal finance magazines tout the top-performing fund of the past year—or even quarter. That is not the time for you to buy into it. And it is not the time to sell a fund you hold just because it appears on the list of worst performers. Investments are cyclical. If you over-emphasize recent past performance, you may be buying funds at the peak. And you may be selling funds that are poised to do well.

Your task as an investor is to set up a portfolio that will do well in all types of market climates. That does not mean each of your funds will be a top performer every quarter. You want funds that complement one another and that perform well in different environments. Sometimes the market favors growth funds, sometimes value funds. Sometimes small-company stocks have a big run, and sometimes the large-cap stocks, like those in the S&P 500 Index, outpace everything else in the market. Overseas stocks, too, have their cycles. All of these asset classes together should create a portfolio that weathers most storms.

A good fund is one that sticks to its knitting. When its style goes temporarily out of favor, that fund underperforms. If you think about it, that is as it should be. You don't want a manager who suddenly changes his style to go where the returns are. You want one with courage and conviction. You've picked him to do what he is good at and to fulfill a specific role in your portfolio.

Consider the Mutual Series funds managed by Michael Price, one of the best-known value investors and one of those managers who knows what he's about and does what he sets out to do. In 1987, when the stock market crashed, Price did just fine. And in 1988, his performance was terrific. Investors who bought that two-year record were probably sorry in the following three years, when value investing fell out of favor. Those who threw in the towel would be sorrier still as Price got back on track. A contrarian investor would probably have bought Mutual Beacon in 1991, reasoning that it was time for a turnaround in value investing.

Look at Price's returns for Mutual Beacon compared with the market in the chart below. Notice that the only year Price actually lost money was 1990. But he underperformed the market for three years running. Still, investors who bought the fund in 1989 because of his recent record and sold after the 1990 loss would have been disappointed, with good reason. Unfortunately, that is exactly what many investors do.

You can see, too, that in 1995, 1996, and 1997, as the S&P Index soared, Price underperformed. His value investing style tends to underperform in a roaring bull market and to outperform the broad market in a bear run or in mediocre market years. Price has been one of the most consistent managers in the market and a favorite among both individual and professional investors. Too bad, then, that he sold his fund group to Franklin Templeton in 1996 and is slowly disentangling himself from the management.

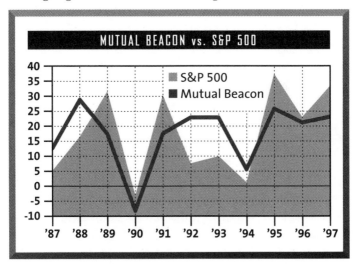

# DO look for consistency.

You want a fund that does what you expect it to do and does it repeatedly, finishing in the top half among funds in its category at least four years out of five. Avoid funds that perform erratically (top quartile one year, bottom the next) compared with their peers, even if their long-term performance is above average.

Thomas R. Ebright, comanager of the Pennsylvania Mutual Fund until the end of 1995, often compares building a mutual fund portfolio to building a baseball team. "You want players who will work together, complement each other's strengths, and cover each other's weaknesses; players who are consistent hitters, and a couple of defensive stars as well," he says. Ebright suggests that you assemble a team of six to 10 players and patiently stick with them, even though each has an occasional off season.

Unfortunately, Ebright's own fund lacked consistency. Ebright and Charles M. Royce bought small-company stocks, which are subject to extreme market cycles, for Penn Mutual. Historically, small stocks have outperformed larger stocks, a fact that gives them an important place in an investor's portfolio. But they can also languish for long periods, as they did for much of the 1980s. During those years, Pennsylvania Mutual was considered one of the top small-company funds, appearing often on "model portfolio" lists.

Look at how it performed compared with the S&P 500 and the Russell 2000. Notice that the only year Pennsylvania Mutual lost money was 1990, which was the turnaround year for small-company stocks. It underperformed the S&P consistently over the last half of the '80s, which is exactly what you would expect of a small-company fund when big-company stocks are doing well. It generally outperformed the Russell 2000 index, yet it was hardly consistent. By 1990, even a patient investor might have begun to wonder.

Look, though, at what happened to Penn Mutual when small-company stocks rallied. Although it did well, it didn't keep up with the Russell index. It was inconsistent, underperforming the small-cap index during three years of a strong rally. Part of the reason is that it held so many stocks—300 to 500.

But Royce, who has been managing the fund since 1973, must have felt something new was necessary as well. In 1991, he introduced Royce Micro-Cap, which invests in tiny companies, and Royce Premier, which skims the best companies from Pennsylvania Mutual. Each got off to a good start, racking up strong three-year records and then plateauing a bit as small-company stocks were eclipsed by the big caps.

In 1996, Royce made changes in Penn Mutual, dropping the number of stocks by more than 50 percent and concentrating on a combination of the styles of Premier and Micro-Cap. Penn Mutual bested the Russell 2000 by two points in 1997. But it's early yet. You want a fund with a proven track record, one with consistency. Penn Mutual didn't have it over the past 10 years. Until Royce proves he can hit the ball consistently, look elsewhere for a small-cap fund.

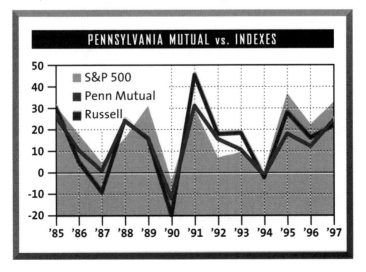

PENNSYLVANIA MUTUAL vs. INDEXES

S&P 500
Penn Mutual
Russell

# DON'T buy a fund with high turnover.

The portfolio turnover rate is a measure of the average buying and selling activity in the portfolio. It refers to the percentage of the portfolio that is bought and sold each year. A turnover rate of 50 percent means half the securities are exchanged each year. A rate of 200 percent means that the portfolio is turned over twice. The turnover rate is disclosed in a fund's annual report and in the prospectus.

Some fund managers trade heavily and frequently. It's not unusual for a small-cap growth fund to trade every security in the portfolio in a year, or even twice in a year. Some of these funds were on a tear in the mid '90s. Think of PBHG Growth, Govett Smaller Companies, and even Brandywine Fund. The managers of these funds play a momentum game, buying stocks as they surge ahead and selling them when they cool off.

There is some evidence that the style itself has cooled off. PBHG Growth ran into a rough spot in 1996 and 1997, and Garrett Van Wagoner also had difficulties when he left Govett and opened the Van Wagoner group of funds. But even if these funds turn around, investors who use them will have tax problems because of the high turnover.

Every time a fund manager sells a security at a profit, investors face both additional transaction charges and a capital gains tax liability. As of 1997, capital gains were lowered to 20 percent on securities held over 18 months. A 1998 law applied the 20 percent rate down to 12 months. But gains on securities held less than 12 months are taxed at your highest marginal tax rate, which can be as high as 39.6 percent. When you add to that state taxes, short-term traders are giving up nearly half their gains.

Worse yet, you may pay taxes even if the fund loses money or lags the rest of the market. That's because a fund that is losing money overall can still sell off its winners at year-end and generate taxable gains. Look at Brandywine Fund, which sports a portfolio turnover rate of around 200 percent. When Foster Friess started moving his portfolio to cash in late 1997, the fund lost 7 percent in December. But Friess generated $7 per share in capital gains. With the fund's net asset value at around $30, that represents one-fifth to one-quarter of the portfolio's value in capital gains. An investor with $100,000 in Brandywine in 1997 would have received a capital gain of around $25,000 and a tax bill on the order of $10,000.

Ditto for T. Rowe Price Science and Technology, another fund that has done some heavy trading. "In each of the four years I have owned this fund, shareholders have had to pay capital gains taxes that more than offset the increase in value," Sarah Oaks of Radnor, Pennsylvania, wrote in a letter to *Smart Money*.

Most portfolio managers don't care about capital gains or turnover. They're trading to post year-end— or quarterly—gains. That's how they earn their bonuses and that's how they get on the cover of *Money* magazine. So you must look for yourself at the portfolio turnover. The average diversified U.S. stock fund has 90 percent turnover. That's too high. What you want is turnover below 25 percent—below 15 percent is better.

One good place to find low turnover is in an index fund. Look at the Schwab 1000, which holds stocks of the 1,000 largest publicly traded companies. Turnover ratios are typically 1, 2, or 3 percent. You can also find a managed fund that sports a low turnover, but it takes some searching. Consider Longleaf Partners, with turnover rates in the teens. A search of the Morningstar data by *Bloomberg Personal Finance* also turned up these low-turnover funds: Oakmark, Baron Asset, Torray, Kemper-Dreman High Return, and Dodge & Cox Stock.

# DO look at income alternatives.

We've been focusing chiefly on looking for growth and on buying stock funds. Some investors do need income. And the low interest rate environment of the late '90s is bad news for them. Most bond funds are bad news, too.

What to do? One option is to buy bonds yourself, direct from the U.S. Treasury with no fees or commissions. The shortest-term Treasury securities, which are called bills, have maturities from three months to one year and carry a $10,000 minimum investment. Treasury notes with maturities of two and three years carry a $5,000 minimum. Longer-term notes and bonds, which have maturities of 10 years or more, carry a $1,000 minimum. You can buy them over the phone by calling Treasury Direct. Or you can buy them on the Web at www.publicdebt.treas.gov. There is no state or local tax on Treasury securities.

Bob Winfield, a planner in Memphis, uses a strategy called "laddering"—buying bonds with staggered maturities—for clients with specific income needs. For example, he recently set up this portfolio for a retired client: One $50,000 bond set to mature in the first year the client needed income and then another bond to mature in each of the following 19 years, with the face amount pegged to inflation. The remainder of the portfolio was invested for growth. "This gives him a certainty of receiving $50,000 in income for each of those 20 years," Winfield says.

Some planners, like Jane King in Boston, don't use bonds at all in income portfolios. "I don't think you have to give up growth to get income," King says. Say a client needs income of $1,000 a month. King invests the money in growth funds like Harbor Capital Appreciation and funds with an income component like Vanguard/Wellesley Income.

In her search for income alternatives, King once tried utility funds but found them too sensitive to interest rates. Now she uses funds with a heavy weighting in utilities, like Robertson-Stephens Partners. "The sector weighting of the S&P 500 is 2.63 percent utilities," King says. "This fund has 7.1 percent in utilities." The income component provides some ballast for her portfolio.

Although these funds have an income element, they won't provide the amount of income most clients need. So King sets aside six months' income—in this case $6,000—in a money market fund. And she regularly trolls through the portfolio to see where she might want to raise cash. For example, when her asset allocations get out of line, she sells something off to raise cash and puts it in the money market fund for income payments. "Or I might look to see whose hands are getting cold and what I might want to sell next," she says. "That way I can have a total return portfolio and still pay a check each month."

Individual investors, too, can craft a portfolio with a strategy like King's to draw income from a growth portfolio. But don't cut it so tight as King does. She's a professional planner with years of experience and large portfolios. I think you need more room to navigate. But you might put 12 to 18 months' worth of income into the money market fund rather than six, for example.

Some funds to consider for an income portfolio include USAA Income Stock, which holds value stocks, REITs, convertible bonds, and utilities and aims to increase its dividend each year. Look, too, at T. Rowe Price Capital Appreciation, T. Rowe Price Equity-Income, Heartland Value Plus, and balanced funds like Vanguard/Wellington and Dodge & Cox Balanced. And if you decide to use such a strategy, remember that you are taking on more risk. If risk scares you to death, use a Vanguard short-term bond fund.

## DON'T invest in a fund that's too big for its britches.

Because brand names matter to consumers when they buy refrigerators or computers, many mutual fund companies have attempted to market brand-name mutual funds. A name means much less in mutual fund investing. Some of the better known funds with household names have left their glory days behind them, chiefly because they've grown too large. Managing a big stock fund is like turning an ocean liner as opposed to a sailboat.

The best example is the biggest: Fidelity Magellan, which approaches $64 billion in assets. Many investors still buy Magellan because of the results garnered by Peter Lynch, the portfolio manager with the best 10-year record in mutual fund history. In fact, the fund has had three managers since Lynch left in 1990, and it has a much different style today.

Peter Lynch made his mark when the fund was going from the millions to the billions of dollars in assets. In other words, he didn't have an overwhelming amount of money to manage until the end of his tenure. That means he could focus on individual stocks. And he did. Lynch paid no attention to where the market was going. He gave little heed to the outlook for different sectors, such as banks or airlines or retailers. He just picked stocks, one here and one there, and was quite good at it.

With all its success, Magellan has changed into a dramatically different fund than it was in Peter Lynch's day. Its huge size means it is no longer a stock picker's fund. Today, the idea of Magellan buying individual stock issues, here and there, is like a lion eating mice. It can be done. But mice won't satisfy this cat's appetite.

So Morris Smith and Jeff Vinik, Lynch's successors, were forced to make sector investments, not just stocks but whole industries. That worked for a while because they bet on the right sectors. In 1995, Vinik piled into technology stocks—and they went up. He dumped them, and they went down. Vinik's next big bet, on Treasury bonds, turned out poorly. The bond market dropped, the stock market kept going up. Many Magellan shareholders were left wondering what they owned. Vinik moved on and Bob Stansky was given the Herculean task of managing Magellan, which underperformed the index substantially in 1996 and 1997.

A better indication that a fund is doing a good job is the decision to close to new investors when there is too much money to invest wisely. Consider FPA Paramount, a growth-and-income fund that closes periodically to help manager William Sams digest the assets. Sams doesn't believe he can get good returns unless he keeps the fund at a manageable size. Notice that only one of the large funds—Washington Mutual—beat the index.

## THE 10 LARGEST STOCK FUNDS

| STOCK FUND | ASSETS | 1997 PERFORMANCE |
|---|---|---|
| Fidelity Magellan | $63.958 billion | 26.59 |
| Vanguard Index 500 | $50.7 | 33.21 |
| Investment Co. of America | $39.99 | 29.81 |
| Washington Mutual | $38.9 | 33.29 |
| Fidelity Growth & Income | $37.769 | 30.17 |
| Fidelity Contrafund | $30.268 | 23.00 |
| Vanguard/Windsor II | $24.524 | 32.38 |
| American Century-Twentieth Century Ultra | $22.558 | 23.13 |
| Fidelity Advisors Growth Opp. T | $21.229 | 28.56 |
| Fidelity Equity-Income | $21.176 | 29.98 |
| Standard & Poor's 500 | — | 33.35 |

## DO buy funds from a single fund family or a discount broker.

Fees are important. Avoiding them is getting trickier. The cheapest way to set up a portfolio is to use a single fund family or to use a discount brokerage that offers funds from a number of fund groups at no transaction cost. The most popular program is Charles Schwab's OneSource, or no transaction fee, program. Jack White & Co. and Fidelity FundsNetwork also offer no-fee programs.

In addition to cutting fees, using a single family or a discount broker makes record keeping much simpler. If you have funds at a number of fund families and you receive reports from each of them, it is very difficult to evaluate the performance of your portfolio or to move money from one fund to another to rebalance your portfolio. That's why most financial planners move their clients' accounts to a discount broker like Schwab. "When a new client comes in with all these bits of paper from different fund companies and brokers, the first thing I do is move everything to Schwab," says H. Lynn Hopewell, a planner in Falls Church, Virginia. If you are a novice investor, it might seem intimidating to be faced with so many choices—more than 2,300 funds are available through Schwab, according to Greg Gable, a Schwab spokesman.

One good place to get help is on the Web. *(See the Resources section for some of the best investing Web sites.)* Don't stop with the information available, either. Try the newsgroups where you can ask the advice of other investors. I participate in a newsgroup at www.moneyinsider.com where we have lively discussions on indexing versus active management, for example, or on the outlook for various funds. One of the regulars, William C. Wood—he calls himself Mr. Indexing—is a finance professor who provides great information to beginning investors.

Look, too, at www.sheldonjacobs.com, where Sheldon Jacobs, editor of *The No-Load Fund Investor* posts and updates his Wealth Builder portfolio. Jacobs reports regularly on single-family investing, including model portfolios for several no-load fund groups in his newsletter. *(See the Resources section for information on his newsletter and how to get a copy.)*

For beginning investors who want to stick with one family, T. Rowe Price is a good choice because it offers solid funds in every category as well as top-notch shareholder information and communications. The chart below shows two of Jacobs's three model portfolios using all T. Rowe Price funds. His third portfolio, which is designed for retirees, modifies the preretirement portfolio by decreasing domestic and foreign stock investments and increasing the percent in Spectrum Income to 35 percent.

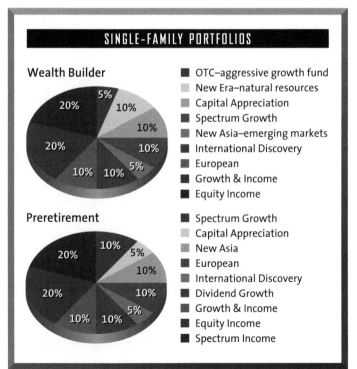

**SINGLE-FAMILY PORTFOLIOS**

**Wealth Builder**

- OTC–aggressive growth fund
- New Era–natural resources
- Capital Appreciation
- Spectrum Growth
- New Asia–emerging markets
- International Discovery
- European
- Growth & Income
- Equity Income

**Preretirement**

- Spectrum Growth
- Capital Appreciation
- New Asia
- European
- International Discovery
- Dividend Growth
- Growth & Income
- Equity Income
- Spectrum Income

# DON'T ignore expenses.

All funds charge expenses. But these charges vary widely. Paying attention to them is critical. Over the long term, expenses have a major impact on investment returns. Here are some of the expenses charged by mutual funds.

**Loads** A load is a sales charge that typically goes to pay the broker who sells the fund. However, some funds that are sold directly over the phone, most notably many of those at Fidelity Investments, also impose loads. A front-end load is subtracted from your money before it is invested. A back-end load, deferred sales charge, and redemption fee all mean the same thing—that a fee is deducted when you are ready to take your money out.

**12b-1 Fees** Rule 12b-1, approved in October 1980 by the SEC, allows funds to charge for marketing and distribution costs. The fee might range from 1 percent to 25 percent. This money comes out of the fund year after year. The National Association of Securities Dealers limits funds sold by its members to a 12b-1 fee of no more than .75 percent plus a servicing fee of .25 percent, or 25 basis points, for a total of 1 percent.

Other expenses include management fees to pay the portfolio manager, certain administrative expenses, and fees to exchange shares from one fund to another. Some expenses, like management salaries and administrative expenses, cannot be avoided. But you should be looking for funds with no load, no 12b-1 fee, and low expenses—under 75 basis points. A 1988 ruling by the SEC made it easier for investors to figure out how much a fund charges in fees. The fund must identify all fees in the prospectus as well as demonstrate how they would affect a $1,000 investment that earns a hypothetical 5 percent after one year, three years, five years, and 10 years.

Consider the example below from the Oppenheimer Real Asset Fund. The total expenses charged by this fund vary from 1.5 percent to 2.5 percent, depending on which class of shares you choose. That compares with 1.4 percent for the average stock fund.

| | CLASS A SHARES | CLASS B SHARES | CLASS C SHARES | CLASS Y SHARES |
|---|---|---|---|---|
| **SHAREHOLDER TRANSACTION EXPENSES** | | | | |
| **Maximum sales charge on purchases (as a percent of offering price)** | 5.75% | none | none | none |
| **Maximum deferred sales charge** | none | 5% first year, declining to 1% in sixth year; eliminated thereafter | 1% if shares redeemed within 12 months of purchase | none |
| **Sales charge on reinvested dividends** | none | none | none | none |
| **Exchange fee** | none | none | none | none |

**ANNUAL FUND OPERATING EXPENSES** (as percentage of average net assets)

| | CLASS A | CLASS B | CLASS C | CLASS Y |
|---|---|---|---|---|
| **Management fees** | 1.00% | 1.00% | 1.00% | 1.00% |
| **12b-1 fees** | .25% | 1.00% | 1.00% | none |
| **Other expenses** | .50% | .50% | .50% | .50% |
| **Total operating expenses** | 1.75% | 2.50% | 2.50% | 1.50% |

**TOTAL EXPENSES** (on a $1,000 investment, assuming a 5% annual return and redemption at the end of the period):

| | CLASS A | CLASS B | CLASS C | CLASS Y |
|---|---|---|---|---|
| **1 year** | $74 | $75 | $35 | $15 |
| **3 years** | $109 | $108 | $78 | $ 47 |

*If you did not redeem your investment, it would incur the following expenses:*

| | CLASS A | CLASS B | CLASS C | CLASS Y |
|---|---|---|---|---|
| **1 year** | $74 | $25 | $25 | $15 |
| **3 years** | $109 | $ 78 | $ 78 | $ 47 |

# DO consider a so-called institutional fund.

The funds we read about all the time—those offered by companies like Fidelity, Janus, and Putnam—are retail funds designed for individual investors. Even though their minimum initial investments may seem high—$3,000, $5,000, or even $10,000—these antes are quite low compared with those of the funds offered to institutional investors such as pension funds and endowments.

Why then should you consider an institutional fund? For the same reason professional managers, with billions of dollars to invest, use them. They have lower expenses—and often more reliable performance—than retail funds. Until recently, they were available only for single investments of $1 million or more. But now they are trying to get a toehold in the retail market by offering their funds at minimums as low as $1,000 through discount brokers like Charles Schwab & Co. and Jack White & Co. This gives you the opportunity to get in on investments that were formerly available only to investors with millions to put in a single fund.

Ten years ago, institutional mutual funds made a decision to ignore the retail market because it is expensive to maintain small accounts. Further, small investors seemed too fickle, moving their money around too frequently. But that decision has come back to haunt them as the retail marketplace has exploded, with $3 trillion in assets.

How to tap into that? They couldn't trade on their names—like Pimco, Pfamco, and DFA—which no retail investor has ever heard of. Advertising wasn't a good option. It's expensive and would boost the fees, canceling out a major advantage of the institutional funds. "Retail is first and foremost a marketing business," says David Booth, chief executive officer of

Dimensional Fund Advisors (DFA), an institutional fund group based in Santa Monica, California. "The skills you need to be successful are more likely to be developed at Procter & Gamble than at a money management firm. We don't know how to market to retail."

So the institutional funds elected to market through discount brokers like Charles Schwab and Jack White. Here retail investors can buy into the funds with low minimums. And the institutional funds treat the discount broker as a single account. For example, Pimco pulled in $750 million from the Schwab account in the first four years. This $750 million is treated like a single account at Pimco, with Schwab as the customer. That means Pimco can maintain its low expenses and avoid marketing and advertising costs. Financial advisers love the Pimco funds, by the way, for their low expenses and reliable, consistent management. Advisers also like DFA, which sponsors a group of small-cap value index funds. These funds invest in different sectors of the small-company market based on company size, an asset class that is difficult to find.

For the individual investors—probably millions of them—who buy these funds, it means they can share in the top management, proven performance, and low expenses enjoyed by institutions. But there is a catch for individuals, too. The companies that sell these funds—such as Federated, Lazard Fréres, and DFA—are not household names. You will not find them on the lists of hot funds in personal finance magazines. If you want to use institutional funds, chances are you will have to find out about them yourself. You can do that by checking with discount brokers who offer the funds and also by looking them up in Morningstar. If you are a serious investor with the confidence to make your own choices and stick to them, investigating these funds is well worth your while.

# DON'T jump in just before a fund closes to new investors.

Closing announcements often pull in huge amounts of cash. Investors who were sitting on the fence or just looking around for a place to put their money believe that they'd better get in under the wire or an important investment opportunity will be lost to them. A fund that is just beyond reach has a certain allure.

In fact, a fund usually closes because it has more money than the manager knows what to do with. That means the opportunity for that fund may have passed, at least for the moment. Awash in money, the fund manager is signaling that he can't find enough good places to put it.

In 1995, reporter Timothy Middleton wrote in *The New York Times* that most funds lagged in performance in the period immediately following the closing. He cited the examples in the chart at right.

Although you shouldn't rush to get into a fund that is about to close, a closed fund that reopens might present a good buying opportunity. Middleton pointed out that when a fund closes, it indicates that the manager is putting investor interests ahead of his own pocketbook. (Because funds make money based on assets under management, the more money in the fund, the more they earn. Consider Fidelity Magellan, the largest mutual fund, $64 billion in assets. The management fee, at .76 percent of assets, is a healthy $283.5 million a year.)

For example, Jean-Marie Eveillard, manager of SoGen International, told Middleton that he closed his fund because the world markets had become so expensive he couldn't put his money to work. The fund's cash level had risen to 30 percent of assets. He said that when prices fell, he would reopen, which he did on March 13, 1995. Similarly, PBHG Growth and

PBHG Emerging Growth closed in March 1995 because the funds had too much money to invest prudently. PBHG Growth, however, reopened on January 2, 1996. The fund continued to grow—to $6.5 billion by the end of 1997.

Excess cash is a particular problem for funds like PBHG, which invest in small companies. Indeed, the Morningstar style box *(see page 151)* shows that PBHG moved from small-cap growth to mid-cap growth in 1996 and 1997 and turned in an extremely disappointing performance. But even a fund that buys medium-size companies, like Longleaf Partners, which doubled in assets from New Year's Day to August 1995, can handle only so much money without sacrificing returns. Longleaf closed on September 15, 1995.

Here's the best strategy: When a fund announces plans to close, put it on your list to watch for a reopening. Monitor the fund's performance while it is closed by looking up its net asset value in the daily newspaper and comparing it with preclosing numbers. Take notes. Watch for news of a reopening in a newsletter like *Morningstar Investor* or *The No-Load Fund Investor.*

A final note here: Fidelity, which in 1996 and 1997 received a great deal of negative publicity focusing, in part, on its willingness to let funds grow too large, began closing some of its biggest and most popular funds. Magellan was closed in October 1997; Contrafund in spring 1998. These funds are already too large. I wouldn't bother to put them on my list.

## RETURNS ON CLOSED FUNDS

| FUND | CLOSED | PRIOR 12 MONTHS | FOLLOWING 12 MONTHS |
|------|--------|-----------------|---------------------|
| Acorn | July 1990 | 6.5 | 2.5 |
| SoGen | February 1994 | 29.3 | 2.1 |
| Windsor | May 1989 | 26.0 | 2.1 |

# DO consider closed-end funds.

When investors talk about mutual funds, they usually mean open-end funds. But there are actually two types of investment companies that pool the assets of investors and buy and sell securities based on the portfolio manager's strategy and outlook.

Here is the difference: An open-end fund sells and buys back shares in the fund each business day. When an investor buys shares, those shares are created; when an investor sells, the shares that are redeemed cease to exist. Thus for an open-end mutual fund, the shares outstanding refer to the number of shares owned by investors.

Both the value of the shares and the number of shares fluctuate from day to day as the value of the securities and the number of investors change. At the end of each day, the securities in the portfolio are valued. That value is divided by the number of investors—or shareholders—in the fund to arrive at a price per share, which is called the net asset value, or NAV. That number is listed in the newspaper the next morning.

The advantages of this open-end structure are numerous and explain the popularity of mutual funds: they are safe, liquid, convenient, and easy to buy and sell.

The closed-end fund is a close cousin. These funds issue a fixed number of shares at an initial public offering. The shares are priced and traded like stocks on major exchanges. The fund company is not responsible for redeeming shares. Here the number of shares outstanding is fixed.

An investor who wants to sell must sell through a broker at the market price. Such a fund's shares do not necessarily trade at its net asset value. They may trade above the NAV, which is called "selling at a premium," or below, called "selling at a discount." The trading price is determined by a variety of things, including supply and demand and the market's perception of the fund's prospects, much like the price of a stock.

Certain types of investments can work better in a closed-end format than in an open-end fund. One good example is one-country funds. Markets in many countries are small and illiquid. The manager of an open-end fund might be forced to liquidate securities to satisfy redemptions in a crisis, such as the devaluation of the Mexican peso in 1994 or the Asian market turmoil in the fourth quarter of 1997. But the manager of a closed-end fund has complete control over its assets.

Consider what happened to Mark Mobius, a top emerging markets manager who manages one open-end and two closed-end funds, in the disastrous fourth quarter of 1997. The open-end fund, Developing Markets, experienced its worst quarter ever. It dropped 25 percent because Mobius used cash inflows to buy into Asia early—in June and July—and then suffered as those markets headed into the tank. So enthusiastic was Mobius that he didn't even keep his typical 10 percent cash buffer, according to Morningstar analyst Kevin McDevitt. "Mobius used that money to buy shares in Asia, reducing cash to 3 percent by the end of September," McDevitt said.

Contrast that with the closed-end Templeton Emerging Markets, which stays fully invested. Emerging Markets does not have idle cash. Nor does it have cash inflows because of its closed-end structure. So in a sense Mobius was saved from himself, and this fund eked out a positive year in 1997. For some years I had envied Don Phillips his wisdom in buying the closed-end Emerging Markets while I had—for the first time ever—paid a load to buy Developing Markets. But 1997 was the first time that the difference really hurt.

# DON'T overlook spiders.

A new option, with the nickname of spider, can make an even better investment than an index fund for some investors who are concerned about tax efficiency. A spider—like its newer sibling, the diamond—is a trust that owns stock positions to match a market index. Both were designed by borrowing here and there—a little bit of mutual fund, a lot of unit investment trust—to make an entirely new instrument.

Mutual funds are open-ended, meaning that shares are created and redeemed every day by the fund company to meet investor demand. In contrast, a closed-end fund issues a fixed number of shares that trade like stocks on an exchange. Historically, a unit investment trust, with both a fixed number of shares and a fixed portfolio, was not a very attractive investment. But these new UITs allow investors to target a specific group of securities and to buy them at a low cost, making them a better investment in some cases than a mutual fund.

The SPDR or spider, which invests in the 500 stocks of the Standard & Poor's index, was the first open-ended UIT, according to Dan Noonan, a spokesman for the American Stock Exchange, which created and sells them. Other issuers are copying or adapting the design to create their own products. For example, Charles Schwab introduced a unit trust that invests in the Dogs of the Dow, or the 10 highest dividend-yielding stocks in the Dow Jones Industrial Average.

Both the spider and the index fund are extremely low-cost: 18½ basis points for the spider and 20 basis points for the Vanguard 500. But the 500 stocks in the S&P are the only investment permitted for the spiders, which must stay fully invested. When a shareholder wants to sell, the shares go back into the open market and are purchased by another shareholder. An index mutual fund aims to stay fully invested, too. But the manager must be ready to redeem shares if investors want to sell. So he typically keeps a small amount in cash. The Vanguard Index 500 is also permitted to buy futures.

The big argument for spiders, though, is their tax efficiency. Shares of the 500 index contain embedded capital gains because the underlying stocks have been held for some time and have appreciated in value. When they are sold, the mutual fund must distribute those gains to all shareholders. Should the market crash and lots of investors bail out, the index fund manager might be forced to sell appreciated stock to raise money to redeem the shares, generating capital gains. "When a large institution sells mutual fund shares, it passes off the gain to everyone else in the fund," Noonan says.

In contrast, spiders do not redeem shares from investors, who buy and sell them on the Amex. Institutional investors are permitted to create and redeem shares. But they must do so "in kind" in lots of 200,000. In other words, if an institution wants to redeem spiders, it would redeem them into shares of the underlying stocks. "They are simply converted by the issuer into stock," Noonan says. This prevents the capital gains from being distributed to all the other investors who continue to hold their shares.

Advisers like Ram Kolluri in Princeton, New Jersey, are replacing the Vanguard 500 with spiders in client portfolios. "My largest position is in spiders," Kolluri says. "I use the spiders as the portfolio anchor and then build value and growth and international positions from there." Kolluri expects more trusts similar to spiders by the end of 1998. "I wouldn't be surprised to see a NASDAQ 100 or a prepackaged commodity instrument," Kolluri says. "Wall Street is finding newer and better ways to package the same old wine."

# DO look for a fund manager with passion.

If most managers trail the market, does it follow that you should never buy an actively managed fund? Not necessarily. But when you do, look for a fund manager with passion. With commitment. With a strategy and a plan.

Most fund managers are timid. They are index huggers. They follow the crowd. And they buy too many stocks. What you want is someone with ideas and with courage. One of my favorites is Mike Price, manager of the Mutual Series funds, which he sold in 1996 to Franklin/Templeton. I've interviewed Price and heard him speak a number of times over the years, and he makes what he does sound so easy. But it's easy only if you have great ideas and the courage to follow them through. He buys the stocks that everyone else fears. Then he puts pressure on the management to make changes that are good for shareholders.

I have a personal story to tell here. At the beginning of 1998, I was growing a bit disenchanted with mutual funds. I decided to buy a couple of individual stocks. I bought Intel at 72, Boeing at 44, Pfizer at 94, and Oxford Health Plans at 14. Oxford, an HMO, was an odd choice. But I'd followed the company almost since its inception and had interviewed Stephen Wiggins, the chairman, on a number of occasions.

I thought Wiggins knew the secret to managed care. He signed up the very best health care providers in the New York area and then offered his members freedom of choice, including use of alternative medicine, if they were willing to pay more. Hospitals and doctors were eager to sign on for the plan. Momentum built for Oxford. When Oxford opened its doors to individuals in 1994 after a change in New York State law, my family and I signed on eagerly. We were happy with the coverage. And I understood the company—I thought.

But Wiggins's secret wasn't really a secret. Investors knew about Oxford and loved it. It was riding high in the bull market of the 1990s. Then on Gray Monday—October 27, 1997—when the stock market dropped more than 500 points, Oxford fell from 89 to 13 a share. Oxford admitted that it was having problems. I pondered it awhile and then—à la Peter Lynch's advice to buy something you understand—I bought it. I reasoned that there was not much downside. Oxford had a large enough customer base to be reckoned with. It wouldn't disappear. Perhaps another company would buy it.

So far, so good. Then I had the chance to do some primary research. I went into the hospital for major surgery. When I got home, I received a notice that Oxford refused to pay all of the bill, leaving the hospital holding the bag. The surgeon was furious, suggesting that Oxford members might be refused at the best hospitals in the future. The physical therapist I worked with didn't like Oxford, either, and he had his own Oxford story. He knew one of the founders of Oxford, he said. The same guy had been involved in starting another HMO in upstate New York. That HMO was now in bankruptcy.

The newspapers were full of reports that Oxford was not paying its bills to doctors and other care providers, too. It seemed that the momentum could turn against Oxford quickly. Besides, there was a lot of emotion involved on my part—all the stuff that the behavioralists love to study. I panicked. I lacked passion and commitment.

I sold Oxford. The following day, the lead story in the business section of *The New York Times* reported that Michael Price had taken a big stake in Oxford. Now that's what you want in a fund manager. Someone who is willing to go against the grain. Someone with more guts than me.

# DON'T confuse a change in the fund's share price with an investment gain or loss.

Does this describe your investment style? You buy a mutual fund and then look it up in the newspaper each day to see whether its share price, or net asset value, increases. If it doesn't move, you sell it and move on to another one. Equating movements in a fund's NAV with investment performance is a common and costly mistake. Consider the Lindner Dividend fund, a solid performer for the past decade even though it hit some difficult times in the late 1990s. Look at its share price, or NAV, and total return *(see graph)*.

If you looked at the change in the NAV from 1986 to 1997 and used that as the sole measure of performance, you would calculate that the fund gained a measly 12 percent in 12 years. In fact, the fund's total return was 298.62 percent, for an average annual return of 12.21 percent over the period.

What's the mystery? Like stocks, mutual funds are introduced at a specific price, or NAV, often $10 for mutual funds. When a stock price moves up from its initial price—or the price you paid for it—it means that your investment is increasing in value. Many investors expect to use the NAV of a mutual fund as the same type of measure. In other words, they think lack of movement in the NAV signals that the fund is a dud. "My own father gives me this problem," says Steven Norwitz, a vice president at T. Rowe Price in Baltimore. "I recommend a fund to him, and then he tells me, 'This fund is going nowhere, and I'm going to sell it.'"

The reason a mutual fund cannot be measured like a stock is that the fund manager buys, sells, and trades securities in the portfolio, producing income and capital gains and losses. For example, Lindner Dividend fund is an income fund, which means it pays out a regular dividend. These dividends should be reinvested in the fund. Although the dividend is part of the return and increases your investment, it does not change the share price.

Portfolio managers also buy and sell securities, generating capital gains and losses for the fund. Once—or perhaps twice—a year, the fund manager pays out capital gains, which you can—and should—reinvest in the fund by buying more shares. The capital gains, too, are part of the fund's total return.

When a fund pays out gains, the share price drops to reflect it. This is called "going ex-dividend." If you look at your mutual fund statement, you will see that you received a capital gains distribution that resulted in a purchase of a certain number of new shares. So your investment will be worth the same amount, but you will have more shares valued at a slightly lower NAV.

What this all means is that you must use the NAV of a mutual fund differently than the share price of a stock. With a mutual fund you need to look beneath the surface to see what the manager is doing to find out how your investment is performing.

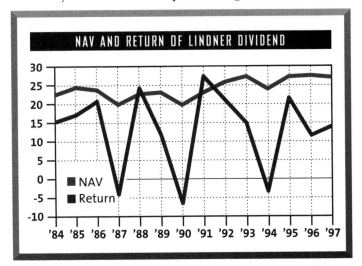

# DO add to your holdings with an automatic-investment program.

Investing is all about discipline: discipline in buying and discipline in selling. The best way to discipline yourself is with a systematic investment program in which you make regular monthly or quarterly investments no matter what is happening in the market.

Professionals have a name for this strategy. They call it dollar cost averaging. This is a method of buying mutual fund shares by investing the same amount of money on a regular schedule regardless of the market price. Studies have shown that investors who do this tend to pay less per share over time than those who purchase shares in a block. It works particularly well when buying volatile funds. That's because the same $100 buys more shares when the fund's price is down and less when it's up. When left to our own devices, most of us tend to do just the opposite: we buy a fund when it's hot and trading at its high, and we dump it when the price sags.

Some pros argue that if you have a great deal of money, you should dump it all into the market at once, because that way you start earning a stock return immediately. Over the past several years, with the stock market heading straight up, getting on that course early had appeal.

But even financial advisers use dollar cost averaging, although they've heard the argument for dumping in a lump sum. That's because they know that there is about a 30 percent chance that a lump sum will decline in value on a market downturn. If a client comes to them with $1 million, they do not want to call the client the following day to report that the portfolio is now worth $850,000.

There's another reason for dollar cost averaging, too. Most investors do not have a $1 million lump sum. But just about everyone can come up with $100 a month to invest. For example, Scott A. McMillin, a knowledgeable investor who participates in the newsgroups at moneyinsider.com, sets up his portfolio in much the same way as he does his 401(k) retirement plan. He arranges for regular monthly deposits from his bank account to the mutual funds he wants to invest in.

Many good fund families will allow you open an account with a minimal initial deposit provided you agree to have $50 or $100 deducted from your bank account to add to your investment program. Of the 533 fund families in the Morningstar database, 220 now offer these programs.

Unfortunately, Vanguard Group is not on the list. Some years ago, chairman John C. Bogle raised minimums on Vanguard funds to $3,000 to hold expenses down. But when a shareholder wrote to complain that the move locked out small investors, Bogle reduced the minimum on STAR, which is made up of seven other Vanguard funds, to $500. STAR makes an excellent core holding. Vanguard will help you arrange for regular $50 investments into the fund.

Likewise, the Spectrum funds, offered by T. Rowe Price, tap into more than a dozen different T. Rowe Price funds, including both domestic and international, growth and income, giving broad diversification within just two funds. This is an ideal portfolio for nearly any beginning investor—and it can be adjusted for your asset allocation needs. For example, you might put $100 per month in the growth fund and $50 in the income fund.

Of course, you can add additional funds to your portfolio, including international players like Scudder International or even emerging markets funds like Scudder Latin America or T. Rowe Price New Asia. Indeed, making small, regular investments is the very best way to move into a volatile asset class like emerging markets or small-cap stocks.

# DON'T ignore a flood of assets.

What happens to transaction costs when fund assets increase? At what point does performance begin to decline? What is the optimum asset size for a mutual fund? John Bogle Jr. analyzed the data from 25,000 trades at his firm, Numeric Investors L.P. in Cambridge, Massachusetts, looking for answers to these questions.

What Bogle found was that across investment styles, in every single instance, as assets increased, performance went down. That prompted Numeric to close two funds when they reached $250 million in assets and to announce plans to close a third when it reaches $200 million—small potatoes in the fund business. Don't expect other funds to follow Numeric's lead, though. Collecting assets is the name of the game in the mutual fund business. Instead, you'll have to decide for yourself when a fund is taking in too much money.

In his research, Bogle broke transaction costs into four pieces: commissions, the bid/ask spread, the market impact of trading, and the opportunity cost, by which he means the inability to execute the entire trade at the price where it first looked good to him.

As a big investor starts buying chunks of stock, the price begins heading up. The larger the fund—and the more stock the manager needs to buy—the higher the opportunity cost. "Opportunity cost is virtually invisible," Bogle says. He studied it by tracking how the stock price moved from the time Numeric identified an idea to the time the entire trade was completed.

The average price minus the "buy price"—or the price where the manager identified the stock as a buy—is the opportunity cost. "That is the cost of not getting into your portfolio the stocks you want because you take too long or assets are too big or someone is taking the stock away from you," Bogle says.

For instance, an investor with a $100 million portfolio who wants 100 names must put $1 million in each stock. "Maybe there is enough liquidity to do that," Bogle says. "But what if I take the portfolio to $1 billion? Now I need to put $100 million in each stock." If the stock trades at 50, that means 2 million shares. Suppose that the stock trades 200,000 shares a day. "I can't be the entire day's volume," Bogle says. "So most of those trades won't get done. Maybe I buy 100,000 the first day and the second day. But soon the price will be well past where I can get a decent return." So perhaps he gets only 40 percent of that money invested in his idea. "That is a cost to my investor," Bogle says, "because the returns will be worse."

Bogle analyzed trades across all four investment strategies used by his firm. They include a core strategy that incorporates value and momentum models; a small-growth momentum strategy; a value hedge that uses both long and short positions; and a hedge strategy that incorporates both value and momentum. All portfolios are managed quantitatively, using computer models. With each strategy, Bogle has identified an excess return—or "alpha"—that Numeric has achieved in the past. That alpha is reduced by transaction costs to produce a "net alpha."

Bogle looked at costs by trading style as well as the trading days needed to complete the order. Not surprisingly, trading costs in the small-cap momentum strategy were highest—more than double the value strategy. "If you are a value manager it is less of an issue," Bogle says. "If you are a large-cap manager, it is less of an issue. For momentum and small cap, it is a huge issue."

Bogle identifies an optimum point at which to close a fund by plotting performance and assets on a graph and looking to see where performance peaks. "You should take your assets up to the peak and no further," he says.

# DO check Bloomberg's good and cheap funds.

You get what you pay for, right? Perhaps. If you're buying skis, audio equipment, an Oriental rug, or a sports utility vehicle. But when you're buying a mutual fund, cheaper is better. That's what *Bloomberg Personal Finance* found in 1997 when it looked at performance across the 15 mutual fund categories tracked by Morningstar. Low-cost funds outperformed high-cost ones in 13 of the 15 groups. When Bloomberg repeated the study in 1998, the results were the same. Only in two categories—small-cap growth and small-cap blend—did the high-cost funds perform better.

So why are companies continuing to offer us high-cost funds? And why are we buying them? "New funds generally carry above-average expense ratios because they're small and have steep start-up costs," Jonathan Burton wrote in the June/July 1997 issue of *Personal*. "But management fees should decrease as funds grow in size and the day-to-day expenses of running the portfolio are spread over a wider base of investors."

Instead, though, fees are heading up, led by the management fees, which represent 75 basis points, up from 60 basis points 20 years ago, Burton says. Add to that the 12b-1 fees that many funds are adding to get their products into more distribution channels. And what you have is a bloated fund that will have great difficulty beating the Standard & Poor's 500 Stock Index, or the broad market.

But Burton found that good and cheap funds do exist. In addition to Vanguard, with its average expense ratio of just .30 percent, he found several other companies that are watching your bottom line: Franklin/Templeton, T. Rowe Price, American Century, Putnam, USAA, and Neuberger & Berman. "While fund expenses should not be the sole determinant behind a purchase decision, they are the single aspect of future performance within an investor's control," Burton says.

Here are some of the top cheap funds from the 1998 survey on good and cheap funds:

| FUND NAME | EXP. RATIO | 5-YEAR RETURN | PHONE NUMBER |
|---|---|---|---|
| White Oak Growth Stock | .95 | 21.63 | 888-462-5386 |
| Harbor Capital Apprec. | .75 | 20.27 | 800-422-1050 |
| Vanguard Index Growth | .20 | 19.46 | 800-662-7447 |
| PIMCO Capital Apprec. | | | |
| Institutional | .71 | 21.34 | 800-927-4648 |
| Fidelity Growth & Income | .71 | 20.92 | 800-544-8888 |
| Vanguard Institutional | | | |
| Index | .06 | 20.28 | 800-345-1172 |
| AARP Growth & Income | .69 | 20.15 | 800-322-2282 |
| Vanguard Index 500 | .20 | 20.12 | 800-662-7447 |
| Dodge & Cox Stock | .59 | 21.12 | 800-621-3979 |
| American Century | | | |
| Equity Growth | .63 | 20.98 | 800-345-2021 |
| Babson Value | .96 | 20.85 | 800-422-2766 |
| Vanguard Growth & | | | |
| Income | .38 | 20.74 | 800-662-7447 |
| Vanguard/Windsor II | .39 | 20.71 | 800-662-7447 |
| Mairs & Power Growth | .89 | 23.69 | 800-304-7404 |
| Nicholas | .72 | 17.98 | 800-227-5987 |
| Neuberger & Berman | | | |
| Partners | .84 | 20.35 | 800-877-9700 |
| Franklin Small-Cap Growth | .92 | 21.54 | 800-342-5236 |
| Lazard Small Cap | | | |
| Institutional | .84 | 20.69 | 800-823-6300 |
| Glenmede Small Cap | | | |
| Equity | .17 | 20.53 | 800-442-8299 |
| Hotchkis & Wiley Int'l. | 1.00 | 17.26 | 800-346-7301 |
| Vanguard Int'l. Growth | .57 | 16.42 | 800-662-7447 |
| Glenmede Int'l. | .18 | 15.94 | 800-442-8299 |
| Janus Worldwide | 1.01 | 19.82 | 800-525-8983 |
| Templeton Growth | 1.08 | 16.15 | 800-292-9293 |

# DON'T get confused by loads.

Once mutual funds came in just two varieties, load and no load. They were easy to tell apart. Load funds were sold by brokers and carried an up-front sales commission. No-load funds charged no commission and were sold directly by the fund sponsor.

Now the distinction has been blurred. There are low-load funds, back-end load funds, and level-load funds, which take the commission out of a higher annual fee. There are also no-load funds being sold by brokers who add their own annual fees. This is essentially a shell game. The one-time up-front load is eliminated and replaced by a permanent load that goes on and on. Instead of paying 5 percent up-front, you can pay 1 percent a year forever. That's not a good trade-off. The reason is that ongoing expenses hurt a lot more than one-time expenses.

Here's an example to illustrate my point. Let's say you invested $10,000 in 1969 in the Standard & Poor's 500 index. No up-front load, no annual fees, and we'll assume no taxes. At the end of 1995 you would have had $170,000. What if you paid a 5 percent up-front load in 1969? In that case, at the end of 1995 you would have had $160,000.

Now, what if you paid no up-front load, but instead paid 1.3 percent a year in expenses? That expense ratio is a bit below average for diversified equity mutual funds. In that case, you would have had just $124,000 at the end of 1995. So how does this stack up? With a 5 percent load, you got 95 percent of the return on your S&P 500 investment. With no load— but 1.3 percent annual fees—you get just 73 percent of the return on your investment, or $124,000 out of the $170,000 total. That's a no-load haircut.

So the lesson here is to look at all the fees. Sure, it's better to pay no load if you're going to do the research yourself and buy your own funds. But just because there is no up-front load doesn't mean you are getting a better deal. You want low annual expenses, too. In fact, as our example shows, low expenses can be more critical than no load.

Based on economies of scale, it would be logical to see mutual fund expenses going down as assets pour into mutual funds. But they are not. In 1980, the average expense ratio for a diversified stock fund was 1.1 percent. In 1995, it was about 1.3 percent; in 1997, 1.4 percent. So the trend is going in the wrong direction—and it's moving rapidly.

One place I suspect investors don't think to look at expenses is in their 401(k) plan. That's too bad, because expenses are creeping up in these plans. In addition to the expense ratio of the mutual fund, many fund companies are heaping on more record keeping and administrative fees. The trend is for the employer to pass these through to employees.

Many fund companies—Neuberger & Berman and Warburg Pincus are two examples—are creating separate classes of shares to offer to 401(k) investors. Although it's not technically a load, it amounts to the same thing. These shares have an extra 12b-1 fee of 25 or 50 basis points that goes to pay a distributor. What this means is that two plan participants might choose the same fund for their 401(k) plan. But one of them might have an extra 50 basis points shaved off his investment every year. That can make a difference of thousands and thousands of dollars over a working lifetime.

Most fund companies believe that investors don't care about expenses. Those that charge high fees encourage investors to ignore them by focusing on performance. But high fees hurt.

You can find out what expenses you pay. And you can refuse to pay out-of-line expenses. Don't pay loads disguised as any other name.

# DO read the prospectus.

Investors have the right to receive certain information from the mutual fund company before they invest, as well as the right to receive regular reports on the fund. Most of this stuff makes for dull reading. But it's worth the effort to find out the fund's objectives, restrictions on the portfolio manager, fees and other charges. You can order the prospectus from the fund company or, in most cases, you can find it on the Internet.

Pay special attention to:

**Summary of Expenses** Look here for any sales load on purchases or on reinvested dividends, redemption fees, and exchange fees (which means you pay when you trade between funds). Ideally, what you want to see in each of these cases is "none" or "0."

Look also for the annual fund operating expenses—the cost of running the fund. These include the management fee, which covers salaries and administrative expenses, and the 12b-1 fee, which covers marketing expenses. Most funds also have a category called "other expenses," which includes miscellaneous fees.

Avoid funds with 12b-1 fees. This is money that will be subtracted from the fund's assets year after year after year. Be cautious, too, if the fund's total operating expenses exceed 1.4 percent, which is the average for a stock fund. Consider Alger Capital Appreciation, the No. 1 performer of 1995, up 78.6 percent. Lots of shareholders were willing to overlook its expense ratio of 3.43 percent to get that kind of return. But in 1996 and 1997, this fund underperformed the market by a wide margin. Yet its expenses held high, in the 2½ percent range. Some funds—such as new funds or those that trade abroad—have a good reason to go higher. You want to know what it is.

Look, too, at the example, which the company is required to provide, of what you would pay on a

$1,000 investment assuming a 5 percent annual return and redemption at the end of the time period. Here's an example from the prospectus of one good no-load fund:

| 1 Year | 3 Years | 5 Years | 10 Years |
|--------|---------|---------|----------|
| **$10** | **$32** | **$56** | **$124** |

When Sheldon Jacobs, editor of *The No-Load Fund Investor,* surveyed about 100 funds, he found that the projected costs on a $1,000 investment, if it were withdrawn after one year, ranged from $4 to $93. The 10-year projections ranged from $35 to $306.

**Financial History** This shows up to 10 years of the fund's performance. Check to see if the fund has cut into net asset value to pay out dividends. Is the expense ratio declining over time or increasing? Is the portfolio turnover rate fairly steady and modest—say under 50 percent? Portfolio turnover became more important in 1997 because of the change in the capital gains tax rate. *(If you hold your funds in a taxable account, see page 46 on portfolio turnover.)*

**Investment Objective** This states where the manager will put most of his money. For example, "the fund will invest substantially all of its assets—but no less than 80 percent—in common stocks." How will the rest be invested? What other options does the manager have? Many funds now say, "The fund can invest up to 33 percent in foreign securities." You will also want to know whether the fund can use derivatives, or products derived from other products, and how they can be used.

**Performance** Look at the fund's total return for the past 10 years, which is calculated according to Securities and Exchange Commission regulations. It will be compared with an index, usually the S&P Index for a domestic stock fund. Compare the fund to the index, and look for consistency.

# DON'T be confused by the profile prospectus.

In early 1998, the Securities and Exchange Commission passed long-awaited rules to simplify and shorten the mutual fund prospectus. Fund companies are now permitted to issue a "profile prospectus" of three to six pages in place of the old prospectuses that could run to 30 pages of gray type. But the fund company is still required to publish a Part B containing all the information that is in the old prospectus and to make it available to investors if they ask for it. Part B is also called the "statement of additional information." The prospectus was first shortened back in 1983 when the statement of additional information was first created, according to John Collins at the Investment Company Institute. Now the prospectus will be shortened again, and Part B will grow longer. You must request Part B from the fund company if you want it.

Two categories of information may be eliminated from the profile prospectus. First is information that is considered secondary to making an investment decision or a comparison between funds. The second category is information that is true for all funds. For instance, the prospectus will now eliminate this type of information: "as a shareholder of the fund you are a percentage owner of a portfolio of securities."

But it must include on the cover page: the fund's name; date of the profile's first use; date of the most recent performance information in profile; a statement identifying the document as a profile; and a legend noting that the profile is a summary document. It must also say that the prospectus contains additional information that you may want to consider before investing and tell you how to obtain additional information.

And it must include these nine specific items, Collins says:

♦ The fund's goals or investment objectives;
♦ Investment strategies, or how the fund will accomplish its goals;
♦ The main risks of investing in the fund including a bar chart of the fund's annual total returns for each of the past 10 years compared to an appropriate index, and a description of the type of investor who might be appropriate for the fund;
♦ Fees and expenses;
♦ Investment adviser and portfolio manager identification;
♦ Information on how to buy shares;
♦ Information on how to sell shares;
♦ Information on distributions and taxation;
♦ Information on other available services.

It sounds straightforward enough. Still, the profile prospectus has been controversial in the industry. Barry Barbash, chief regulator for mutual funds at the Securities and Exchange Commission, is proud of the new prospectus and says he believes that it will help investors who did not take the time and trouble to read the old one.

But Don Phillips, chief executive at Morningstar, has been a staunch critic. For one thing, Phillips doesn't like the idea of separating necessary information into two parts. Even worse, he believes, it continues the trend of treating fund investors like consumers rather than owners of mutual funds. The Investment Act of 1940, which laid down the regulations for the mutual fund industry, was based on the concept of investors as owners. The new prospectus doesn't mention it. "The most salient fact is omitted from the profile prospectus," Phillips says. "And that is that you are becoming a shareholder and that you have rights. I dislike the whole notion that it has turned into a consumer-information thing."

## DO get help over the phone or on the Web.

Until recently, investors who needed advice on buying mutual funds had little choice but to go to a stockbroker and pay a load or commission for the fund. That's no longer the case. As funds that are sold directly over the phone, by mail, or on the Internet have gained market share, they, too, are beginning to offer advice. "The direct-marketing companies have recognized that, with the increasing complexity of financial markets and the hundreds of fund offerings, people need much more assistance in selecting funds and in determining a suitable asset allocation strategy," says Steven E. Norwitz, a vice president at T. Rowe Price.

This is happening at the same time that advice offered by brokers is coming under increased scrutiny. Brokers face potential conflicts of interest that pit their own compensation against the needs of their clients. For example, they typically receive higher commissions for selling funds that are sponsored by their brokerage firms. Or a firm might offer a sales-incentive program in which a broker can win a free trip by selling a certain investment.

There are a couple of advantages to getting information from no-load companies. The obvious one is that it's free. Second, the advice from a no-load company is arguably more objective than advice from a brokerage firm. The phone sales representative, who earns a salary, has nothing to gain by pushing you into a particular fund. In fact, your conversation is recorded, and the rep knows that if you make a decision you regret based on his advice, he stands to lose. Still, he does want you to pick a fund from his company rather than take your money to a competitor.

As an experiment, I called a dozen good no-load companies to see what kind of information investors could expect. Not once was I pressured to buy a fund or even asked for my name and telephone number. But you should know that not all the advice is as complete as you might need. And you should reject simplistic answers, such as "Our best fund is our international fund." Clearly, the same fund is not right for every caller. A good phone rep will ask you something about your goals and investment experience.

Here are some tips for obtaining information by telephone:

◆ **Don't worry about sounding unsophisticated.** This is a good place to ask the most basic questions you can think of: What does equity mean? What is a long-term bond? What does a growth-and-income fund do? Which emerging markets does your fund invest in?

◆ **Provide a thumbnail sketch of what you want and ask for recommendations.** For example, you might ask which is the company's best middle-of-the-road fund for a core holding. Or you might ask for the most aggressive fund or the best new fund.

◆ **Ask which of the company's funds is most highly regarded in the press.**

◆ **Ask the rep for his personal favorite and why.** Some reps are chatty. You might learn more than you expect.

◆ **Don't buy a fund based only on the information you receive from the fund company.** But do consider it of value. In many cases, it is more valuable than what you will get from a broker with a vested interest.

It's probably safe to say that each mutual fund company has a Web site, too, which is often the source of great information. For example, www.vanguard.com posts information about new fund offerings as well as investor education articles and portfolio holdings of its funds. Check www.mfea.com, the Mutual Fund Education Alliance site, for links to fund Web sites as well as fund news.

# DON'T ignore the vested interest of the seller.

The other day, a friend who works on Wall Street told me about the fabulous weekend she'd just spent. A limo picked her up from work on Friday and whisked her to an elegant spa with a lavish room dominated by a big four-poster bed. She took early morning hikes through the mountains, followed them with yoga and aerobics classes, and enjoyed two daily massages, an herbal facial, body wraps, and marvelous spa food. Expensive? Not for her. She won the weekend in a contest for selling the most mutual funds from a particular load-fund company.

As it happens, the company was a fine one. And my friend is a fine person. She would never intentionally misguide someone. It didn't occur to her that her clients might not be well served by the funds she sold. Yet hers is one of the more innocent stories. Brokers are subjected to multiple pressures all the time to push certain funds. The incentive might be a vacation in Hawaii. Or it might be keeping their job or getting a promotion. Most large brokerage firms reward brokers based on commissions generated. It's not always so bald as the contest to see who could sell the most mutual funds that my friend won. Some fund companies sponsor lavish golf outings, sailing trips, or other perks to "build a relationship with the brokers." However you measure it, though, the pressure on brokers is intense.

Investment houses serve too many masters, too. If a company is an investment banking client of the brokerage firm, it might be difficult for a research analyst to be candid about the company's stock outlook. If the brokerage is helping to bring a new stock issue to market, it puts pressure on the analyst who is supposed to provide an objective outlook on the stock. The brokers

THE DOS AND DON'TS

themselves have a number of conflicts, too. When the brokerage brings a stock to market, they may be given a certain portion of that issue to unload. That's part of their job. Or the firm might buy big blocks of investment products for inventory. Then brokers are told to push these products.

Brokers also typically get bigger commissions for selling "house products," such as mutual funds marketed by their own firm. And they get bigger trailing commissions, or ongoing commissions, for these products. For example, a broker might get 25 basis points, or one quarter of 1 percent of assets, for each year you stay in a mutual fund he sold you. But if he sells you a house fund sponsored by his brokerage, he might get 35 basis points. If he sells $10 million in mutual funds, that's a difference of between $25,000 and $35,000 a year in additional income. Add to that contests and the desire to stay on the right side of the boss.

It's very difficult to determine whether a broker is giving you objective advice. If, say, a Dean Witter broker recommends a Dean Witter fund, is it because it is the best fund for you? Or because he will get a larger annual trailing commission? Perhaps it's just the fund that he knows best.

Whether the motivation is ignorance or greed, you don't want to be stuck with a lemon so that your broker can win a trip to a spa. If you intend to take a recommendation for a fund, ask to see some backup. Why should you buy this fund? Does it meet your objectives? How does it compare with its peers? What was its best year? Its worst year? How does its annual return compare with a benchmark like the S&P 500 Index? To know an average annual return is not enough.

Of course, this is not an issue for fee-only planners, which is one of the very good reasons many planners have converted their businesses to fees: to avoid this conflict of interest. A fee planner is paid by you, the client, not by a brokerage firm.

## DO elect reinvestment of dividends and capital gains.

When you buy a mutual fund, you probably hope that its share price—or net asset value—will increase over time, because that means your money is growing. But for many funds, it is the reinvestment of earnings that is the real powerhouse. Mutual fund earnings come from the dividends paid by stocks and the interest paid on bonds and money market funds. Funds also generate capital gains and losses when a manager sells securities in the portfolio.

When you open a mutual fund account, you will be asked what you would like to do with these dividends and capital gains. You can either have them reinvested in your account or you can have the money sent to you in a check. For some investors, such as a retiree who is using a portion of investment income for living expenses, electing a payout is OK. But most people should choose reinvestment.

The ability to reinvest income and capital gains automatically by buying additional shares is one of the clear advantages a mutual fund offers over investing directly in common stock. That's because the bulk of the long-term growth in the stock market, particularly in large-company stocks, comes from this reinvestment rather than from the stock price appreciation.

If you invest in a stock directly, the dividends that stock pays might be paid in cash, which pays no further interest. Or they might be deposited into your money market account at the brokerage, where you earn money market rates on the dividends rather than plowing them back into the stock market.

If you have the opportunity to reinvest stock dividends, you should definitely take it. Many companies offer reinvestment programs, but there is often a fee. Some discount brokers are also beginning to offer automatic reinvestment of stock dividends. If you are buying individual stocks, though, one of the best ways to do it is with a dividend reinvestment plan, or DRIP. These plans allow you to buy stock from the company for as little as $50 per month and to have all dividends automatically reinvested. As these programs have grown in popularity, there are now a number of Web sites with information on getting started. *(See the Resources section on page 285.)*

Reinvestment is critical. Consider this: If you had invested $1 in large-cap stocks—those that make up the S&P 500 Index—in 1925 and reinvested all the dividends, you would have had $1,828.33 at the end of 1997. This is called the total-return index. But if you did not reinvest earnings, your return would be based only on the appreciation in stock prices, and you would have had $76.07 at the end of 1997. This is called the capital-appreciation index. Small-cap stocks typically do not pay dividends, so the total-return and capital-appreciation indexes are the same. If you had invested $1 in small stocks in 1925, you would have had $5,519.97 in 1997. Small-stock funds do generate capital gains when the portfolio manager trades, and these, too, should be reinvested.

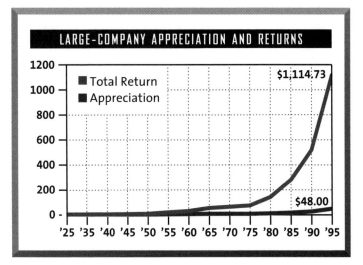

LARGE-COMPANY APPRECIATION AND RETURNS

■ Total Return
■ Appreciation

$1,114.73

$48.00

'25 '35 '40 '45 '50 '55 '60 '65 '70 '75 '80 '85 '90 '95

# DON'T buy a market-timing fund for your portfolio.

Countless studies have proved that no one is able to time the market effectively. You should not try to do it yourself. And you certainly shouldn't be paying someone else to do it.

One of the most well-meaning managers of a market-timing fund is Paul Merriman, manager of the Merriman Asset Allocation Fund, based in Seattle. Merriman travels the country meeting with the press and talking at conferences about the advantages of market timing.

Unfortunately, the results of his market-timing decisions have not been entirely positive for his fund. Consider its performance during its first eight full years of operation compared with both the S&P 500 Stock Index and the Lehman Brothers Aggregate Bond Index, a measure of the bond market *(see graph)*.

Merriman argues that being out of the market when it falls apart is worth a lot. But the performance of his fund is mediocre at best. On January 1, 1992, even Merriman made something of a concession to the negative image of market timing by changing the name of his fund from Merriman Timed Asset Allocation to Merriman Asset Allocation, although he still moves among domestic stocks, foreign stocks, and domestic and foreign bonds and cash. He often moves to high cash positions—75 percent of the fund was in cash at the beginning of 1995, according to Morningstar.

Market-timing funds have a number of problems. The most obvious one is that it's difficult to time the market. Second is the high expenses incurred in attempting to do so. For example, the Merriman fund had a turnover of 450 percent in 1994. Its turnover of 205 percent in 1997 helped to produce an expense ratio of 1.82 percent. That number is dwarfed by the

2.17 percent at Righttime Blue Chip, though. So when you buy a market-timing fund, you are paying a great deal of money for a strategy that is not successful.

Righttime, a market-timing fund with a longer record, provides a clear example of why that investment strategy doesn't pay. It outperformed the market three years—1987, '90, and '94—when the market did poorly. But it underperformed in the years the market did well, often by a big margin. The reason, according to Morningstar analyst Lori Baron, is the computer model that manager David J. Rights uses to decide whether to invest 100 percent in blue chips or to put all the assets in cash.

Though the model has been successful in predicting the downturns, it misses the uptrends. For example, Rights started the boom year of 1995 all in cash. The model gave the buy signal in February, but the fund never caught up with peers that started the year fully invested. So Righttime gained 29 percent compared with 37 percent for the overall market. The fund also carries a 4.75 percent load and a 50-basis-point 12b-1 fee. Morningstar's Principia shows that $10,000 invested in 1987 would have grown to $26,084 by the end of 1997 compared to $41,286 for the S&P 500.

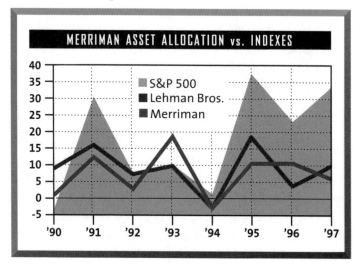

# DO look at what the pros use.

Professional investors use academic tools to measure risk and to analyze and compare the performance of different mutual funds. The most common measurement of risk—and perhaps most useful to individual investors—is *standard deviation,* which shows how far the return of a mutual fund might be expected to deviate from its average return, based on its history.

Think of a bell curve with the average—or mean— in the middle, with a wide band above and below the mean. A standard deviation is an equal number of returns above and below the average. Statistics tell us that we can expect the returns of a fund to fall within one standard deviation from the mean two-thirds of the time. And returns can be expected to fall within two standard deviations 95 percent of the time.

For instance, let's say the average, or mean, return for Fund X over a period of three years is 10 percent. The standard deviation is also 10. So one standard deviation encompasses returns from 0 percent to 20 percent; two standard deviations range from –10 to 30 percent. If you looked at such a fund, you might say that there is almost no chance that you will lose more than 10 percent or gain more than 30 percent in a year with this fund, based on its history. If the same fund had a standard deviation of 15, the range of your expected returns would fall between –20 percent and 40 percent.

Let's look quickly at the three tools of modern portfolio theory. *Beta* measures risk or the volatility of a fund relative to the market; *alpha* attempts to measure the value added—or subtracted—by a portfolio manager by showing the performance of a fund relative to the risk it took. And *r-squared* attempts to show how much confidence you can put in a fund's beta and alpha by showing you how similar the fund is to the market. We'll start at the bottom.

R-squared shows the percentage of movement in a particular security or mutual fund that is explained by the movement in an index, ranging from 0 to 100. So a stock or fund that moves in tandem with the S&P 500 would have an r-squared of 100, because 100 percent of its movement is explained by the movement of the S&P.

So it is that the Vanguard Index 500 has an r-squared of 100. All of its movement is attributed to changes in the index itself. But the T. Rowe Price Japan fund has an r-squared of just 2 to the S&P because this fund invests in Japan. A better fit for it is the Morgan Stanley Capital Index-Pacific. Here it has an r-squared of 73, according to Morningstar.

Beta measures the volatility of a fund by comparing its return to the return of a benchmark, which has a beta of 1.0. A fund with a beta of 1.0 tracks the movement of the index exactly. A fund with a beta of 1.25 has 25 percent more volatility. That means you can expect it to rise 25 percent more in an up market and sink 25 percent more in a down market. A fund with a beta of .75 is less volatile than the market. You can expect it to get a return 25 percent lower than the overall market when the market goes up and to lose 25 percent less when the market falls.

Beta is neither good nor bad. And it is meaningful only if the r-squared is high. For instance, the T. Rowe Price Japan fund has a beta of .23. But its r-squared of 2 shows that its movements don't correlate with the U.S. market. When measured against the Morgan Stanley Pacific index, it has a beta of .83.

Alpha is an attempt to measure the value a manager adds—or subtracts. A positive alpha implies the manager delivered more return than could be expected given the risk that he took. A negative alpha implies that the portfolio was not compensated for the risk it took.

# DON'T overlook the Roth IRA.

You can't get away from the hype about the new Roth IRA. Even driving down a country road in rural America, you're likely to see a sign at the local bank: "We have the new Roth IRA." I did. It became common as weeds in less than a year. Still, there's good reason to take note of it.

This account, named for Senator William Roth of Delaware, a long-time campaigner for retirement accounts, permits taxpayers within certain income limits to contribute up to $2,000 a year to what is referred to as a "back-ended retirement account." That means there is no tax break on the money going in. But it is not taxable when it comes out.

Here are the advantages:

**1 Withdrawals from the account are completely tax-free.** Taxpayers who can leave the money untouched for a long period of time will almost always do better with this open-ended savings vehicle than with a regular IRA, thanks to the power of compounding.

**2 There is no mandatory withdrawal schedule.** You need never take the money out during your lifetime. It can continue to grow tax-deferred. "If you live to 80 or 90, you don't have to take anything out, and you can keep contributing," says Gregory Kolojeski, a tax attorney who is developing software to compare the Roth IRA to the deductible IRA.

**3 There is no 10 percent penalty made on early withdrawals before age 59 ½ provided you withdraw the contributions you made, not the earnings.** That means your money is not out of reach until retirement.

**4 You can continue to contribute to the account as long as you continue to earn employment income.** With the traditional IRA, you cannot contribute after age 70½.

**5 The money is not included in taxable income when you withdraw it.** That can be important, for example, for those who receive Social Security income. Money from a traditional IRA *is* included in taxable income, which can make Social Security benefits taxable for some people.

"When you have distributions from a regular IRA, it is taxable income, which pulls your income up," says Robert S. Keebler, a financial planner in Green Bay, Wisconsin. "So $1 in IRA income might increase your taxable income by $1.85 because it pulls your Social Security benefits into the equation." But that's not the case with distributions from a Roth IRA.

The tax bill left intact the traditional, deductible IRA, with a couple of improvements, and the old, nondeductible IRA. The income limits to contribute to the deductible IRA will be increased gradually to $50,000 to $60,000 in 2005 for single filers and $80,000 to $100,000 in 2007 for joint filers, giving many more people the opportunity to use these plans. For 1998, the limits are $30,000 for the full contribution for singles, which is gradually phased out until it disappears at $40,000. For couples filing jointly the 1998 limit is $50,000 for a full contribution, phased out until it disappears at $60,000.

The maximum contribution that can be made to a Roth IRA is phased out for single filers with adjusted gross income between $95,000 and $110,000 and for couples filing jointly with adjusted gross income between $150,000 and $160,000.

Contributions may be split between the three plans. But no taxpayer is permitted to make more than $2,000 in total IRA contributions per year. Most experts who have examined the Roth IRA say that it is a better deal for nearly every taxpayer who has a choice between a traditional, tax-deductible IRA and the new Roth. "The Roth IRA is almost always better," says Steve Norwitz, a vice president at T. Rowe Price & Associates in Baltimore, who has run models comparing the various types of retirement accounts.

# DO read the proxy statement.

A mutual fund is not required to hold an annual meeting each year. However, it must do so if it wants to make changes in investment policy or in the investment advisory contract, or sometimes if it needs to elect new directors. In these cases, it must issue a proxy statement announcing the meeting and the agenda. Proxy statements make heavy reading. Take the trouble, though, to look for these things, which you should vote against if you are opposed to them.

**Changes in Investment Policy** When the Strong Funds sent out proxy statements in spring 1995, the group asked for sweeping changes in the way its funds are permitted to invest. Among them: a fund may purchase real estate–related securities; it may trade commodity future contracts; it may leverage up to one-third of the fund's assets (up from 5 percent); it may borrow from or invest in other funds. Strong also asked to make some "fundamental" policies "nonfundamental." A fundamental policy cannot be changed without a vote by the shareholders or owners of the fund. Not so with a "nonfundamental" policy, which can be changed by management. So this change takes future decisions out of the hands of the fund's shareholders.

Strong argued that it was merely following a trend. In fact, Fidelity Investments and T. Rowe Price had already made such changes, which they called simple bookkeeping. "We had a situation where funds had different investment provisions, not as a matter of intent, but depending on when they were brought out," says Henry Hopkins, chief counsel at T. Rowe Price. "We were trying to standardize our funds."

All of the Strong Funds changes passed. Still, many professional investors decided to drop the Strong Funds because they thought the changes gave its managers too much investment leeway. Financial advisers who use mutual funds to invest for their clients want to know exactly what a mutual fund is doing. "One of the biggest problems we have with a portfolio manager is we don't know what's underneath his jacket," says H. Lynn Hopewell, an investment adviser in Falls Church, Virginia. "Everybody's got a reason for asking for more freedom. But who cares?" As an investor in the fund you should be particularly vigilant for requests for changes that will send the fund in a different direction.

**Changes in Investment Management Fees** Every fund charges shareholders for certain expenses, including fees to pay the portfolio manager. Changes in these fees must be spelled out. Increases must be approved by shareholders.

For example, in 1995, the Third Avenue Value Fund announced that it would pay manager Martin Whitman 90 basis points, or nine-tenths of one percentage point, up from 50 basis points, or one-half of one percentage point.

Although the fee was not exorbitant, it seemed unfair to shareholders who had invested on the promise of decreasing fees. For example, Don Phillips, CEO of Morningstar Mutual Funds, had invested when the fund first opened with an expense ratio of 2.5 percent, roughly double the average.

New funds typically have high management fees because they have few assets. But Third Avenue said it would decrease the fee as assets grew. At first it did. But Phillips felt the fund broke its commitment to early shareholders with the 1995 increase.

"For four years, I paid substantially above-average fees," Phillips says. "Now they're renegotiating the contract." Although Phillips says he won't dump the fund, he feels less enthusiastic and says he'll contribute less money in the future.

# DON'T buy gimmicky funds.

There are more than 9,000 mutual funds available today. Are there 9,000 good fund ideas? Hardly. The good funds are the ones that don't try to get fancy. They do something you can understand, like buy small-company stocks. The bad ones are usually developed by fund companies during a bear market, when there is little investor enthusiasm for stocks, or during a time of low interest rates, when conservative investors feel they're losing ground with their money in the bank.

Here's an example: Option income funds were developed in 1977, when stock funds were very much out of favor after a long bear market. Mutual fund assets were declining; investors were bored. Sumner Abramson, a portfolio manager at Colonial Management in Boston, hit on a way to give a stock fund a little kick by writing options to provide extra income.

Abramson didn't buy options, though. He used them conservatively, by putting together an equity portfolio and selling options on all of the stocks. If the stocks went up in value, the option holders could call them away. But if they didn't, he could pocket the money from the option sales, adding some income to his stock fund.

Unfortunately, these funds proved to be poor performers in both good markets and bad. After a couple of years, they disappeared. But the gimmicks did not. In 1986, Dreyfus Investments introduced a group of funds that relied on market timing and derivatives to exploit market volatility. The funds shot the lights out in 1987, turning in high double-digit returns as the market crashed. Since then, returns have ranged from mediocre to dismal. Worse yet, heavy trading racks up tax bills that eat up what returns there are.

Add to your gimmicky list the bear-market funds

that debuted in 1994, such as Lindner Bulwark, Robertson-Stephens Contrarian, and Rydex Ursa. These funds are designed to feed investor fears of a stock decline and to do well when stocks do poorly. But since stocks do well most of the time, these funds will usually lag.

I would also add to the gimmick list market-timing funds, lifestyle funds, asset allocation funds, and any other type of fund in which the manager proposes to do something other than buy a portfolio of securities that he expects will appreciate.

The market-neutral funds introduced in 1998 belong in that category, too *(see page 158)*. Funds in this group, which would not have been permitted before the changes made in the 1997 Taxpayer Relief Act, promise to deliver a return no matter what the market does by both buying stocks and shorting stocks—or borrowing them, selling them, and waiting for them to go down in price in order to buy them and pay back the loan. When you consider that few portfolio managers beat the market even when they do something straightforward like buying stocks, this type of fund ups the ante considerably. The manager has to be right not once but twice: He must know which stocks will do well and which stocks will do poorly.

Your goal is to set up a portfolio that does well in all types of market environments. The best way to do that is by choosing good funds that invest in different classes of assets or that employ different investment styles. There are a number of legitimate types of funds that can be used to hedge against declines in the stock market. These include real estate funds, natural resources funds, energy funds, and funds that invest in stock markets around the world. But do not buy into a portfolio manager's promise that he can go against the grain of the market and save you from losses.

# DO invest internationally.

Just one generation ago, U.S. stocks represented two-thirds of the value of all the stocks outstanding in the world. Today that statistic has neatly flip-flopped: two-thirds of all stock value is to be found outside the United States. Investing only in this country is far too limiting. Investors should always be looking for different asset classes that perform well in different environments, and one of the arguments for investing overseas is that stock markets in different parts of the world tend to hit their peaks and valleys at different times because of varying economic conditions. Although some researchers have found that the negative correlation—or the tendency of two assets to perform differently in the same environment—between foreign and domestic markets has lessened as the world has become a global marketplace, it has not disappeared.

Look at the graph of returns of large-cap U.S. stocks compared with foreign stocks, as measured by the Morgan Stanley Europe, Australia, New Zealand, Far East Index (EAFE). There is no clear-cut pattern showing that foreign investments appreciate in value when U.S. investments decline. Still, it is clear from the 12-year totals that investing overseas is worthwhile. "When you put somewhere between 30 to 40 percent of a U.S. portfolio in international stocks, you both increase the rate of return and decrease overall volatility," says Mark Holowesko, director of global equity research for the Templeton Funds in Nassau, the Bahamas.

The U.S. economy is mature, although that did not stop the domestic market from roaring through 1995, 1996, 1997, and early 1998 fueled by the hot economy made possible partly by corporate downsizing. Over time, though, most professional investors believe that economic growth in the Pacific Rim, Latin America, and other emerging markets will outpace growth in the United States.

These emerging markets do not yet move in sync with the U.S. stock market. "The correlation here is zero or negative," says Campbell R. Harvey of the Fuqua School of Business at Duke University. "These markets provide a good hedge against the U.S. market." Investing in emerging markets requires iron discipline, though.

Look at what happened in 1997 for emerging markets' investors. The year started out well enough with the typical fund up 20 percent by midyear. In the second half of the year, though, they hit the skids. Thailand's currency devaluation in July gradually spread, leading to a case of Asian flu that eventually affected all developing markets. Emerging markets funds did poorly in the third quarter and much worse in the fourth quarter when the Korean government required a bailout by the International Monetary Fund. It would have been easy to swear off emerging markets after that. That's what *Wall Street Journal* columnist Roger Lowenstein announced that he was doing in his "Intrinsic Value" column at the beginning of 1998. Most investors should still make room in their portfolios for this asset class, though.

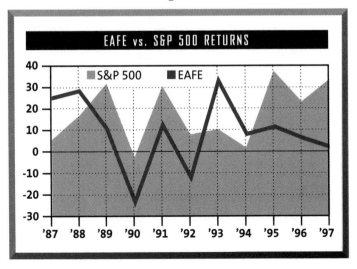

EAFE vs. S&P 500 RETURNS

# DON'T buy global funds.

Diversifying your portfolio by investing some of your money internationally is an important goal. Buying a global fund is not the best way to do it.

There is a key difference between global funds and international funds. International funds invest exclusively outside the United States. Some invest only in developed countries; some only in emerging markets. Some exclude particular areas of the world, such as Japan. Some focus on specific areas, such as Europe or the Pacific Rim.

In contrast, global funds are permitted to invest anywhere in the world, including the U.S. A global manager may move money into U.S. markets if he feels that they present the best opportunity. If you have put together your portfolio carefully, you will already have a fund that invests in U.S. stocks. Better yet, you will have one for large U.S. stocks and one for small U.S. stocks; one for growth and one for value. You do not want the manager you've chosen for your international fund to duplicate your efforts in domestic stocks.

That means that international funds are the best way to invest overseas, because they offer a pure play on foreign stocks. For the same reason, they are more volatile than global funds. If foreign markets do poorly, you can expect international funds to do worse than global funds. One interesting example is in the two Janus funds managed by Helen Young Hayes. Janus Overseas, an international fund, closed in spring 1998 because Janus said lack of liquidity in foreign markets made it difficult to invest additional assets. Yet Worldwide, a global fund with 25 percent of its assets in the United States, remained open.

Consider the total returns of international funds, global funds, and the S&P 500 over the past 10 years, as measured by Morningstar *(see graph)*. You can see that in the years that foreign markets did really well—particularly 1986 and 1993—the international funds outperformed the global funds by a wide margin, presumably because the global funds were dragged down by U.S. investments. On the other hand, in the years foreign markets did poorly—like 1990 and 1992—the global funds did better.

In this case, though, you are not looking for the least volatile fund. You should be looking for funds that provide a good deal of diversification and, of course, growth over the long haul.

One exceptional global fund may tempt you, though. It is Templeton Growth fund, one of the oldest of the funds that invests around the world, including the United States. This fund, set up in 1954 by the legendary value manager John Templeton, has been managed since 1987 by Mark Holowesko, his protégé. Holowesko follows Templeton's value style of management and includes stocks from emerging markets as well as developed countries. Because he combines consistent performance with low risk, this fund could provide a solid portfolio core. Of course, you would need to adjust your U.S. holdings to account for the fact that the Templeton fund invests in the United States.

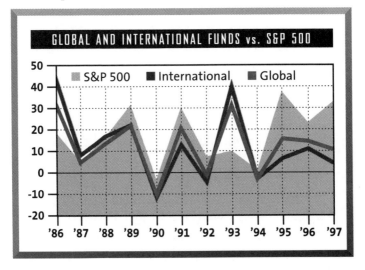

GLOBAL AND INTERNATIONAL FUNDS vs. S&P 500

# DO look to see how a fund uses derivatives.

Newspapers and financial magazines were filled with talk of derivatives during the mid 1990s, thanks largely to some spectacularly bad bets on interest rates—and some big losses—by municipalities like Orange County, California, and large-company pension funds like Gibson Greetings and Procter & Gamble.

As a result, many advisers warned against using them at all. If big investors can lose a lot of money in derivatives, small investors don't belong in them, the reasoning went. Another important principle is at work here, too: never invest in anything you don't understand. And who can understand derivatives? Certainly not most individual investors.

T. Rowe Price, a mutual fund company based in Baltimore and known for the high quality of its communications to shareholders, included in a 1995 newsletter a definition of derivatives that is all but impenetrable. When asked about it, Steven E. Norwitz, the T. Rowe vice president responsible for communications, said: "I'm going to be honest with you. I don't understand them myself. That's probably why we didn't have such a good story." And Norwitz is hardly a novice. He's been with T. Rowe for more than 20 years and is one of the most knowledgeable observers of the industry.

So there is a good argument for avoiding derivatives. But there are two problems with that approach. First, derivatives are part of the investment scene. Avoiding them is akin to avoiding foods that need refrigeration. You could do it, to be sure. But what you have left would be pretty limited and perhaps even unpalatable.

A derivative is any instrument whose value is "derived" from the movement of a stock, interest rate, market index, or commodity such as wheat, sugar, or coffee. Many common types of investments, such as pools of home mortgages that are sliced up and sold to investors as collateralized mortgage obligations, or CMOs, are technically derivatives.

The second problem is that most fund prospectuses are written broadly to allow the use of derivatives. Even though the manager may not currently use them, he could change his policy at any time. For example, James A. Engle, comanager of the Winthrop Small Company Value, uses no derivatives. But that is just his personal policy. The fund is permitted to use them. And another portfolio manager might see things differently. Even Engle might change his mind—and he is entitled to do so.

A better option is to find out how they are used. Call your fund company, and ask when, how, and why it uses derivatives. Although the aggressive derivatives get the attention, many derivatives are used to protect against big fluctuations in share price. For example, they might be used by funds that buy securities based in other currencies to hedge against swings in the dollar-exchange rate. This is certainly an acceptable practice.

You do want to know whether your foreign-stock fund uses derivatives to hedge, though, not because it is good or bad, but because the performance results can differ greatly. If you want a more stable foreign-stock fund, you might prefer that it be hedged. But if you want to diversify into other currencies, you don't want the fund to hedge back into the dollar. Much of the return of a foreign fund can come from fluctuations between the dollar and the foreign currency. Of course, these same fluctuations can also produce a loss.

So the best approach is to become informed about how your mutual fund uses derivatives and how much of the fund's assets are invested in these instruments. Then you'll avoid unhappy surprises.

# DON'T rely too much on ratings.

The easiest way to pick a mutual fund is to look at the star ratings, right? With this strategy, you just eliminate all the funds except those in the top one or two categories, which vary depending on which system you use.

Morningstar rates funds from one to five stars, five being tops. Value Line, another rating service, does it the other way. One is the top rating and five is the lowest. Morningstar's ratings are based on risk-adjusted returns. The Value Line numbers come from a formula that measures the timeliness of investing in a particular fund.

The data and comparative statistics provided by these services are a great benefit to investors. Indeed, they have revolutionized the fund industry. Fifteen years ago, we really didn't have a way to make an apples-to-apples comparison of funds, as we can with these services.

Be careful, though. While ratings have some usefulness, the problem is the emphasis they give to recent past performance. The better the performance, the better the rating. As a result, they are backward looking, measuring something that has already happened. Yet what matters in investing is what happens tomorrow, not what happened last quarter or last year. In that sense, the ratings are like the articles and cover stories in most personal finance magazines. They tend to highlight the hot fund categories and downplay laggard groups whose performance may be about to turn around. Let's take an example.

I looked in Morningstar's guidebook one day and compared the star ratings for two categories of mutual funds. The first category was growth-and-income funds. This type of fund invests in stocks of large U.S. corporations—big, solid companies like General Electric, Exxon, Ford, DuPont, and Merck. Of the 125 funds listed, 58 had four- or five-star ratings. That's 46 percent with either the highest or second-highest rating from Morningstar.

The other category was international stock funds. They invest in big companies based outside the United States. Of the 68 funds listed, there were just *four* with four-star ratings and *none* with five stars. In other words, only 6 percent of the funds in this category had one of the top ratings, while 46 percent of the growth-and-income funds had top ratings.

Now, why is that? Is it because the growth-and-income fund managers are better investors than the international stock managers? No. It's because the stocks of big U.S. companies have rallied tremendously in recent years. The growth-and-income funds that invest in those stocks have done very well in terms of recent performance, so their ratings are higher. Foreign stocks have lagged, and so have the ratings of the international funds that invest in them.

Which would make a better investment—a five-star growth-and-income fund, or an international fund with a lowly two or three stars? If, as some strategists were saying, the U.S. market had had a pretty good run and values were better overseas, the international fund may be a better choice. Or maybe not. The star ratings simply don't help you make that decision.

When Alice Lowenstein, a Morningstar analyst, gave a presentation on using the Morningstar services in mid 1998, she acknowledged this point and said, "the star rating should be only an introduction." In fact, Lowenstein said, 80 percent of the mutual funds sold in 1996 had four or more stars, indicating that they are used as a decision point. So do look at the star ratings. Use them to compare funds within a category, say one large-cap growth fund with another large-cap growth fund. But don't use them to compare funds across categories.

## DO check to see if the manager buys his fund.

Whether the manager invests in his own fund is one of the most important and useful pieces of information you can obtain about a mutual fund. And it is one of the most difficult to get. Certainly you want to know whether the manager believes in his own ability to manage money. When a manager invests his own money in a fund, the fund is likely to have lower risk scores. It is likely to be more tax-efficient. It is probably also likely to be a fund where the manager puts his heart into picking stocks—where he does it with a passion. After all, it's his money.

Unfortunately, there are no rules that require disclosure in any coherent, consistent way. The Securities and Exchange Commission and other regulatory groups don't care whether a manager invests in his own fund. Nor do most fund companies care. And, given that many fund companies set the rules on how their funds are invested, it's not surprising that the manager doesn't want to invest in the pool he manages.

However, many fund companies advertise the fact that their managers invest in their funds. For example, the Davis family has $500 million invested in its funds—like Davis New York Venture. When Shelby Davis retired in 1997, lots of investors—including professional investors like financial advisers—felt comfortable that his son, Chris, would continue in the same fine tradition, thanks to the family money that is now his responsibility.

Look, too, at Longleaf Partners. O. Mason Hawkins and G. Stanley Cates, the fund's comanagers, invest all their own equity money in the fund. So do their employees. "If we're going to invest in equities, we think we should do it through our funds," Hawkins says. "It's the same principle that we look for in the managements of the companies we buy for the fund. That is, we want a commitment to the business. If we think we're picking the right stocks, that's where we should put our money."

That makes a lot of sense, doesn't it? And it makes you wonder why you should want to invest in a fund if the manager doesn't. Where can you find funds whose managers invest their own money? The least likely place to find them, I think, is at a big mutual fund company like Fidelity Investments. Think about it. At Fidelity, a talented young manager might be assigned to one of the Select portfolios and then moved on to a more diversified fund. He will certainly do his best to pick good stocks in each category. But his options are limited by his assignment. Perhaps he wants a more diversified portfolio for himself.

Then look at a fund like Third Avenue Value, where manager Marty Whitman runs the show. In addition to serving as portfolio manager, Whitman is chairman, CEO, and chief investment officer at Third Avenue Funds. With this kind of clout at his small firm, Whitman can clearly buy whatever he likes. And he does. A "vulture investor," Whitman looks for stocks trading at a 50 percent discount to their market values and with lots of cash relative to liabilities. That includes some quirky, unusual stuff. In 1997, he bought Tejon Ranch and other agribusinesses with undeveloped land. With all the trouble he goes to to find companies, it's not surprising he invests in them himself.

There also seems to be a correlation between funds that are concentrated *(see page 140)* and those with big investments by management. These funds are worth looking for. They typically represent managers with conviction, with passion, and with minds of their own. One way to use them is as accent funds. You might index your core portfolio and use funds like these to give it spice.

# DON'T ignore your mutual fund statements.

Most investors glance at their statements to determine the value of their accounts and then toss them in the trash. But you can use them as an investment and tax-planning tool. "There's been a big change in statements over the past couple of years," says Steven E. Norwitz of T. Rowe Price. "Instead of just providing account value, they include a great deal of information that is helpful in planning."

Bond funds typically send a statement each month to show you the reinvested dividends. Stock funds send a statement when you buy or sell shares, as well as a quarterly or annual statement.

When you get the statement, look to see the change in the value of your account over the period. You don't want to sell a fund just because the price is down, of course, but you should be monitoring your funds.

If you own more than one fund in the same fund group, or if you own your funds through a discount brokerage, you can look at the overall value of the account and at the asset allocation. Check your current statement against your previous one to see how the allocation has changed.

For example, a T. Rowe Price statement for an investor holding more than one fund breaks down your investments into stocks, bonds, and cash. It shows what percentage of your total portfolio is allocated to each fund. And it shows what percentage is in stocks, in bonds, and in cash. You should not be changing your asset allocation with each statement. But you should rebalance once a year (see page 132). Looking at your statement will help you decide how to do that.

If you've sold any shares during the period, take note of the price for tax purposes. Either keep the statement for your records or note the price of the shares in your tax files. Many statements will provide the gain or loss for tax purposes, calculated using the average cost per share.

Some fund statements, such as those provided by Neuberger & Berman, show the current value of your shares as well as your cost basis, which is the amount the shares originally cost, for the purposes of calculating taxes.

That might help you decide which shares to sell. If you wish to sell specific shares, you must notify the company before you make the sale. For example, the statement might say that your shares of XYZ fund are worth $10,000 and that the cost basis is $7,000. Perhaps the shares of ABC fund are also worth $10,000. But their cost basis is $5,000. That means if you sell XYZ, you will owe capital gains tax on $3,000. But if you sell ABC, you will owe tax on $5,000.

The bottom right-hand corner of the Vanguard statement provides a box called Portfolio Allocation, which looks like this:

**PORTFOLIO ALLOCATION**

| | |
|---|---|
| Money Market | **10%** |
| Fixed Income | **10%** |
| Balanced | **0%** |
| Equity | **80%** |
| Total | **100%** |

This information can help you see quickly what you need to do to rebalance.

Before long, expect to see mutual fund statements that provide your personal performance in a fund. Rather than telling you what the fund has done over the past year, the statement will tell you what the fund has done since you began contributing to it. "That's the next thing coming in fund statements," Norwitz says.

# DO read the annual report.

Like a company that makes cars or toothpaste, an investment company that manages money is required to send out a report to shareholders each year with details of its performance. These reports can make for dull reading, and they're easy to ignore. Don't do that, though. One of the key differences between buying a product—like a tube of toothpaste—and investing in a mutual fund is that your mutual fund investment makes you a shareholder or owner of the company. There's an important distinction between being a consumer and an owner. Owners have special rights—to vote on changes in company policy, for example.

Here are some things to do:

◆ **Compare the fund's annual performance with a performance index.** If it is a large-company fund, compare it with the Standard & Poor's 500 Stock Index. If it is a small-company fund, compare it with the Russell 2000. If it is an international fund, compare it with one of the Morgan Stanley international indexes. The benchmark index should be included in the annual report. If not, you can look it up in *Barron's,* the weekly financial newspaper.

◆ **Compare your fund with its peer group by looking at the Lipper categories published by Lipper Analytical Services.** These figures are also published in *The Wall Street Journal* and *Barron's.* If the fund did poorly, you want to know whether the same was true of the entire group. You should expect your fund to be a consistent performer, ideally in the top quartile of funds in its peer group.

◆ **Look at the table that gives year-by-year performance going back 20 years.** This is the only place you will get this type of snapshot of the fund's performance history. It helps you determine whether the fund has been a consistent performer or whether its performance is changing over time.

◆ **Read the portfolio manager's explanation of the fund's performance and his market outlook.** This is particularly important if the fund's performance was different from that of its peer group. Look for a candid appraisal of the market and an explanation of the fund's performance in it. The Vanguard Group has been particularly good in this area, even going so far as to warn investors when a particular industry or market has done extremely well and noting that its bull run might be nearing an end. If the fund did poorly, you want to see what the portfolio manager plans to do about it and when he expects a change.

◆ **Check the fund's portfolio holdings.** Many of the materials you receive about a mutual fund will provide only its 10 largest holdings. But the annual report lists all the fund's holdings, as well as the percentage allocated to different industry groups. This information is particularly helpful during a period when many mutual funds concentrate in a single industry. During the mid to late 1990s, many funds bought heavily into technology, bio-tech, and health-care stocks. Check to see that your various funds are not all overweighted in the same industry.

◆ **Look at the financial-highlights table, which provides such data as the fund's expense ratio and portfolio turnover rate for the past five years.** You want to see whether they are consistent, increasing, or decreasing. The expense ratio should be trending down rather than up. A portfolio turnover rate of under 30 percent is low; 40 to 60 percent is typical; 100 percent or more is high—that means the manager is turning over the entire portfolio each year. If the turnover rate was 40 percent two years ago and it is now 100 percent, you should find out why.

Don't sell your fund based solely on something you see in the annual report. Call the fund on its toll-free number and ask for details.

# DON'T neglect the buying opportunity in new funds.

Traditional advice to mutual fund investors is this: do your research, buy a fund with a good track record, and then stick with it through thick and thin. For most, it's good advice. But for the more adventuresome, there's an argument to be made for investing in new funds.

Here it is: Many of the top-performing funds specialize in small companies or emerging markets. These two areas have great growth potential. But they require a money manager to be nimble, moving quickly into good stocks. When cash pours into a fund, it can grow too large to be invested efficiently. In fact, a 1998 study by Morningstar found that ballooning size affects small-cap growth funds first and most. Size doesn't reduce cost. But it does make the fund far less nimble. "The benefits that small-cap growth funds derive from economies of scale are minimal," says Morningstar's Tricia O. Rothschild, "and by the time the manager of a fast-growing fund manages to establish a position in a given stock, he or she has probably missed out on a significant portion of the issue's gains."

Some experts also suspect that fund companies pack small funds with their best stock picks, including hard-to-get initial public offerings, to give them an advantage out of the starting gate. The Value Line Mutual Fund Investor, a mutual fund rating service, conducted a study in 1994 to see if new stock funds did outperform their peers.

The study looked at the first-year performance of new funds compared with other funds in the same group. The result: first-year stock funds had a clear advantage over their peers. The opposite was true of bond funds, though.

As the chart below shows, the results were most impressive in the small-company category, which is precisely the category where it is most difficult to pick winners. New small-caps outperformed their peers by nearly five percentage points in their first year and continued to outperform—although by only 1 percent—in subsequent years. The performance of new small-company funds was consistent over a 10-year period, the only exception being 1987, when the market crashed. Many professional investors take advantage of this opportunity. "I believe there is a real incentive to uncover a winner early," says Sheldon Jacobs, editor of *The No-Load Fund Investor* in Irvington-on-Hudson, New York. "Once a fund gets big, a few good selections don't mean as much.

The Morningstar study found that size affects value funds least. In fact, when a large-cap value fund—say Windsor II or Dodge & Cox Stock—attracts additional money, the risk-adjusted returns stay positive and fees fall sharply, which gives performance a boost, according to the Morningstar study. In the value category, even small-cap funds can do well as they grow, the study found. But in the growth category, things can fall apart quickly as the fund grows.

## PERFORMANCE OF NEW FUNDS RELATIVE TO PEERS

| FUND TYPE | FIRST YEAR | SUBSEQUENT YEARS |
|---|---|---|
| Aggressive Growth | 1.38 | 0.75 |
| Growth | 1.63 | 0.27 |
| Foreign | 1.59 | −0.60 |
| Income | 2.74 | 0.39 |
| Small Company | 4.50 | 0.76 |
| General Bond | −0.21 | −0.13 |
| Government Bond | 0.36 | 0.41 |
| International Bond | 1.17 | −1.76 |
| Municipal Bond | −0.28 | −0.13 |

## DO think about how to sell your funds when you need the money.

As you move closer to the time when you need to take your money out of your mutual funds for a major expense, like college tuition or your own retirement, you need a strategy for moving out of the stock market by selling shares of your funds.

You have several options. You can have it transferred to your bank or mailed to you, or you may be able to write a check for it. But if you sell the proceeds of a large account all at once, you must pay tax on all your gains. And if you sell when the stock market is off, you will have defeated your purpose of riding out the market ups and downs by investing for the long term.

Instead, you want to plan in advance how you will transfer your money from the markets and into a liquid account like a money market fund. Your strategy will depend, too, on how much risk you want to take. During the roaring bull market of the 1990s, one young couple decided to invest the money they wanted to use for the down payment on a house in just three years. They knew the market might turn down and that they would then be forced to delay their home purchase. But they were willing to take the risk. You don't want to take that kind of risk with college money, though. Here it makes more sense to start moving the money gradually into a money market fund three years before you must begin paying tuition, leaving money for later tuition bills in the stock market for growth.

If you are retiring and you have to begin to use the money you have saved, you might take out what you need and allow the rest to keep earning income for you. You can do that with a systematic withdrawal plan.

With a systematic withdrawal plan, you can redeem a specific dollar amount from your mutual fund account at regular intervals, such as monthly, quarterly, or annually. You can have the check made out to you and use it for living expenses, or you can request that it be paid to a third party, such as your son in college or the bank that holds your mortgage.

Consider this example. Let's say you are ready to retire and you have accumulated retirement savings of $200,000 in a mutual fund that is growing at 9 percent a year. Now you need some of this money to supplement your income. Perhaps you decide you need $20,000 a year. You can ask the mutual fund company to send that to you, paid out in monthly installments, if you like. If your money continues to grow at the same rate, it will last for 26 years.

The Magic Triangle *(below)* shows how long your money will last, depending on how much it is earning and how much you withdraw each year. The percentage of your principal that you will withdraw is on the left; the earnings are on the right; and the number of years your money will last is where the two intersect. If the intersection of the two lines is off the chart, your money will last forever, provided it keeps earning the same return. For example, if you have $500,000 in an investment that is earning 8 percent and you withdraw $35,000 a year—or 7 percent of your original principal—your money will never run out.

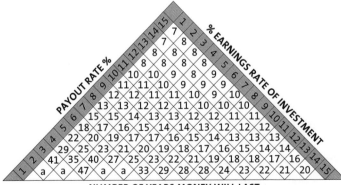

NUMBER OF YEARS MONEY WILL LAST

THE MAGIC TRIANGLE

# DON'T be fooled by so-called diversified funds.

One of the benefits of buying mutual funds is that you buy broad diversification across a number of market sectors, right? Sometimes. The Investment Company Act of 1940, which regulates mutual funds, classifies them as either diversified or nondiversified. A diversified fund must spread out 75 percent of its assets by investing no more than 5 percent in any one company. So it must have at least 15 companies in that portion of the fund. The remaining 25 percent may be invested in a single company. So the minimum number of companies a fund could hold to qualify as diversified is 16.

Some funds choose instead to be nondiversified, allowing them to take a larger stake in a particular stock. For example, in 1995, the Clipper Fund changed its charter from diversified to nondiversified. Janus 20 is another fund that is registered as nondiversified. Indeed, in 1998, opening focused, concentrated shops was something of a trend with funds like Yacktman Focus, Oakmark Select, and CGM Focus coming to market *(see page 140)*. But this technicality masks the real issue: many funds that qualify as diversified actually concentrate heavily in whatever market sector is currently hot.

The first half of 1995 provided an excellent example. The market exploded in one of the most spectacular rallies in its history, led by the large-company stocks that make up the S&P 500, which was up 20.19 percent for the first six months. I asked Barbara Gertz at Morningstar to compile a list of the diversified stock funds that beat the index, thinking that there might be some lessons to learn from them.

We eliminated sector funds, or those that invest in a particular industry, because some industry segments always do better or worse than the market averages.

Gertz found 243 diversified stock funds that beat the S&P 500 Index. When we looked at these funds, though, we found that they looked a lot like sector funds. The two hot market sectors in the first half of that year were technology and financial services. Gertz ran the list of winners to see how much each had invested in these sectors. The answer? A lot.

Market weightings can be measured by looking at the S&P index, which has about 10.7 percent in financial services and 9 percent in technology. Most of the funds that beat the index had at least double that weighting in one or the other sector. For example, Alger Capital Appreciation, the No. 1 performer with a return of 45.36, had more than 62 percent in technology. The No. 4 fund, Robertson-Stephens Value+ Growth, had nearly 80 percent of its assets in technology! And Retirement Planning Growth, another top performer, had triple the market weighting in technology and more than double the weighting in financial services stocks.

Making big sector bets means taking on additional risk. If you owned just three funds and they were all on the winners list, you might feel pretty smug about your investments. But if they were all buying the same stocks, you might have more than half your portfolio invested in technology. So, rather than three diversified stock funds, what you really have is one big technology sector fund. Investors in that situation were sadder but wiser when technology funds headed the list of losers in 1995's fourth quarter, as semiconductor stocks took a dive.

One good place to get information is on www.morningstar.net, where you can find the mutual fund portfolio's exposure to different regions—like Asia and Europe—and to different industry sectors, such as technology or financials. Some of the information is available free; some of it comes from Morningstar's premium subscription service.

## DO make your 401(k) the core of your mutual fund portfolio.

For many investors, a 401(k) plan *is* their mutual fund portfolio. Without this retirement plan at work, they would have no mutual funds—and no portfolio. Whether you are just starting out with a 401(k) plan or you have substantial investments outside the plan, you should take care to make your 401(k) an integrated part of your portfolio.

◆ **Invest as much as you can.** For most Americans, a 401(k) plan represents the single best investment opportunity they have. The money is taken out of your salary before you pay tax on it. If you are in the 30 percent bracket (including state and local taxes), putting $1,000 in a 401(k) saves you $300 in taxes—before your investment has earned a penny.

◆ **Most employers match a portion of your 401(k) contribution.** For example, your employer might kick in 50 cents for every dollar you contribute up to 6 percent of salary. If you contribute $3,000, you get $1,500 in employer money that would otherwise be lost to you.

◆ **Most plans permit loans.** That means your money is not out of reach if you need it. You repay the loan with withdrawals from your paycheck. The interest you pay goes into your account.

Once you've decided to make the contribution, how should you invest it? Diversify. If it is your only investment, choose at least three funds. If your plan offers an index fund that follows the S&P 500 Stock Index, that is a good core holding. You might put 40 to 50 percent of your money there.

To diversify, you should have one fund that invests in small-company stocks and one international fund. If you are extremely concerned about variations in your principal, put a portion—perhaps 15 percent—

in a fixed-income investment such as a short-term bond fund, a guaranteed investment contract, or a money market fund.

Remember to think in broad terms about your investment portfolio. That includes your spouse's 401(k), college accounts for the kids, and other tax investments. All of these accounts should be coordinated if you are to get the most out of investing.

Consider what Don Phillips, CEO of Morningstar, did with his 401(k) money. Because the company is in the mutual fund business, it took great care in selecting mutual funds for the 401(k) plan, putting together a group of top funds from a number of different mutual fund families.

Some of them were a bit too aggressive for Phillips, who considers himself a conservative investor. For example, he says he would never invest in emerging markets on his own. But he took the plunge with his 401(k) plan, splitting his contributions equally among the 10 funds offered. He reasoned that a retirement account is the best place to make aggressive bets. He keeps his more conservative choices for the rest of his portfolio, which includes money he might need in the shorter term.

If your plan offers aggressive funds, check out their records before investing. During the '90s, most employers have been revamping their 401(k) plans, thanks to government regulations that suggest offering three diversified options with different levels of risk and potential return. Employers are also upgrading education programs to help employees understand their choices. Take advantage of that and do some research into the funds.

Remember that 401(k) investing allows you to take advantage of dollar cost averaging *(see page 68),* so it is the best way to invest in more volatile funds. Also remember to rebalance your 401(k) once a year *(see page 132).*

# DON'T mistake commodity funds for mutual funds.

I often see postings on the Web suggesting that trading commodity futures in your spare time is a sure-fire way to get rich. What baloney! Commodity futures are traded on a number of exchanges around the country, including the Kansas City Board of Trade, the Chicago Board of Trade, and the New York Mercantile Exchange. Commodities are bulk goods, such as metals, oil, grain, and livestock. The exchanges trade contracts for the future delivery of these goods. For example, a farmer who wants to hedge the price of his fall wheat crop could sell a contract guaranteeing him a certain price. If the market goes down as he begins planting or harvesting, he still gets the contracted price.

The traders on the other side of the deal do not plan to take delivery of this farmer's crop of wheat, though. They are speculators who buy and sell commodity futures, hoping that they will earn a profit by guessing which way the price is going. For example, a drought might drive the price of wheat futures up. Excess capacity will drive the price down.

Futures prices are very volatile, often moving swiftly and erratically in a single day, simply on rumors of changes in the outlook for that commodity. A speculator will trade in and out of the commodity, unwinding his position before it is time to take delivery. It is important to understand that the trader does not actually have anything of value underlying his trades. He is simply buying and selling a binding agreement to take delivery of the commodity at some future date. If he guesses wrong, he can lose all the money he invests—and more because his investment is leveraged.

Commodity traders also trade for investor accounts, using pools of investor funds to buy and sell commodity and financial futures such as those based on Treasury bills or stock market indexes; they, too, are traded on a commodities exchange.

Investors become interested in these funds for two reasons: First, they hear about the sometimes spectacular returns—200 percent, 300 percent, or 400 percent—which dwarf those from investments in any type of stock mutual funds. Second, some studies have indicated that commodities have a negative correlation with stocks and bonds, meaning that when stocks and bonds do poorly, commodities do well. It's true that investors should always be looking for investments that have a negative correlation to their core holdings in stocks.

Most investors don't belong in commodity funds, though. Their risk is too high. With a commodity fund, you could lose everything.

Commodity funds are set up as limited partnerships, not mutual funds. Like the real estate limited partnerships that were popular in the 1980s, they are sold in units. A general partner sets up a fund, collects the money from the limited partners, and assigns a trading manager to trade commodity futures.

Unlike mutual funds, commodity funds are not a short-term, liquid investment. Although the funds do post a NAV daily, there is no secondary market for them. You must buy your units from the general partner, and you must sell them back to the general partner.

Many funds impose a stiff exit fee, and they pay the manager a very high fee—perhaps 5 percent or more a year. In addition, the fund is charged with all the trades made, which might rack up expenses of 20 to 25 percent a year. That compares with less than 2 percent on a typical stock fund.

Most of us do not belong in commodity futures. If you have a very large portfolio—several million dollars—and you are looking for an aggressive investment for a small portion of it, commodities might qualify.

# DO think about the impact of taxes on your investments.

There are two ways taxes can bite into your performance. Most investors know that when they sell or trade shares of a fund, they must pay taxes. But many do not know that when the portfolio manager buys and sells securities, the investor must pay taxes on any capital gains generated by the sale.

Mutual funds do not pay taxes on their earnings. The earnings are passed on to you and the other shareholders, and you are responsible for paying taxes as if you owned the securities yourself. These earnings might be paid out to you as income, or they might be reinvested in your account. Either way, you owe the taxes.

At the end of each year, your mutual fund company will send you IRS Form 1099-DIV, reporting your income for the year. The fund company also files a copy with the IRS. And you must, too. Even if you have invested in a tax-free fund, you will receive a form and you must report the tax-free income on your tax return.

There is something you can do to reduce taxes on the shares you trade. It requires careful record keeping. If you sell shares at a loss during the year, you can use the capital loss to offset any taxable capital gain. If losses exceed gains, you are allowed to deduct the excess loss from your regular income, up to $3,000. To track your capital gains and losses, you need records of when you made your investments, how much you invested, the price you paid for each share, and how many shares you bought. Reinvested dividends are the same as purchases for record-keeping purposes. Be certain to add these to your cost basis when calculating taxes.

Good records allow you to reduce your taxes in another way. You can instruct the mutual fund company to sell the shares you paid the most for first, reducing your capital gain, and so your current tax bite. Perhaps you bought 100 shares of a fund at $10 a share some years ago. Last year, you bought another 100 shares at $20 per share. Now the fund is selling at $25, and you need to raise some money. You want to sell 100 shares, which will net you $2,500 at today's price. If the fund company redeems the 100 shares that you bought at $10 a share, your cost basis—the price of an asset that is used to calculate capital gains tax—is $1,000 and your capital gains $1,500. But if you ask the fund company to redeem the 100 shares that you bought at $20 a share, your cost basis is $2,000, and your capital gain for tax purposes will be only $500.

Some companies require their managers to use this method—called the specific identification method—when they sell securities in order to reduce taxes for shareholders. Unfortunately, though, most fund managers pay no attention whatsoever to tax consequences when they trade. They leave that to you.

To sell the highest-priced shares first, you must write to the mutual fund company in advance and identify the shares you want to sell. For example, you might write: "On October 1, 1998, I plan to sell the 100 shares of XYZ fund that I purchased on March 1, 1995, for $20 per share."

In order to use the long-term capital gains rate, which is currently 20 percent, you must have held the shares you sell for at least 18 months. If you held them between one year and 18 months, the rate is 28 percent, although Congress is talking about lowering the rate for securities held between one year and 18 months. Those securities held less than one year are taxed at ordinary income rates, which go as high as 39.6 percent.

# DON'T neglect an annual performance review.

You know that you shouldn't be looking your funds up in the newspaper every day, panicking, selling, trading, churning. But you should take stock once a year. This is the time that you determine how your funds have performed and rebalance your portfolio so that you maintain the asset allocations you have set up.

Collect all your statements, including those from the end of the previous year. If all your funds are in the same family, or if you bought them all through a discount brokerage such as Charles Schwab, Jack White, or Fidelity Investments, you will have a single statement. That will make things easier. Some fund groups even show you what percentage of your account is in each fund and what portion is in stocks, bonds, and cash. If you have your portfolio on the Web at www.bloomberg.com, or www.morningstar. net, or www.investor.com, or any other Web site that offers portfolio monitoring, you will have a head start.

If your statement does not break your investments into asset classes, do it yourself. Then look at your actual asset allocation to see how it has diverged from your target strategy. Even if you made no investments during the year, your allocation has probably been altered by movements in the markets.

If it has, you must rebalance, which simply means selling off the portion that has performed well and buying more of the asset class that did poorly. This is perhaps the most difficult thing for most investors to do, because it is counterintuitive.

But if you have selected your funds carefully and they are each doing the job they were chosen to do, you will be putting money into those that have underperformed because they were out of favor in the market. This is the disciplined way to "buy low and sell high."

This is also the time when you should make certain that each fund is doing what it is supposed to do. Calculate the overall performance of your portfolio and compare it with market indexes.

The report will provide the value of each fund. But calculating the change might require some work on your part. Look at the value of accounts at the beginning and end of the year and determine the difference.

If you did not buy or sell shares during the year, the calculation should be fairly simple. But that's rarely the case. If you took money out of the account during the year, you might just subtract that amount from the beginning value. Although it will not be accurate to the penny, it will give you a rough idea of the change in value.

Calculate the performance of your stock, bond, and cash portions. If the value of your stock account is up 10 percent and the market is up 15 percent, you want to know why.

This is a way to spotlight funds that are not keeping up. If you selected extremely aggressive funds, you might have one or two that pulled your account down. Examine those funds and make certain that their performance is still within limits you feel comfortable with. Compare them to their peer group, too.

Look at the fund's annual report to read what the portfolio manager says about performance and expectations. Was this one bad year for the fund, or the second or third year in a row that it lagged?

Does the fund have a new manager? Has the strategy shifted? Research the fund in Morningstar Mutual Funds to find the objective comments of an analyst. You should not plan to sell a mutual fund just because of one year's underperformance. But you should keep an eye on it.

# DO consider real estate funds.

Real estate can be an important asset class to balance a portfolio, because it tends to have a negative correlation with stocks. In other words, when stocks do poorly, as in times of inflation, real estate does well. However, most pros have been unhappy with the vehicles available to invest in it. For example, the real estate limited partnerships sold so actively in the mid 1980s burned a lot of investors when Congress changed the tax rules.

Real Estate Investment Trusts, or REITs (pronounced "reets"), are companies that are traded on stock exchanges and that manage portfolios of real estate. Some, called equity REITs, buy real estate and pass on income and capital gains to shareholders. Others, called mortgage REITs, lend money to developers and pass on interest income to shareholders. Some REITs mix the two.

Until recently, the mutual fund industry has not had much to offer in the way of real estate funds. The Fidelity Real Estate Investment Portfolio, set up in 1985, is the oldest and largest fund. But recently companies such as CGM, Crabbe Huson, and Selected/Venture Advisers have offered new funds.

These funds have a low correlation with stocks, as measured by a tool called r-squared *(see page 88)*. The average real estate fund has an r-squared of 13.8 to the S&P 500 and an r-squared of 8.6 against the Lehman Brothers Aggregate index. "These are really tiny numbers and show a strong negative correlation," says Jim Raker, a Morningstar analyst. And real estate funds are not particularly volatile. One of the things that prevents volatility is their income. REITs are required to pay out 95 percent of their net income to shareholders.

Although real estate funds are one logical choice for a portion of your portfolio that provides an inflation hedge, picking a fund from the dozen or so offerings has not been an easy task. In 1995, Morningstar took note of the funds as a subset important enough to deserve its own category. That will make picking one from the group easier.

Many financial planners use real estate as an asset class. An early favorite was Cohen & Steers Realty. But many planners believe that fund is now too large. Lou Stanasolovich, a planner in Pittsburgh, prefers Cohen & Steers Special Equity, Heitman Real Estate, Longleaf Partners Realty, and CGM Realty.

Planners look for pure REITs rather than funds that mix REITs with construction stocks and other securities that would do well when the real estate market booms. As the demand for REITs grows, that is becoming more difficult to do. For example, when Kim Redding, REIT portfolio manager at American Century, spoke to a group of financial planners at the beginning of 1998, he told them that many REITs are adding real estate operating companies to their holdings. That makes them look less like real estate and more like a stock.

Although some investors buy the REITs themselves, financial planners typically use the mutual funds. For example, Deena Katz, a financial planner in Coral Gables, Florida, says, "I buy real estate mutual funds instead of REITs for the same reason I buy stock mutual funds instead of stocks: I want a diversified portfolio."

Note: Not everyone agrees that REITs are a separate asset class. Some investors worry that because REITs are relatively new and are growing so rapidly, the comparative performance figures are skewed. Barry Vinocur, editor of the *Realty Stock Review*, views REITs as a sector, like technology or health care. But he still considers them a good investment.

# DON'T stick with a bond fund that is maintaining its payout by returning your principal.

There was a time when investing in bonds was straightforward. You invested your principal—say $1,000—at a set interest rate of perhaps 5 percent and collected $50 a year in interest income. The value of the bond might change between the time you purchased it and maturity. But that didn't matter to you unless you wanted to sell it. If you held on until maturity, you got your $1,000 back.

Bond funds have changed all that. When interest rates rise, the value of bonds in the fund declines. Bond fund managers may not hold the bonds until maturity, so they may not get the full principal back. These complications can plague the best of funds.

But some bond funds virtually guarantee that you won't get your whole principal back at bond maturity because they juice up the income payments by returning a portion of your principal. Here's how that works. Suppose you are a retiree who invests $100,000 in a bond fund that is paying out 7 percent. You need this money to live on, so you elect to take the income in quarterly checks, receiving about $1,750 each quarter.

Remember that a bond fund is different from an individual bond. It does not have a maturity or a set interest rate. Income is determined by changing conditions in the bond market and in the value of the bonds in the fund. Suppose bond market conditions change and the fund generates less income. The fund should pay you less, right? That's what the best of them do. But many funds—including some of the largest ones—continue to pay the same $1,750, bolstering the decreased income with a portion of your principal.

The problem for you, the retiree, is that you are

spending what you believe to be income. Only when you cash in your bond fund do you discover that you have spent some of your principal. To determine how common the practice is, John Rekenthaler at Morningstar Mutual Funds studied bond funds over two periods. One started November 1, 1986 and the other October 1, 1991; both ended September 30, 1994.

The periods were selected because interest rates were similar at their beginnings and ends, and so they represented what Rekenthaler called a "neutral" environment. When interest rates rise and fall, the underlying value of bonds in a fund rises and falls, too, sending the NAV up and down. But with steady rates, in theory, a fund's net asset value should be about the same at the beginning and end of the period. In practice, investors who spent their distributions during those periods lost about 1 percent a year. Many lost more than twice that.

Unfortunately, it is very difficult to determine which funds are paying out principal. "It is simply not possible to understand a fund's accounting practices from its publicly available documents," Rekenthaler says.

He did identify nine bond funds that did a good job of preserving principal: Federated Intermediate, Benham Treasury Note, Vanguard F/I Long Treasury, Columbia Fixed-Income, Scudder Income, Vanguard F/I Long Corporate, Strong Government Securities, Princor Government Securities, and Fidelity Mortgage Securities.

One good way to select a bond fund, though, is to check the expenses. Rekenthaler suggests that investors who wish to use bond funds stick with funds that have low expenses. Expenses are particularly critical for bond funds. A fund with high expenses is more likely to turn to accounting tricks to boost payout. "Those who purchase a fund with an expense ratio of less than 0.5 percent can rest fairly secure that the fund will pay out just what it earns," Rekenthaler says.

## DO consider a "fund of funds" for a specific purpose like a college account.

A fund of funds is one mutual fund that invests in a number of other funds, providing an entire portfolio in a single fund, sometimes for an investment as low as $500. Too bad, then, that most of them are not worth considering.

During the 1920s, the fund-of-funds concept was used to create confusing layers of funds that allowed the managers to take the money while the investors weren't looking. Likewise, Bernard Cornfield set up an investment vehicle called the Fund of Funds—in capital letters—in the 1960s, which made millions for the managers at the expense of the investors. Because multifund investing has such a checkered past, the SEC looks very carefully at new proposals for such funds. Those introduced are carefully scrutinized. But they are not necessarily good investments.

Three good ones are Vanguard STAR, Spectrum Growth, and Spectrum Income.

The advantage of these multifunds is instant diversification. You probably know by now that one fund does not provide adequate diversification. A fund of funds spreads your money across six to 10 funds.

The disadvantage is high fees. In most cases, you pay two layers of management fees. First you pay the fees for the funds themselves, then you pay another manager to assemble the group of funds. Consider the Righttime Fund, set up in 1985 to invest in other mutual funds. The fund initially had expenses of 3.19 percent, more than twice that of the average stock fund. Although the expenses have trended down over time, they are still in the 2.5 percent range. Worse yet, the fund's performance rarely beats the S&P 500 Index. You would be better off in a low-cost S&P index fund.

Similarly, in 1995, Robert Markman, a Minneapolis money manager, set up three MultiFund Trust funds, each with a different objective: conservative growth, moderate growth, and aggressive growth. Markman said he would cap his own management fee at 95 basis points. But that still cuts nearly 1 percentage point off the returns you could get by investing in the funds directly.

That's not to say that either Righttime or Markman funds are doing anything sneaky. Of course they're not. They've been examined by the SEC and passed muster. It's simply that they cost too much, just like many other mutual fund strategies. The bottom line is, if you plan to build a portfolio of funds yourself, you do not need a fund of funds. If you can't bear to pick your own funds or if you have a single purpose, such as a college account, that you don't want to spend time with or that is too small to diversify properly, you might be well served by these:

◆ **Vanguard STAR fund, which is made up of nine Vanguard stock, bond, and money market funds, is a very steady performer with low volatility.** Equally important, Vanguard does not add a second layer of expenses. You pay only the underlying expenses of the funds.

◆ **T. Rowe Price took the concept one step further with Spectrum Growth and Spectrum Income.** Growth invests in six stock funds, including an international one. Income invests in seven income funds, which are spiced up by an international bond fund, an equity income fund, an emerging market bond fund, and a junk bond fund. These funds do not add a second layer of fees. Their advantage over STAR is the inclusion of foreign funds and the opportunity to pick either growth or income—or to put both together. The income fund is also a good choice for a mostly stock portfolio that needs a little income exposure. Indeed T. Rowe bills the income fund as "the only bond fund you need," and that's not far from the truth.

# DON'T stick with a fund if the manager doesn't.

You should always be on the lookout for change at a fund that you own or one that you are considering. If the portfolio manager leaves, you leave, too—with him, if you can. A fund's track record belongs to the portfolio manager, not to the fund. There is no reason whatsoever to stick with a new manager.

One notable exception is a fund that has a true committee approach, with no one lead manager. Dodge & Cox is one good example of that strategy. Another is the American Funds group, which sponsors funds like Washington Mutual and Growth Company of America. If you invest with either of these fund groups, chances are you don't even know the name of the fund manager or how long he's been with the fund. These companies have decided that continuity, discipline, and method are key.

But at most funds, the portfolio manager is the star. Can you imagine PBHG without Gary Pilgrim? Brandywine without Foster Friess? How about Mutual Shares without Michael Price? The reason investors stick with a fund when the manager leaves is that it represents to them a brand name, like KitchenAid or Whirlpool. Some investors worry: what if I sell and the fund continues to outperform? Forget about that. When the manager leaves, you are buying a new fund. Unless the manager who takes over is a proven winner, you can do better elsewhere.

Even if the fund company replaces the departing manager with a big name, tread carefully. For example, when Elizabeth Bramwell left Gabelli Growth in 1994, Mario Gabelli took over the fund himself. Not to worry with a manager like Gabelli, right? Actually, Gabelli is a value manager, and the fund Bramwell managed was set up as a growth fund, so it was a poor fit. In 1995, after mediocre results, Gabelli found a new manager for the growth fund.

A fund typically stumbles during the first year under a new manager even if he is great, chiefly because the new manager is forced to clean out the portfolio to set it up to match his own style. But sometimes change creates opportunities. When Donald Yacktman left Selected American Shares to set up the Yacktman Fund in 1992, loyal fans moved along with him, eager to get in on the ground floor with a tested manager.

In this case, there was reason to take a second look at Selected American Shares, too. After two different interim managers in a short time, the management company assigned Shelby Davis, a portfolio manager who had built a stellar record at New York Venture, to the fund. New York Venture has a 4.75 percent sales charge; Selected American Shares is a no-load. That allowed careful observers their first opportunity to get Davis's management without paying a load.

Investment pros follow the careers of top managers to see when they might get such an opportunity. For example, Don Phillips, Morningstar's CEO, watched Martin Whitman develop a unique value or "vulture" investment style, picking at securities that no one else would touch. When Whitman opened Third Avenue Value Fund in 1990, Phillips jumped at the opportunity to invest with him. By the end of that year, Whitman added a sales charge to the fund. Then in 1995, he removed the load again, creating another window of opportunity.

One final note here: When Shelby Davis retired from Selected American and New York Venture in 1997, many savvy shareholders did *not* leave those funds because they had confidence that his son, Christopher Davis, who took over the funds, had learned his lessons well and that the funds would continue to be good investments. It didn't hurt that the Davis family money is invested in the funds, either.

# DO rebalance.

Once you've considered your goals and carefully put together a portfolio, including different types of funds, is your work is finished? Not quite. Even if you are a buy-and-hold investor (and you should be), your portfolio has to be tended. Think of it as weeding a garden. You've selected the plants well, now you must control their growth. For many investors, this is the toughest part.

If you pick a winner and it takes off, chances are you feel proud of your investment prowess. Why prune it back? Because it's not giving the other investments a space in the sun. When you put together your portfolio, you selected different types of funds that would do well in different market climates. Left untended, your portfolio will grow toward the market sector with the best recent performance.

Want a simplistic example? Suppose you have 50 percent in an S&P index fund, 25 percent in a small-cap fund, and 25 percent in an international fund. If international funds doubled last year while U.S. stocks had a pretty miserable year, perhaps you now have 50 percent in international funds, 20 percent in the S&P index, and 30 percent in small-company funds (because they did better than the larger funds in our example).

It's tempting to stick with your winners. But it is this emotional attachment to investments that trips up most investors. If you understand market cycles, you know that what goes up comes down. International funds, too, will have their down cycles.

Rebalancing—if it is done rigorously and unemotionally—helps you to do what all investors want to do: buy low and sell high. It encourages making contrarian plays because you are selling the investments that have done well and buying those that have done poorly. In our example, the U.S. stocks will have their run-ups, too. If you rebalance, you will catch them before they start to move.

Consider what Brian Ternoey, a principal at Foster Higgins, benefits consultants in Princeton, New Jersey, did with his 401(k) portfolio when his employer offered only two options: a stock fund and a guaranteed investment contract, or GIC. Ternoey, whose specialty is 401(k) management, knows that stocks have the best return over time. So he knows that a retirement portfolio should be chiefly in stocks. But he also knows that diversification is important.

Ternoey put 75 percent in the stock fund and 25 percent in the GIC. Once a year, he rebalances his portfolio. If stocks have had a good year and have grown to 85 percent, he sells off a bit, bringing the stock portion back to 75 percent. If they've had a bad year, he adds to the stock fund to bring his portfolio into line.

The key to rebalancing is to remove all emotion from it. Don't try to guess when it's time to sell one fund and buy another or to redirect your investments. That amounts to trying to time the market, which cannot be done successfully. Instead, pick a date, perhaps the first day of the year, and ruthlessly sell off the winners and add to the losers.

Ternoey squeezed the most out of his limited options. You can follow the same strategy whether you have two investments in your plan or a dozen. You have two basic choices: You can either sell off a bit of your winner and put that money into your biggest loser. Or you can redirect your contributions so you are putting more money into the worst performer. Psychologically, many investors prefer the second choice. Either way, develop your plan at the beginning of the year and then put it on automatic pilot so you don't second-guess yourself.

# DON'T own more than a dozen funds.

If three funds is something of a minimum in order to achieve a diversified portfolio, then 12 funds is something of a maximum. Even an investor with significant assets can put together a diversified portfolio with a dozen funds.

Owning more causes problems in a couple of ways. First, experts say that most investors who own dozens of funds have not thought through a strategy. They simply add new funds as they see an advertisement or read a newspaper or magazine article about a fund. Some investors choose a new fund each year for their retirement money, disregarding what they already have and how the new fund fits in.

The second problem with holding scores of funds is that many of the investments will overlap. That means you will not achieve real diversification. And you will pay more, because you will be paying expenses on each of the funds.

To be well diversified, you want a group of funds that will perform differently in any given type of market. Investors refer to the way funds perform relative to one another as their correlation. If two funds correlate 100 percent, they always move in lockstep. That is expressed as a correlation coefficient of 1, or perfect positive correlation. For example, the Vanguard Index 500 always moves in lockstep with the Standard & Poor's 500 Stock Index, although the Vanguard Index 500 has a slightly lower return, because of expenses.

Perfect negative correlation is expressed as a correlation coefficient of –1. Of course, few pairs of investments move either in lockstep or in totally opposite directions. Most are somewhere in between. But the closer their correlation coefficient is to 1, the more they move together. Investment professionals consider investments with a correlation coefficient higher than .75 to have a high positive correlation. Such investments would not be used together in a portfolio because there is too much overlap between them.

Most individual investors are not familiar with the concept of correlation. They buy a group of well-known funds believing they have achieved good diversification. What they don't know is that large funds are all likely to hold the same well-known stocks that are touted by research reports. So an investor might buy a group of 10 funds, spreading them out among different fund companies, and still have done little to diversify.

Let's take a look at how a group of well-known funds correlate with one another. A correlation coefficient measures the movement of two investments relative to one another, not to an entire group. Consider the correlation of several other large funds to the Janus Fund for the period of March 1990 to March 1995:

| | |
|---|---|
| Fidelity Asset Manager | **.79** |
| Fidelity Contrafund | **.96** |
| Fidelity Growth & Income | **.95** |
| Fidelity Magellan | **.89** |
| Fidelity Puritan | **.70** |
| American Century/ | |
| Twentieth Century Ultra | **.89** |
| Vanguard Index 500 | **.95** |
| Vanguard/Wellington | **.92** |
| Vanguard/Windsor | **.75** |

Clearly, in terms of diversification, none of these funds would make a particularly good match with Janus. Nor would owning all 10 of them give you much more diversification than owning Janus alone.

The high correlation between Janus and the Vanguard Index 500 is interesting, too. It raises the question of whether Janus adds any value over the index.

# DO use a mix of investment styles.

As you diversify your portfolio, make sure you include both large-company and small-company stock funds and that both growth and value stock-picking styles are well represented. These different styles perform well in different environments.

**Value Investing** A value stock picker attempts a rough valuation of companies by taking apart their balance sheets, looking at their various businesses, and estimating their breakup value.

Some of the best-known value investors are Warren Buffett; John Neff, who retired at the end of 1995 from managing the Vanguard/Windsor fund; Bob Sanborn at Oakmark; Mason Hawkins and Stanley Cates at Longleaf; and Michael Price, who manages the Mutual Series funds. Price doesn't hesitate to buy companies in bankruptcy. He took a big position in R. H. Macy & Co., the New York–based department store, in 1990, when it went into bankruptcy. When the company turned around, Price was well rewarded. In 1997, he took a stake in Oxford Health Plans, the New York–based HMO, after that company's stock had plummetted from 89 to 13 a share.

Value investors, like Price, never buy on instinct, only on the numbers. "This puts a floor under the company," Price says. "If you buy a company that is seriously undervalued, you really can't get hurt too badly." Value investors also typically have a formula for selling a stock. When a stock reaches some predetermined measure of value, they dump it.

**Growth Investing** Growth managers look for companies that are growing much faster than the rest of the economy, never mind how much they cost. They are willing to pay a higher price for a rapidly growing company because they believe the stock price will appreciate much more rapidly, too. Mark Seferovich, manager of

United New Concepts, sticks with small-company growth stocks because he thinks that's where he can get the biggest appreciation.

"The revenue growth rates should be 25 percent or more if I find the right companies," Seferovich says. "The sin of paying too much can be overcome if you're in the right part of the growth curve and you can ride it to the top." Growth managers don't care if a company is cheap. They believe that it's cheap for a reason and may well stay that way.

Of course, neither the growth nor the value formula is a guaranteed success. United New Concepts has badly lagged the indexes in the mid 1990s. Still, as you build your portfolio and diversify, you should include at least two growth funds—one that invests in small companies and one that invests in large companies— and two value funds.

Here are some top funds to consider:

**Small- to Mid-Cap Growth**
◆ Acorn Fund
◆ Baron Asset
◆ Franklin Small-Cap Growth

**Large-Cap Growth**
◆ Harbor Capital Appreciation
◆ Montag & Caldwell Growth N
◆ Vanguard Index Growth

**Small-Cap Value**
◆ Fidelity Low-Priced Stock
◆ Oakmark Small Cap
◆ Neuberger & Berman Genesis
◆ T. Rowe Price Small-Cap Value

**Large-Cap Value**
◆ Clipper
◆ Dodge & Cox Stock
◆ Longleaf Partners
◆ Oakmark
◆ T. Rowe Price Equity-Income
◆ Vanguard/Windsor II

# DON'T buy a load fund without determining that there is something special to justify it.

Numerous studies show that there is no difference in total return between load funds (those that charge a commission) and no-load funds (those that are sold direct over the phone or by mail without a commission) when they are adjusted to reflect the load. The load is not used to hire a better manager; it goes to pay a commission to the salesperson. The most obvious reason to consider a load company, then, would be to get advice on which funds to buy. Many top financial planners consider the funds offered by American Funds in Los Angeles and Putnam Investments in Boston to be the finest load offerings for this purpose because they are consistent performers with low fees.

When you buy a load fund, the commission is subtracted right off the top before your money is invested. If you invest $1,000 in a fund with an 8.5 percent load, $85 is subtracted as a sales charge, and only $915 is invested for you.

Not long ago, 75 percent of the funds sold were load funds. As investors have become more sophisticated and refused to pay commissions on mutual funds, that proportion is shifting closer to 50-50. That means there are many good funds available without loads, and most experienced investors prefer to do their own research and buy those funds.

There are still some instances, though, when you might consider a load fund. For example, Fidelity Investments, which sells its funds directly over the phone and by mail, has nonetheless added loads of 2 percent and 3 percent on many of them. These loads go to the fund company rather than to a salesperson. Many confirmed no-load investors pony up for these funds, even though they may resent it, because Fidelity offers specialized funds that they cannot find else-where. Good examples are the sector funds that invest in particular industries. These funds, which carry a 3 percent load, are often the hottest performers in the market and the only way to make a bet on semicon-ductors, electronics, or the entertainment industry, for example.

Other investors are willing to pay a load for an out-standing portfolio manager. For example, many mutual fund investors paid 5 percent to buy Colonial Newport Tiger because they believe manager John Mussey is the finest stock picker available for the Pacific Rim. It is the only mutual fund that Joe Mansueto, founder of Morningstar Mutual Funds, chooses to invest in. All of his other investments are individual stocks. Even though T. Rowe Price offers a no-load New Asia fund, many professional investors don't think it has the depth of management of Newport Tiger.

One other thing to consider is that studies show that load funds contain less "hot" money, or money that moves in and out. Stability of assets is food for a fund and advisers who help clients buy a fund tend to encourage them to stay put, whereas individual investors typically trade too much.

One fund category where I think it might make sense to consider a load fund is small-cap growth. This is an important asset class and top funds in this cate-gory are limited. Worse yet, some follow a hot streak with a long, dismal period, making the pickings even thinner. Size matters, too—a lot. So you might want to throw your net wider here, adding funds like Franklin Small-Cap Growth as possibilities.

The bottom line is to look carefully at alternatives before paying a commission for a fund, particularly if you are doing the research yourself. Consider a load fund only to get the talents of a unique manager or to get a toehold in an industry or part of the world that is not represented in the no-load market.

# DO look for concentration.

We know that the average U.S. stock fund doesn't beat the stock market index. That's hardly surprising if it contains 100 to 200 stocks. Concentration, on the other hand, *can* provide index-beating returns. It can also deliver more risk, as Jonathan Burton notes in the March 1998 issue of *Bloomberg Personal Finance.* "A big bet that goes bad can bring down an entire portfolio just as quickly as a good bet boosts it," he says.

Still, you want a fund manager with conviction. If he knows how to identify a good security—and he's got some confidence—he should be willing to put some money into it. That translates into concentration in a few good investment ideas. "We find it difficult to understand why you would want the 50th best investment," O. Mason Hawkins, comanager of Longleaf Partners Fund, told me a couple of years ago. "We're looking only for the very best investments, the top 20 or 30 that we believe have the best chance of outperforming all the others." And that's what they put in the fund.

The argument for concentration is indeed a strong one. But it's hardly typical for a mutual fund. As Burton pointed out, the average diversified stock fund has at least 130 stocks. Burton cited a study by professors Lawrence Fisher and James Lorie, formerly at the University of Chicago's graduate school of business. The two constructed portfolios ranging from one stock to 500 stocks. What they discovered, not surprisingly, is that adding securities reduces the portfolio's risk. However, that diversification begins to diminish after the portfolio reaches 16 stocks.

Hawkins maintains that a portfolio can be adequately diversified with just 12 names as long as they're in different industries. "We believe you can get 90 percent of company risk diversified away with 20 names or so," Hawkins says. "It's very difficult to fully understand a larger number of companies. We certainly don't want to buy the ones we don't understand. And once we understand a business and it meets our criteria, then we want to make a big bet on it."

Burton identified a number of top funds that focus in a select number of stocks and also have three-year track records. Several new funds—like Yacktman Focus, Oakmark Select, and CGM Focus—were too young to be included but bear watching. Here are some of Burton's picks that have 50 or fewer holdings:

| | TOTAL HOLDINGS | 3-YEAR ANNUAL RET. | 800 NUMBER |
|---|---|---|---|
| **LARGE CAP** | | | |
| Torray | 46 | 33.9 | 443-3036 |
| Clipper Fund | 20 | 27.7 | 776-5033 |
| Janus Twenty | 25 | 27.9 | 525-7048 |
| Vontobel U.S. Value | 19 | 27.3 | 527-9500 |
| Oppenheimer Quest Opportunity Value | 43 | 25.3 | 525-7048 |
| Hilliard Lyons | 25 | 25.1 | 444-1854 |
| **MID CAP** | | | |
| Gintel | 41 | 28.6 | 243-5808 |
| Advantus Cornerstone | 39 | 26.3 | 655-6005 |
| Oak Value | 25 | 26.3 | 622-2474 |
| Chicago Trust Talon | 20 | 26.2 | 992-8151 |
| First Mutual | 27 | 24.7 | 257-4414 |
| **SMALL CAP** | | | |
| Weitz Hickory | 29 | 32.6 | 232-4161 |
| Wasatch Growth | 35 | 27.2 | 551-1700 |
| Flag Investors Emerging Growth | 48 | 25.5 | 767-3524 |
| Royce Total Return | 50 | 25.1 | 221-4268 |
| Ariel Growth | 33 | 22.6 | 292-7435 |

# DON'T use gold funds.

Not every type of investment is suitable for use in a mutual fund. The idea behind gold funds is to offer an inflation hedge—something that does well when stocks and bonds do poorly. Unfortunately, gold has not proved to be a very good hedge over the past several years.

Here's the story behind gold: Gold has its own fan club, a group of fervent believers dubbed "goldbugs," who think it is the only true source of value and the time is always right to own it. Reality is a bit different. The price of gold was fixed at $35 an ounce in the United States from 1934 to 1971, and individuals were prohibited from owning it. When the fixed price was lifted, the price tripled in two years. In 1974, the ban against private ownership was lifted, and speculation drove the price up still higher, to about $200 an ounce. Then the price fell back to the $170 range until the roaring inflation of the 1970s, when the price of gold skyrocketed, hitting $875 an ounce on January 21, 1980. But when inflation cooled, gold dropped back to the $300 to $500 range.

As this history shows, the price of gold is volatile and unpredictable. Gold is not a growth investment, like stocks or real estate, that increases gradually, albeit unpredictably, over time. In fact, there is an old saw that throughout history an ounce of gold would buy a decent man's suit. During Roman times, it bought a toga. And today, it will buy a decent department-store suit. That doesn't argue much for it as a long-term investment.

Not so long ago, it was thought that gold protected a portfolio against inflation. But there is no longer evidence that gold acts as an inflation hedge, either. A good test of an inflation hedge is whether a commodity increases in value when bonds decrease in value.

That's because bonds do poorly during times of inflation or fears of inflation. During the 1990s, gold did
not perform well during bond bear markets. By the
late 1990s, many investors questioned whether gold
had any value at all. It has been replaced by paper
money as a store of value and by inflation-indexed
bonds as an inflation hedge.

So the value of gold as an investment is question-
able at best. But investing in gold mutual funds pre-
sents yet another problem. Gold funds do not offer a
pure play on gold. Most gold funds are managed to
move in and out of gold-mining stocks and other precious metals as the manager sees fit.

Even if you do like the outlook for gold, investing
in a gold fund is no guarantee that you will be investing in it. Consider this: In 1982, the price of gold
dropped more than 15 percent. But the average gold
fund was up nearly 50 percent. What this means is
that gold-fund managers attempted to move their
assets out of gold to more attractive investments.
That's not what you want as an investor. You want a
pure play on a particular asset class. That is difficult
to find with gold.

Gold and precious-metals funds used as an asset
class to hedge against inflation are losers. So, too, are
their records as a long-term investment. Consider the
10-year annualized returns of the top metals funds
ranked by Morningstar through 1997. They were
erratic, and most were dismal. The top performer,
Oppenheimer Gold, had an average annual return of
.43 percent for the period. The worst fund, U.S.
Global Investors Gold Shares, had an annualized
return of –17.48 percent.

So gold funds simply don't merit your attention.
Every so often, you'll see a story in one magazine or
another urging you to consider gold. Just remember
that magazines have to fill up their pages with something and move on to the next story.

## DO consider natural resources funds as an inflation hedge.

You should not be moving into the stock market when you think it will go up and out of it in anticipation of a downdraft. But you might consider putting a small portion of your portfolio into an asset class that does well when stocks do poorly. Although there is no perfect hedge against inflation, it's still worth looking for something to help insulate your portfolio. Natural resources funds are one possibility.

John Rekenthaler, who is back at Morningstar after a stint in the corporate world, makes the argument for natural resources funds, which invest in stocks of companies that own or develop natural resources, such as paper, metals, or energy, or companies that supply natural resources companies, such as energy-service companies. He reasons that these basic commodities will increase in price during times of inflation.

To prove his point—that this group acts as an inflation hedge—Rekenthaler looked at nine quarters when the bond market had a negative total return. Inflation—or fear of inflation—drives the bond market down. So Rekenthaler wanted to see how gold and natural resources funds performed during the periods when bonds did poorly. His reasoning was this: a fund that does well when bonds do poorly works as an inflation hedge.

Rekenthaler used the Vanguard Bond Index fund, which follows the Lehman Brothers Aggregate Bond Index, as a proxy for the bond market. The Vanguard Bond Index fund began in 1987. Rekenthaler identified nine quarters when the bond fund had a negative return. Then he looked at the performance of the Vanguard Gold fund, which he considers to be a very good gold fund, during these periods. He also looked at T. Rowe Price New Era, set up in 1969 and the granddaddy of the natural resources funds. New Era is a diversified resources fund; it includes some gold. Finally, he looked for a natural resources fund without gold. He chose Fidelity Select Industrial Materials, which invests in chemicals, metals, building materials, but no gold whatsoever, because he considered it more of a pure play on resources. The results of his study are shown in the chart below.

As Rekenthaler notes, there is no perfect hedge against inflation. But the natural resources funds are a much better option than gold, which performs erratically and had a positive return in only three of the nine quarters when bonds were down. New Era did much better, with a gain in five of the nine quarters. But Fidelity Select Industrial Materials, which contains no gold, was by far the best hedge, showing a positive return in seven of the nine quarters that bonds were off.

So if you are looking for a place to put a small portion of a large portfolio—say 5 to 10 percent—consider an investment in natural resources as a hedge.

## NATURAL RESOURCES FUNDS vs. BONDS

| QUARTER | VANGUARD BOND | FIDELITY INDUSTRIAL | VANGUARD GOLD | T. ROWE NEW ERA |
|---------|---------------|---------------------|---------------|-----------------|
| 2Q '87  | −2.21 | 3.75  | −3.45 | 2.14  |
| 3Q '87  | −3.11 | 14.66 | 21.48 | 13.26 |
| 1Q '90  | −1.08 | −3.22 | −7.59 | −1.52 |
| 1Q '92  | −1.27 | 7.54  | −4.02 | −5.60 |
| 4Q '93  | −0.20 | 11.74 | 31.20 | 5.64  |
| 1Q '94  | −2.71 | 2.88  | −6.99 | −1.38 |
| 2Q '94  | −1.02 | 3.71  | −0.94 | 1.95  |
| 1Q '96  | −1.91 | 8.73  | 15.59 | 9.71  |
| 1Q '97  | −0.62 | −4.51 | −3.79 | −0.46 |

# DON'T hold on to a fund that has changed direction.

If you've taken care in putting together your portfolio of mutual funds, you've selected funds that complement one another. Now you want all the portfolio managers you've chosen to do their job. Unfortunately, many of them tend to change direction when returns fall off in their own arena. For example, in the 1990s, many U.S. growth funds began moving their assets overseas to boost returns. By 1995, these five funds had 20 percent or more of their assets overseas: Janus Fund, Strong Opportunity, Twentieth Century Growth Investor, Fidelity Retirement Growth, and Fidelity Contrafund.

Investment advisers dump funds that stray from their objectives. You should, too, if you've taken the trouble to select one fund to do one job, like invest in domestic growth stocks, and another to do something different, like invest overseas. "There are three things we look for in a fund," says Harold Evensky, an investment adviser in Coral Gables, Florida. "Philosophy, process, and people. If they change their philosophy, their process, or their people, we're out."

When a fund company announces that it plans to take a fund in a new direction, that should be your signal to leave. You don't know that it won't work out. But you do know that the fund is no longer doing what you chose it to do.

Look what happened when Ryback Management took over the portfolio of the highly rated Lindner Fund in 1993. Eric Ryback, who had been assistant manager of the fund, said that he would make some changes, namely that the fund would move from small-company stocks to medium-size companies and that it would concentrate its holdings in fewer companies. If you had been a shareholder in the successful fund and liked the role it played in your portfolio, you probably wouldn't have been pleased at that news. But what actually happened was worse. Over the next couple of years, the opposite occurred, according to Morningstar. The fund actually moved to even smaller companies and doubled the number of holdings. It also moved more heavily into foreign markets. So the fund changed direction in an unpredictable and unheralded manner. Beginning in 1994, the fund underperformed the market—often substantially—for four years.

It shouldn't matter to you whether the changes affect the performance of a fund, though. A change in direction alone merits action on your part. So does a request for a change in investment operations. For example, if a fund asks for more investment leeway, including the ability to trade illiquid securities or to borrow to make investments, that should raise a red flag.

Evensky dumped the Strong Funds in 1995 when they requested broad changes in the way they were permitted to invest. He dumped the Janus Fund when it began buying foreign securities. He dropped Lindner because of its request to use illiquid securities. When a fund wants to alter what has been a successful recipe, wise investors get out.

You need to look beyond the individual fund to get a broader perspective of what is happening, too. The fund industry is beginning to consolidate. So be aware that mergers and acquisitions of funds can make a difference, sometimes bringing in a flood of new assets. When the Colonial Funds bought Newport Tiger, which invests in the Pacific Rim, Evensky dropped it, even though he was happy with its performance. He was concerned that the big load-fund group was going to bring too much money into the fund and make it more difficult for the manager to maintain his performance.

## DO leave room in your portfolio for a special manager.

One of the hottest controversies among professional investors in the 1990s is over "style drift" or "style slippage," which means a fund's drifting from one objective, such as buying U.S. small-company stocks, to another, such as buying small-company stocks around the world. Often it's far less clearcut than this. A manager might start picking up stocks here and there in many different asset classes.

Many investment advisers hate style drift because they feel they lose control of their portfolios. Take Harold Evensky, a Coral Gables, Florida, adviser, who is chairman of the CFP Board of Governors. A former engineer, he looks at investing quantitatively. He wants each part of his portfolio in a specific box, such as "small-cap value," "emerging markets," or "small-cap growth." That typically leads Evensky to index funds where the securities are determined by an index rather than an active manager.

But other investors, like Don Phillips, CEO of Morningstar Mutual Funds, feel just as strongly that a talented manager can add value—even if he strays out of the box. In fact, Phillips, who was a literature major at the University of Chicago, picks his funds based almost entirely on the talent of the managers. Although he thinks indexing makes good sense, to him it lacks romance.

If even the professionals can't agree, what's an average investor to do? You should pay attention when a fund changes direction. In other words, if a manager like Gary Pilgrim at PBHG, who has spent his entire career picking small-company growth stocks, announced that he would become a value manager, you would have little reason to stick with him. You know Pilgrim has lots of experience as a growth manager and little or none picking value stocks.

On the other hand, I think some special managers offer something an index fund cannot. There is a place in your portfolio for them. I like the approach of Eleanor Blayney, an investment adviser in McLean, Virginia, who uses indexes for a portfolio's core—perhaps 10 percent of assets. But she still looks for active managers to give a portfolio kick. Even Evensky makes some exceptions. He set up a special box just for Jean-Marie Eveillard, manager of SoGen International, admitting that he couldn't justify it intellectually. "But Eveillard is just a great manager," he says.

Whom does Phillips pick as great managers?

◆ **Eveillard.** "You can't get this kind of talent in an index," Phillips says.

◆ **Ralph Wanger,** manager of the Acorn Fund, a small-company growth fund that looks around the world for offbeat ideas. When Wanger opened the Acorn International fund in 1992, Phillips signed up for a monthly investment plan. After a spectacular 1993, the fund had a couple of troubled years. But Phillips hung in there, and by 1996 Wanger was back on track and Phillips's patience was rewarded.

◆ **John Templeton,** former manager of the Templeton Growth fund, Phillips's first mutual fund, given to him by his father for Christmas when he was a child. Although Sir John no longer manages the funds, Phillips has held—and added to—his stake, which is now managed by Mark Holowesko.

◆ **Peter Lynch,** who established the great record of the Fidelity Magellan fund.

◆ **John Neff,** who retired at the end of 1995 after more than 30 years as manager of the Vanguard/Windsor fund.

◆ **Michael Price,** manager of the Mutual Series, a value manager with a great record.

◆ **Shelby Davis,** retired manager of Selected American Shares and New York Venture, who uses a large-cap value approach.

# DON'T sell all your stock funds when you retire.

How to reposition an investment portfolio for retirement is one of the most important decisions investors must make. You have saved throughout your working years, and now is the time you must make certain your assets will last for the rest of your lifetime.

Unfortunately, many retirees are advised that the best course of action is to sell stocks or stock mutual funds and put the money in fixed-income investments. For most people, that's a mistake.

Inflation is one of the biggest risks all investors face. It doesn't end when you retire. But your earned income does. That makes the risk of inflation much greater for retired people on a fixed income than for workers, who can hope for a pay increase, overtime, or even a higher-paying job. At age 65, you could easily have 25 or 30 years to live—and invest—but perhaps no more time to earn a salary.

Retirees don't have much flexibility in terms of generating earned income. But they do have flexibility in allocating their unearned or investment income. Even during retirement, a good portion of your investments should be in stocks for growth. The average return on stocks is about 10 percent a year; for bonds it's about 5 percent.

If you can leave a good chunk of your money in stocks, you'll have more money to live on in retirement. Money that you will not need for living expenses for five years or more is a prime candidate for the stock market. Conservative blue-chip funds are a good choice. So is the Vanguard Index 500. "Our clients who are in their 60s are still 60 percent invested in stocks," says H. Lynn Hopewell, a financial planner in Falls Church, Virginia.

If you need to receive income from the money you've accumulated, you must move a portion of it into income-paying securities. But they need not be bond funds, which have problems of their own. You could choose a diversified income fund like Spectrum Income, which invests in a variety of foreign and domestic bond funds and in an equity-income fund. Or you might put a portion into an equity-income fund itself, which invests in stocks that pay high dividends, preferred stocks, utilities, and REITs, in an effort to pay out a steady income. Equity-income funds are one of the best-performing groups of stock funds.

In addition to growth and income, most offer a steady, stable performance without much volatility. T. Rowe Price, Fidelity, and Vanguard all offer consistent good performers in this group. Check, too, a relative newcomer, Marshall Equity-Income, which has established a good performance record with low risk in its first five years.

Sheldon Jacobs, editor of *The No-Load Fund Investor,* an investment newsletter based in Irvington-on-Hudson, New York, compiles suggested portfolios of no-load funds for investors at different stages of life. His retirement portfolios contain a healthy dose of stocks, though they are a bit more conservative than the portfolios for workers.

Some of the funds Jacobs has recommended for retirees are: Vanguard Index 500, Mutual Beacon, T. Rowe Price International Stock, Spectrum Income, T. Rowe Growth and Income, T. Rowe Equity-Income, Vanguard/Wellesley Income, and Vanguard/Wellington.

As always, resist the urge to trade too much. Don't sell your stock funds if they dip—or even if they languish in the doldrums. Keep the money you need for income over the next five years liquid and leave the stocks to grow.

# DO check the investment style.

Investment style is one of the most controversial subjects among professional investors. Some argue that each money manager should be a purist; that he should choose to buy a single asset class, such as small-company growth stocks.

The problem is that most managers drift to where the action is. If a manager of a small-company fund sees that the real gains are to be made overseas, for instance, he might start buying foreign companies. There are two ways to look at what the professionals call "style drift": One school says that you must insist that your manager adhere to his style. The other says that you pick a truly great manager—and there are only a handful—and let him choose whatever he likes.

Both arguments have merit. But I think you should still check to see how the fund adheres to its investment style. One good way to do that is to look at what Morningstar Mutual Funds calls its style box, printed on each fund-analysis page. This is a simple grid with nine small squares that shows whether the fund uses a value or growth approach to stock picking or whether its style is a blend of the two, and whether it invests in large-, medium-, or small-cap stocks.

In 1996, Morningstar made it even easier to determine a fund's style by changing fund categories to broad groupings based on investment style. So now, for example, all small-company growth funds will be grouped together. Still, you'll want to check the style box to see how closely the fund adheres to the style.

For example, Harbor Capital Appreciation fund is a large-cap growth fund. That means you can compare its performance with a market index like the S&P 500. Few large-cap funds manage to beat the index over time. Harbor Capital Appreciation is one that has most years since portfolio manager Spiros Segalas took over in May 1990, beating it by 24.20 in 1991, by a little over 2 percentage points in '92, '93, and '94, and just barely in '95. In '96 and '97, though, Segalas lagged the index—by 3 points in 1996 and almost 2 in 1997.

If you were researching the fund, you might want to know how Segalas manages his impressive record. If he is buying small-company stocks or going overseas, for instance, he would be adding risk to the fund to get a higher return.

To help you determine that, check the investment-style history. Harbor Capital Appreciation fund has been fairly consistent since Segalas took over, slipping out of large-cap growth in only one year, 1993. That's what you want to see. What you don't want to see is a fund that moves from small-company growth to large-company value and back. Look to see what portion of the fund, if any, is invested overseas. For instance, the Morningstar analysis notes that Segalas invests more than 10 percent of the portfolio in foreign-based companies. That's information you want to know.

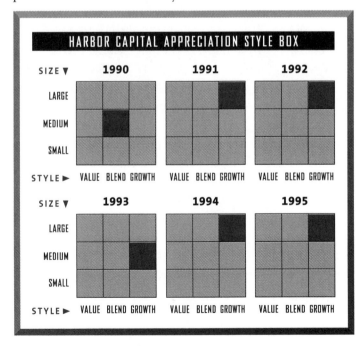

# DON'T overlook "social" funds.

Socially responsible funds represent a small group that is difficult to analyze, much less to put together in a portfolio. Many investment professionals consider them part of the group of gimmicky funds that rely on marketing tricks rather than investment performance to attract investors. That said, if you are an investor who feels strongly about how your money goes to work and whom it helps—and hurts—read on.

First the negatives:

◆ There are just a handful of these funds, hardly enough to make a portfolio.

◆ Performance is erratic.

◆ Many are load funds.

◆ Some use their "conscience" as a marketing tool.

◆ There is no precise definition of what a social fund is.

For example, one fund might say only that it will invest in the more responsible companies of an industry group. That still leaves a lot of room for practices that the purists might object to. Others, like the Pax World Fund, the oldest of these funds and the most austere in its restrictions, will not invest even in U.S. Treasury bonds, because some of the money is used for defense.

That's why many investors—like Sheldon Jacobs at *The No-Load Fund Investor*—suggest that you pick the best mutual funds available and then pick the charities you wish to give money to, and not mix the two.

But not everyone agrees. "Socially responsible investing eliminates a mental roadblock that some people have to investing," says Don Phillips. "Many people—some teachers and artists among them—are suspicious of the business world and see all the evils done by big business. They don't want to be party to that, so they simply don't invest at all."

That was the case with Sarah Carpenter, co-owner of Grandy Oats Granola, a breakfast-food company in Farmington, Maine. When Carpenter inherited money from her father that was invested in the defense industry, she insisted on a change. "I want to feel good about what I do in this world. That means both in creating a good product and in doing what is good for me and for the environment," Carpenter says.

If she couldn't find socially responsible investments that she felt comfortable with, Carpenter simply wouldn't invest. Certainly hers is a valid viewpoint that is shared by others. Like Jacobs, I think that choosing from a broad array of funds is much better than limiting yourself to a dozen or so. That's my best advice. But if you, like Carpenter, will not invest at all if it means some of your money will go for things you cannot tolerate, consider a fund that uses "social screens," which means the managers screen stocks based on some social criteria. But be careful when you do it. Parnassus Fund was a highly touted "social" vehicle until it lagged the market by 31 percentage points in 1995.

Perhaps the best bet is the Domini Social Equity Trust, which combines indexing with a social conscience. Amy Domini started with the S&P 500 and then screened out companies that she considered polluters or those that had alcohol, tobacco, gaming, nuclear power, or weapons interests. "I lost half the S&P stocks," she says. Adding 150 companies "with strong social profiles" brought her index total to 400. "When you eliminate IBM, Exxon, DuPont, you're eliminating companies with lower financial quality than companies like Coca-Cola, Merck, and Wal-Mart," she says. So she argues that investing in "good" companies makes for good investing.

The fund has a very fine record, too. In 1997, the Domini Social Equity Fund was among the 8 percent of U.S. stock funds that outperformed the S&P 500 Index.

# DO vote against fee increases.

As the popularity of mutual funds grows and grows—
and grows—many fund managers and management
companies have lost sight of the shareholders they are
supposed to be serving. One of the pieces of evidence
is the way that mutual funds keep hiking their fees.
What other business could get away with ignoring
economies of scale and just continue to charge the
customer more? We wouldn't pay more for many
other consumer products. But in the case of mutual
funds, many shareholders simply don't pay attention
to fee increases.

So if your fund company asks you to vote for an
increase in fees, vote no. It's a fairly common request
today. But one of the more outrageous instances was
outlined by Edward Wyatt in a "Market Place" column in *The New York Times* on January 15, 1998.
Here's Wyatt's story. In 1997, the Securities and
Exchange Commission charged the manager of the
Parnassus Fund, a "socially responsible" fund, with
violations of federal securities laws, including mis-
pricing a security. Manager Jerome Dodson claimed
the charge had no merit. But he also argued that he
needed to raise the fee investors pay him to manage
the fund so that he could do a better job of complying with the laws.

"I don't look at it as asking shareholders to pay the
costs of our defense," Dodson told Wyatt. "I started the
Parnassus Fund years ago on very limited resources, and
I didn't like the idea of hiring lawyers. So I did all of the
administrative work on my own." Now, though, he said,
because of the cost of the SEC hearings and other com-
plexities of running a growing fund, he needed to put
more money into legal and administrative work.

So Dodson asked shareholders to approve a new
management contract, raising his fee. Under the old

contract, his fee went down as assets grew, which, one could argue, is as it should be. Once you're managing money, adding new money to the pot doesn't cost a great deal of effort on your part. Wyatt went on to discuss the performance of Parnassus Fund in a manner that was quite generous to the fund. In fact, its performance has been spotty. For 1997, the fund gained 29.7 percent, putting it in the top third of growth funds, Wyatt reported. But for the past three years, it ranked 501st out of 511 growth funds tracked by Lipper Analytical Services.

The SEC also claimed that Dodson's management company used credits from the fund's trading account to acquire computer equipment to benefit Dodson personally rather than to benefit the fund and its shareholders. Although Dodson did not acknowledge that the equipment was for his benefit, the management company repaid the money to the fund, Wyatt reported.

Not to belabor Parnassus and Dodson. It is but one example of a fund company asking shareholders for more money. "Mutual fund shareholders rarely vote against the recommendation of the board and the Parnassus board has advised shareholders to approve the pay increase," Wyatt wrote.

That is something that should definitely change. We should all be reading carefully the proposals we are asked to approve. I don't think we should ever approve fee increases.

Sometimes fund companies argue that an increase in fees will benefit current shareholders. That usually doesn't play out, though. Instead, you pay more now to attract new shareholders and then you pay more later as well. Rarely does a fund decrease its fee—that probably won't happen until investors find a more attractive investment and mutual funds begin losing shareholders.

# DON'T ignore the demise of the short-short rule.

What in the world does that mean? And why should you pay attention if it no longer exists? Here's why: This rule prevented mutual fund managers from doing a lot of short-term trading and excessive short selling—or borrowing stock and selling it, betting that the price will recover so the loan can be paid back with cheaper shares. Both of these things can be bad for your financial health. With the end of the rule, experts expect mutual funds to do more of both beginning in 1998. That's bad news for investors. "I think the repeal of the short-short rule will lead to the development of the next round of ill-conceived funds," says Don Phillips, Morningstar's CEO.

As part of the clean-up of securities regulation in the 1930s, Congress passed the short-short rule, which prohibited mutual funds from generating more than 30 percent of gross income from stock held for less than three months or from short selling. But the Tax-payer Relief Act of 1997 eliminated that rule. That leaves money managers free to trade as much as they like and to use the extremely risky short sales.

Stanley W. Angrist discussed the rule change in an article in the January 26, 1998, issue of *Business Week*. Angrist noted that the rule change will give existing managers more latitude and the ability to respond quickly to market conditions. He also pointed out that the change had resulted in the introduction of mutual funds that are more similar to hedge funds. These funds attempt to generate good returns in both up and down stock markets. How do they do that? They invest in stocks but limit their risk—and their upside potential—by investing a similar amount of money in short selling other stocks. As an example, he mentioned the Barr Rosenberg Market Neutral Fund, introduced in December 1997.

Making money in both up and down markets is appealing, of course. But it's extremely difficult. And it costs a lot. Remember that the 1997 tax law also changed the capital gains rates. Capital gains taxes were reduced to 20 percent on long-term gains. But short-term gains—those on securities held less than 12 months—are taxed as ordinary income, and the rate goes as high as 39.6 percent. So the active trading of these portfolios will increase both fees and taxes. A 1998 change in the capital gains law eliminated an awkward period of 12 to 18 months when gains were taxed at 28 percent.

Further, history shows us that doing more is seldom better than doing less. The simplest mutual funds are the ones you want. Look for a fund that does something straightforward like picking undervalued stocks, setting a sell target, and selling them. Funds with too many bells and whistles inevitably blow up.

For example, one of the funds on Angrist's list of stock market hedgers is Crabbe Huson Special. Manager James Crabbe beat the market by 25 points in 1992 and 1993. He did just fine in 1994, too. But in 1995, Crabbe believed that tech stocks were overpriced and he sold them short, betting that they would come down. That year, he trailed the market by 25 points.

Market-neutral funds and others that trade excessively and rely on short selling belong to a category I call "gimmicky funds." That's not what you want in your portfolio. If you invest in stocks, you should expect your fund to go down when the market goes down. Hiring a manager to shield you from downturns amounts to hiring someone to engage in guessing. Lou Stanasolovich, a financial planner in Pittsburgh, expects dozens of these funds to be introduced before the end of the century. En garde!

# DO use mutual funds as a launch pad.

If you didn't think mutual funds were a good investment, you wouldn't be reading this book. If I didn't think so, I wouldn't have written it. But mutual funds have grown troublesome. They're expensive. Many are unreliable. Fund companies are growing arrogant.

Most investors will always have a portion of their assets in mutual funds. Some will use mutual funds entirely. But many investors are beginning to move beyond mutual funds. For instance, Judy Shine, a planner in Denver, creates her own index fund for clients with 10 large-cap stocks. They are: Intel, Coke, General Electric, Boeing, Amgen, Computer Associates, Hewlett Packard, Countrywide Credit, Merck, and Ford.

Shine prefers holding the stocks themselves for several reasons. First, it's cheaper. Second, her clients can control taxes. If they don't sell the stock, they don't realize capital gains and they don't pay tax. If a mutual fund manager holds them, he may decide to sell and force her clients to realize capital gains. Third, individual stocks are great for estate planning. If stocks are left to heirs, they are inherited at current market price and no capital gains are due.

Many mutual fund managers focus on the short-term need to dress up their portfolios and turn in good performance numbers. Their need for good numbers can translate into high costs for you. If you are a long-term stock investor, you can arguably do better holding the stock yourself.

Some asset classes will never lend themselves to investment in individual stocks, of course. Small investors cannot invest in developing markets around the world. Nor can they really diversify internationally by buying individual stocks. Mutual funds work best for these things.

You could make a good argument for using a mutual fund to buy undervalued companies, too. Look at how Michael Price, Bob Sanborn, Mason Hawkins, Marty Whitman, and other value investors poke around in bankruptcies and pull an investment out of the rubble. Most of us won't feel comfortable doing that.

But what about growth stocks? This is where it seems that mutual funds cost the most and add the least value. Suppose you were planning to tuck some money away for 10 years or more. You want to identify solid companies that are expected to do well over that period.

What sectors and names come to mind? Technology and drugs certainly. Perhaps names like Intel and Microsoft? Maybe Lucent Technologies and the Norwegian company Nokia. What with the aging of the boomers and the great leaps in medicine, you'd probably focus on drug companies like Pfizer and Merck. You might look for companies with a monopoly. Boeing, perhaps. And some good consumer products companies like Procter & Gamble and General Electric. We're not talking about beating the index; only about matching it while avoiding the costs of mutual funds and gaining more control.

After the market crash of 1987, I vowed to stick with stock mutual funds and stay out of individual stocks. I kept my promise for a decade. But in early 1998, I began looking at—and buying—a few stocks again. I can't claim to have found bargains. But I did find a couple of new advantages. Investors are no longer penalized with higher prices for buying an odd lot— or less than 100 shares. And they are permitted to reinvest the dividends in most cases, which adds power to the compounding.

Mutual funds will still make up the bulk of my portfolio. But I don't want ho-hum growth funds that buy 200 stocks and then hug the index.

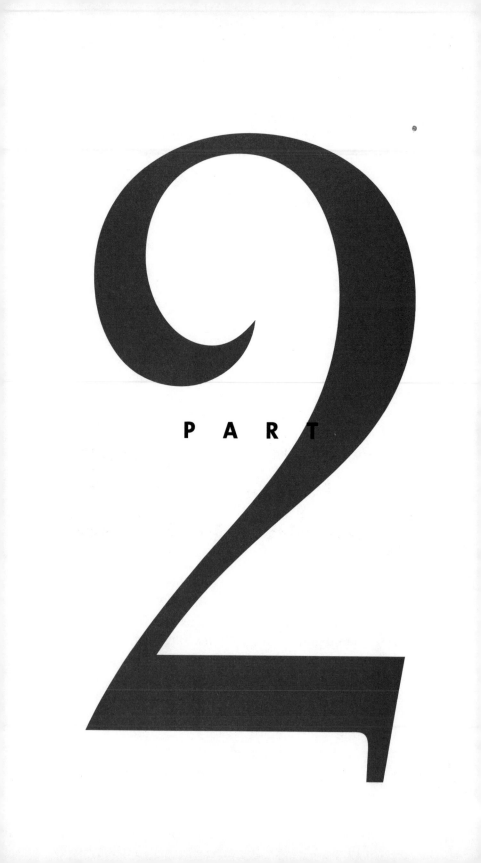

PART

# Building
# BLOCKS

F YOU ALREADY KNOW the nuts and bolts of how mutual funds work, you can skip this section. Most investors do not. So here are some mutual fund basics, including how funds work, where they came from, and why some funds charge commissions. There are also some tips on buying, selling, monitoring, and paying taxes on funds.

More than 63 million Americans own mutual funds, according to the Investment Company Institute, the fund industry's trade group in Washington. Yet surveys show that most Americans still do not know what a mutual fund is or how it works. My own unscientific research shows the same thing. When investors write letters or post questions in on-line newsgroups, they inevitably want to know the most basic things about funds. That's really not so surprising. Most Americans own cars, too, and yet they probably don't know how to repair them. There are some good reasons for understanding mutual funds, though. The best one is that you can save money if you choose the funds and maintain your portfolio yourself.

So here are the basics. A mutual fund is an investment vehicle that pools the money of hundreds or thousands or even millions of different investors and uses it to buy securities, such as stocks, bonds, short-term loans in the money markets, foreign securities, or even gold or real estate. Each fund has an investment objective, which is stated in the *prospectus*. It might be something like "this fund seeks current income," which means the fund is designed for investors who need regular income from their investments. Or it might be "this fund seeks capital appreciation," which means it is designed for investors who want their money to grow over the long term. The fund company hires a professional money manager to make investment decisions, trade securities, and accomplish what it is that the fund sets out to do. The way he plans to accomplish this is outlined in the prospectus.

Each investor buys a slice of this investment pool, which is called a portfolio. Investors share in the gains, losses, and expenses, according to the amount of their investment. Every day the mutual fund company calculates the value of all the assets in the portfolio. Then it deducts expenses, which include management fees, administrative costs, advertising expenses, and servicing fees, which are used to pay brokers and others who service the account. The remaining assets are divided by the number of shares outstanding to come up with the value of a single share of the mutual fund. This is called the net asset value, or NAV.

You can look up the NAV in the morning newspaper. Except in the case of closed-end funds, a fund company is obligated to buy and sell shares at the current price, or NAV, on every business day, although some funds add sales charges or redemption fees. Mutual funds pass on all their gains or losses to the shareholders. The shareholders receive two types of income from mutual fund investments: dividends and capital gains. And they pay taxes on this income as if they owned the securities outright. A mutual fund is just that simple.

Mutual funds have been around for a long time. But 15 or 20 years ago, few Americans talked about them or used them. Mutual funds have exploded on the American investment scene for several reasons. Most important is the 401(k) plan. Twenty years ago, Americans looked to their employers to provide them with a pension. Today they must look to themselves. The 401(k) plan, which is a company retirement plan funded and controlled by the participant, uses mutual funds as its chief investment vehicle. Whether they contribute to these plans or not, most employees have come to understand that retirement is their own responsibility. Add to the changing pension system the growing concerns about the inadequacy of the Social Security system and the uncertainty of future benefits. The result is that nearly every American knows that he or she must invest for retirement. Whether they do it or not is, of course, another question. But mutual funds now have a place on center stage in American life. Go to any newsstand and you will see as many cover stories about mutual funds as about diets, sex, exercise, and politics.

Mutual funds do offer investors a number of advantages. Here are some of them:

**Instant Diversification** No matter how much or how little money you have to invest, diversification is important. You shouldn't keep all your money in the same security or even in the same market. You should have some in the large U.S. companies and some in small companies, some overseas, and perhaps some in a hedge against inflation. You should probably have a little in the money markets. (These are simply short-term loan obligations of governments, banks, and corporations. They include Treasury bills and overnight borrowings between companies.)

Most of us don't have enough money to invest in so many different securities. With a mutual fund, you can get instant diversification even if you have only $500 to invest. That's because your $500 goes into the portfolio, or pool, of money with the dollars of lots of other small investors. Even with a small investment, you might own a piece of 100 different stocks.

**Marketability** There is a ready buyer for your mutual fund shares—the fund itself—when you decide to sell. Many investments, including many good ones, are not readily marketable. That means you can't get your money out when you need it. For example, your house may be the best investment you've ever made. But if you need money to pay an emergency medical bill, the investment in your house won't help. Mutual funds can be sold quickly and conveniently. Each open-end fund is required to establish a daily price for shares. You can redeem your shares at that price and have the money wired to your bank by the following business day. Or you can transfer the sale proceeds from a fund into a money market fund in the same fund family and write a check on it.

**Convenience** You can buy mutual funds by mail and by phone, or from a broker, a bank, or an insurance agent. To make automatic, regular purchases of mutual fund shares, you can arrange to have deductions made from your paycheck or bank account. You can also elect to have your dividends and capital gains automatically reinvested in new shares of the fund. By contrast, when you buy stocks or bonds directly, earnings may sit idle in an account that earns no interest. Reinvestment, and the power of compounding, help your mutual fund investment grow much more rapidly.

**Flexibility** Just as you can buy and sell your funds easily, you can also move your money from one fund to another within a mutual fund family. If you choose to invest in funds through a discount brokerage, you can move from one fund family to another without penalty. You can do the same thing in your 401(k) plan. You can readjust your portfolio and adapt your investments to your own changing needs or to the changing economic environment, usually with a phone call.

**Professional Management** The companies that sponsor mutual funds hire professional money managers to oversee your investment. It's true that investing is more complex today and that many of us don't get information quickly enough to know when to buy and sell individual stocks. Professional money managers can do this for us. They work with teams of researchers and analysts who have direct contact with thousands of companies.

**Variety** There are more than 9,000 mutual funds offered by about 700 mutual fund groups or families, and the number is constantly growing. You can pick conservative, blue-chip stock funds; funds that aim to provide income with modest growth; or funds that take big risks in the search for capital gains. If you're looking for regular income, you can pick from a huge variety of income funds that range from very conservative to those that invest in low-rated "junk" bonds. You can pick a fund that invests in a single industry, in a single country, in dozens of countries around the world, or in natural resources or real estate.

Of course, there are disadvantages to investing in mutual funds as well. Here are some:

**No Guarantee** Your investment in a mutual fund is not guaranteed to provide a specific return. Nor are you guaranteed that your principal won't decrease in value. There is no federal or state agency that backs mutual fund investments, for example, in the way that the Federal Deposit Insurance Corp. guarantees bank deposits. The mutual fund industry is extensively regulated by the U.S. Securities and Exchange Commission, which requires mutual funds to disclose information about their fees, past performance, and portfolio investments. But this does not guarantee that you won't lose your money in a mutual fund.

**Minimum Investment** Most mutual funds require an initial investment that ranges from $2,500 to $100,000, and sometimes more. That represents a real barrier for small investors. To make it easier, some funds waive their initial minimums and let you start with as little as $100 if you agree to make regular deposits of, say, $50 a month. Many funds also drop their minimums for special kinds of accounts. For example, minimums are typically lower—perhaps $250 or $500—for individual retirement accounts and custodial accounts for minors.

**Sales Charges and Ongoing Fees** Another drawback of mutual funds is the complex structure of sales commissions and other fees. Up-front sales commissions can range up to 8.5 percent, which is more than brokers charge to sell individual stocks. Some funds charge stiff redemption fees when you sell your shares, or ongoing fees to cover sales expenses. In response to consumer resistance to sales charges, many fund companies have attempted to hide their commissions and other fees, making it more difficult to compare different funds.

**Keeping Records and Tracking Performance** Careful record keeping is important. Investors who don't keep complete records of their mutual fund purchases may find themselves paying higher taxes than they would otherwise have to pay when selling some of their shares. Also, tracking how well your mutual funds are performing requires some extra effort on your part, beyond just looking at the quoted share value in the newspaper.

**No Local Branch Offices** Most mutual fund companies do not maintain local branch offices. Instead, they deal with customers by mail or telephone from central or regional service centers. Even funds that sell shares through representatives in your community—stockbrokers, banks, or insurance agents—are likely to have their service offices elsewhere. If questions or problems arise concerning your account, you will have to handle them by mail or phone, not face-to-face.

## WHERE THEY CAME FROM

MUTUAL FUNDS HAVE been around for a long time, at least since King William I set one up in the Netherlands in 1822. They flourished later in the century among the thrifty Scots. At about the same time, the British embraced them. Investment companies, along with the stock market, boomed in the United States in the Roaring Twenties. The first mutual fund, or open-end fund, the Massachusetts Investors Trust, was started in this country in 1924. It still exists, offered by MFS Corp. in Boston. But during the bull market of the 1920s, mutual funds were eclipsed by their sister investments, the closed-end funds. Mutual funds were often used and abused during the 1920s stock market frenzy. For example, some portfolio managers borrowed heavily against the securities in the portfolio. When the market crashed, these funds were ruined.

Their collapse tarnished the entire industry. It also attracted the interest of the SEC, which began investigations into how mutual funds were marketed and operated. The result was the Investment Company Act of 1940, a federal law that regulates the industry today. It requires registration with and regulation by the SEC. The act is intended to provide investors with complete and accurate information about mutual funds and to protect them from abuses. The mutual fund industry today is one of the most heavily regulated in the financial services industry.

The SEC requires that the mutual fund company provide you with a prospectus that lists all the details of its investment offering. You must also be sent complete and accurate information about your investment. The SEC mandates that all mutual fund shareholders be treated equitably and that no major changes in operation be made without their approval. Investment companies must also disclose fees, commissions, and other charges.

The SEC cleaned up the mutual fund industry. And the stock market performed well during the 1950s. But it wasn't until the 1960s that the mutual fund industry really took off. This was the decade when a different type of money manager, with a "go-go" approach to stock picking, delivered returns of 50 percent and even 100 percent to mutual fund investors. Then came the 1969-70 bear market. Investors again deserted mutual funds in droves. But this time mutual fund companies began looking around for alternatives to funds that invested only in stocks. Fund companies knew that they had to offer different kinds of funds for all kinds of market environments if they wanted to prevent investors from taking their money back to the bank every time stocks took a downturn.

One of the mutual fund industry's most brilliant innovations—the money market fund—was introduced in 1971. The money market fund offered a safe, liquid alternative to banks. It paid a current market rate of interest. And it kept investors in mutual funds even if they did not want to invest in the stock market. Even though the stock market did not take off again until much later, investors started coming back to mutual funds. Many of them were small investors who had never trusted their money to anything but a bank or a savings and loan.

In the '90s, the chief source of growth in mutual funds came from the 401(k) market. As Americans began to mind their own retirement money through company-sponsored 401(k) plans, mutual fund companies rightly saw this market as the growth area. By the spring of 1998, assets in 401(k) plans passed the $1 trillion mark, according to Catherine S. McBreen at the Spectrem Group in Chicago. Because many studies show that 401(k) participants are less likely to move their money around than those who invest in the retail market, 401(k) plans are expected to be a source of stability for mutual funds.

## WHAT'S IN A LOAD?

THE FINANCIAL SERVICES industry is going through a revolution in the way it offers products for sale. Banks, insurance companies, brokers, and mutual fund companies are all offering the same products. It's up to you to decide what to buy from whom. How do you buy insurance? If you're like most of us, you buy it from an agent. Or perhaps you buy it on the Web. How do you

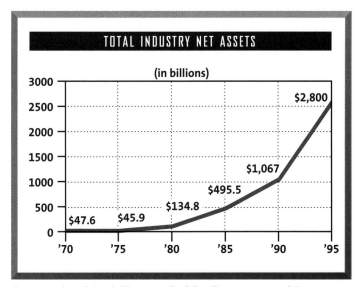

**TOTAL INDUSTRY NET ASSETS**

(in billions)

| | | | | | |
|---|---|---|---|---|---|
| $47.6 | $45.9 | $134.8 | $495.5 | $1,067 | $2,800 |
| '70 | '75 | '80 | '85 | '90 | '95 |

do your banking? You probably slip your card in an ATM machine and collect the cash. What about your mutual funds? You can buy them from banks, insurance companies, brokers, discount brokers, the mutual fund companies themselves, or through your 401(k) plan.

Fidelity Investments, the largest mutual fund company, played an interesting role in the evolution of how funds are offered to investors. Fidelity, founded in 1946, grew out of the fertile money management business that began in Boston in the 1920s. "By 1948, there were about 100 such companies in existence, with combined assets of about $1.5 billion," according to Wiesenberger Investment Companies Services. Most of them, like Massachusetts Financial Services, Putnam Investments, and the Keystone Group, sold their products through brokers and charged investors a one-time sales commission, or "load." Scudder, Stevens & Clark was "pure no-load" from its beginning in the 1920s.

Fidelity began as a load group, offering its funds strictly through a network of broker-dealers. The story of how Fidelity came to offer its products direct differs depending on who's telling it. One source close to the company says Fidelity management became frustrated with broker-dealers' inability to sell its funds during the difficult market environment of the early 1970s and decided it could do better by selling its funds directly to the public. The pivotal event, though, was when Fidelity first offered a money market fund with check-writing privileges in 1973.

When Fidelity presented its idea to brokers, they wanted to know what the commission would be. The answer? Nothing. "The idea was to bring assets back in after the 1973 market crash," says William T. Ryan, a former Fidelity vice president, "not to pay commissions." Ryan says that when brokers rejected the no-load money fund, Fidelity decided to offer it direct. "When the dealers said they weren't interested, we put an ad in the paper," Ryan says. "That was the inadvertent beginning of Fidelity as a direct distributor."

Although Fidelity offered its money fund direct, it was not until 1979 that it dropped the 8.5 percent load on its equity funds. Then Fidelity began to see that it could impose small loads—2 or 3 percent—even though the funds were sold direct, and the money would go straight to the fund company. It began adding loads to its most popular funds, knowing that investors would buy them anyway. In fact, the loads even gave them more cachet.

A story about its Magellan fund, which at its height had more cachet than any other mutual fund, with its $64 billion–plus in assets and strong performance history, illustrates this point. Fidelity management thought too much money was pouring into the fund in the mid 1980s. So it decided to raise the load to 3 percent. The result? The cash inflow nearly doubled. Investors apparently reasoned that if it cost more, it had to be better. And in 1986, Fidelity introduced a new group of broker-sold funds called the Plymouth group (later renamed the Advisor series).

Fidelity is the best example of the blurring of the

line between load and no-load groups, according to Catherine Voss Sanders at Morningstar Mutual Funds. "It sells funds a number of ways: directly to the public without a sales charge, directly to the public with a sales charge, through registered representatives, and through its own fee-based advisory service."

Does this story have a moral? I think it is this: The idea that you "get what you pay for" does not apply to mutual funds. There is no evidence that funds with loads have anything extra to offer.

Numerous studies bolster that insight. For example, Morningstar divided its mutual fund universe into two groups in mid 1995 to study the difference between load and no-load funds. The study obviously found that load funds had a higher annual expense ratio— 1.62 percent, on average, compared with 1.11 percent for no-load funds. It also found that no-load funds are a bit less aggressive, on average, in investment style. As for performance, the no-load funds outperformed in

## BROKER-SOLD vs. DIRECT-SOLD FUNDS

| | % DIRECT | % SALES FORCE |
|---|---|---|
| 1984 | 32.6 | 65.8 |
| 1985 | 22.9 | 75.6 |
| 1986 | 23.1 | 74.9 |
| 1987 | 27.8 | 69.3 |
| 1988 | 28.5 | 68.2 |
| 1989 | 32.6 | 63.5 |
| 1990 | 35.0 | 60.0 |
| 1991 | 34.9 | 59.4 |
| 1992 | 35.2 | 58.9 |
| 1993 | 35.8 | 56.8 |
| 1994 | 40.4 | 51.3 |
| 1995 | 36.9 | 53.9 |

Numbers do not add up to 100 because they do not include mutual funds that are sold in variable annuities.

the short run when the load-fund performance was adjusted to account for loads. As the graph shows, the two groups were neck-and-neck after 10 years.

What are you to make out of this? Clearly, if you hold shares for less than 10 years, you are better off with a no-load fund. But money managers do not decide whether a fund will be load or no load. That decision is made by the marketing people. The fund business is extremely profitable. The more assets under management, the more money a company makes. With this in mind, fund companies structure their funds in whatever manner they feel is most likely to bring in the cash. Many funds have changed from load to no load or vice versa. It didn't change their performance a whit.

There are two reasons to choose a load fund: you need investment advice or you have found a very special money manager who is available only in a load fund.

If you have any interest in investing, though, picking your own funds is very doable. That's partly because there is so much information available, much of it developed by Morningstar Mutual Funds, which started operations in 1984. The availability of infor-

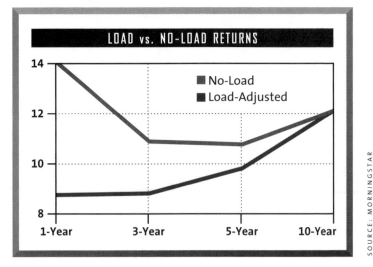

LOAD vs. NO-LOAD RETURNS

■ No-Load
■ Load-Adjusted

SOURCE: MORNINGSTAR

mation and heightened consumer interest have shifted the balance from broker-sold funds toward funds that are sold direct.

## BUYING A FUND

HERE ARE 10 questions to ask before you buy:

1 What are the expenses and fees?
2 What is the fund's ranking within its peer group for one year? Five years? Ten years?
3 Does it have a Morningstar rating? What is it? Has it changed recently?
4 What is the fund's style? Is the manager a growth picker or a value picker? You can check by looking at the "style box" in Morningstar Mutual Funds (see page 153).
5 Is the fund permitted to use derivatives? If so, how?
6 If it is a domestic fund, is it permitted to invest overseas? What percent of assets?
7 How long has the manager been with the fund?
8 How much of the assets are permitted by prospectus to be in cash? How much is currently in cash?
9 How big is the fund? Have assets increased significantly in recent months?
10 Has anything about the fund's operation changed recently—load to no load; expenses; 12b-1 fee; investment objective; investment parameters?

## KEEPING UP

ONCE YOU'VE INVESTED in a group of mutual funds, you'll need to keep tabs on them. One of the best places to get information is your daily newspaper. You'll be able to find out how the stock and bond markets moved the previous day. You'll be able to see what the short-term interest rates are doing and what money market funds are paying. And you'll be able to see how your mutual funds did, as well.

To check on your fund, look under the "Mutual Funds" heading in the back of the business section. Major newspapers like *The New York Times* and *The*

*Wall Street Journal* now provide different information on various days of the week. For example, on one day, the *Times* provides the fund's return for the past three months; on another, the four-week return; on yet another, the five-year average return or the Morningstar five-star rating.

First, find the name of your fund family. Let's say it's Kemper. Then find the name of the particular fund. Suppose it's Blue Chip *(see example below)*. The "x" following the fund's name means it paid a distribution on the previous day. The "f" means it has a front-end load, or commission. The next column, which is headed NAV, shows the fund's share price at closing on the previous day—in this case, $14.01. You can see in the next column that the fund lost 1.6 percent in the previous day's trading. But it gained 29.4 percent in the year to date. That number doesn't mean much in isolation. Check to see how the U.S. stock market as a whole is doing for the year by looking up the Vanguard Index 500 *(see example)*, which on this particular day was up 35.3 percent for the year. That means

| Fund Family / Fund Name | NAV | Dly % Ret. | YTD % Ret. | Sales Chg. |
|---|---|---|---|---|
| **Kemper A** | | | | |
| AdjRtUS xf | 8.30 | ... | + 8.1 | 3.50 |
| BlueChip xf | 14.01 | −1.6 | +29.4 | 5.75 |
| DivrInc xf | 6.00 | −0.5 | +17.4 | 4.50 |
| DremHiRet xf | 20.78 | −1.5 | +42.0 | 5.75 |
| GlobInc xf | 9.52 | +0.1 | +19.6 | 4.50 |
| **Vanguard Index** | | | | |
| 500 | 57.39 | −1.5 | +35.3 | NL |
| Balanced | 12.78 | −1.2 | +26.2 | NL |
| ExtMkt | 23.76 | −2.1 | +28.3 | NL |
| Growth | 13.93 | −1.6 | +37.2 | NL |
| Inst | 57.79 | −1.5 | +35.5 | NL |

your Kemper Blue Chip fund is lagging the index. The
final column shows that the sales charge is 5.75 percent for the Kemper fund. The "NL" for the Vanguard
fund means it is no-load.

You already know that the net asset value is akin to
the price per share of a stock. It is a figure that is recal-
culated daily by toting up the value of all the assets in
the fund, subtracting the expenses, and then dividing
the result by the number of shares in the fund.

Changes in the NAV might show you if the value of
the underlying assets is increasing or decreasing. But
there are other reasons for the share price to change
*(see page 66)*.

The NAV may drop when the fund declares a distribution of dividends or capital gains, or when it
declares a split or dividend. This does not mean that
your investment's value will drop. Instead, you will
have more shares. When a fund makes a capital gains
distribution, an "x" or "e" will appear after its name in
the fund table. A stock dividend or split is indicated by
an "s." After a distribution, you will receive a new statement. To figure the value of your investment, take the
new NAV and multiply it by the number of shares you
now have.

Example: Your statement shows you have 252.301
shares. The newspaper shows that your fund is trading
at $15.22 per share.

$$252.301 \times 15.22 = \$3,840.02$$

Pay attention to the letters that pertain to sales
charges and other fees, such as a 12b-1 plan. These
plans make use of assets from the fund to pay for distribution and marketing charges. They might be used
for advertising or to pay additional compensation to
salespeople. Either way, the money comes out of the
fund before you receive your earnings.

An "r" means that the fund has some kind of

redemption fee. That means that when you sell your shares, the fund company charges you 1 percent or 2 percent. For example, let's say you invested $10,000 in a fund, left it there for 10 years, and saw it grow to $25,000. If you want to take your money out and the fund has a 1 percent redemption fee, $250 will be deducted before you receive your balance. In many newspapers, a "t" means the fund has both a 12b-1 plan and a redemption fee.

If you've chosen good funds and you're investing for the long term, you don't need to check on your funds every day. And you shouldn't be concerned if the net asset value drops a bit. Nor should you plan to sell if it gains a few cents. If you've done your homework, you should understand that the markets move up and down from day to day and that different factors affect their performance.

But you do want to check from time to time to see that your fund is meeting its objectives. Looking at the daily price is not the way to do that. A better time to check up on your funds is each quarter, when the quarterly statistics are published in newspapers and magazines.

Look at the total return on your funds. Compare it with a couple of benchmarks. You might be interested in how the return of a large-company stock fund compares with that of the Standard & Poor's 500 Stock Index. If it is consistently below the index, you may as well buy an index fund and save money. But if you've diversified carefully, your funds are probably more specialized. You want to know how they performed compared with their peer groups.

## SELLING DOS AND DON'TS

EVEN THOUGH YOU buy for the long term, there does come a time to sell. Here are 10 tips:

**DO** sell when it's clear that the fund is no longer doing what you bought it to do. I bought Pennsylvania Mutual

Fund in 1990 because I wanted a small-company value fund and it was one of the most highly regarded. It did not do well that year, which was a bad year for small-cap stocks. I held on. The following three years, its returns were quite respectable by absolute standards. But it underperformed other small-company funds. By 1994, I had decided that it was not performing the role of a small-cap value fund, and I sold it.

**DON'T** set a "target price" to sell. This is a strategy that many investors use with stocks, buying when the stock hits a low and then selling when it hits a target price. Some investors do the same thing with mutual funds, believing that the fund has "peaked out." But mutual funds don't work that way. The portfolio manager is using his own buy/sell discipline. If you did your job right, you researched the fund. Then you should buy and hold.

**DO** sell when you're within three years of needing your money. For example, if you've saved money for your child's college education, begin to move out of stocks and into cash three years before you will need it for tuition.

**DON'T** sell when the market declines. Expect the market to move up and down.

**DO** sell when the portfolio manager leaves. For example, when John Neff retired at the end of 1995 after nearly 35 years as manager of Vanguard/Windsor, Vanguard rightly pointed out that his successor, Charles Freeman, had 20 years' experience on the fund and the transition would be smooth. Nonetheless, as an investor, I would have sold Windsor when Neff left.

**DON'T** sell on impulse. If you are becoming disenchanted with one of your funds, do some research. Compare its return with other funds in its group and with a suitable index. Read the Morningstar analysis. Try to determine if the manager had a temporary streak of bad luck.

**DO** sell if the fund changes the investing rules and you're not comfortable with the new ones.

**DON'T** sell a diversified stock fund because you think it's about to end a hot streak. A diversified stock fund should be a long-term hold. This advice does not apply to a sector fund. Industry sectors go in and out of favor. Investors who use them must be able to estimate when sectors will take off and decline.

**DO** sell if the fund moves into a different type of security and you already have another fund in that area.

**DON'T** sell when the Morningstar rating goes down. The rating may well have to do with the performance of the entire class of assets. If it is a class you want in your portfolio, hold tight.

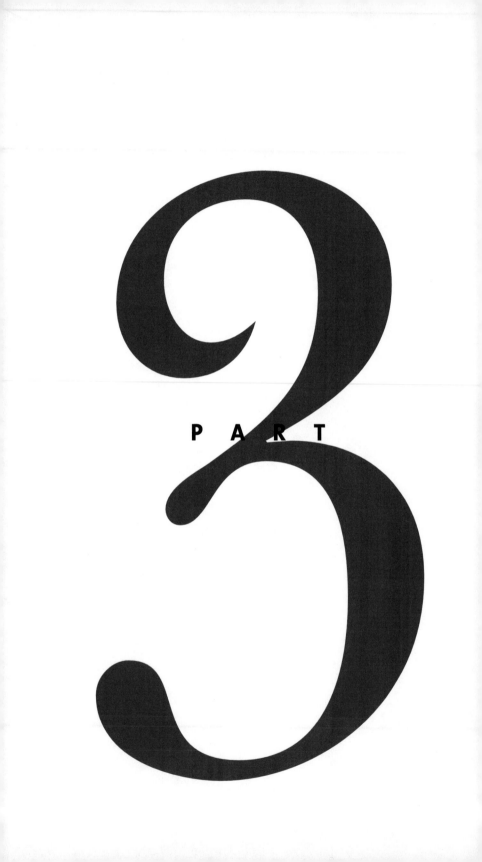

PART

3

# Risk and Asset
# ALLOCATION

OW MANY TIMES have you read that earning a good return is important, but not as important as being able to sleep at night? Investment guides typically advise you that feeling comfortable with investing is as important as earning a good return. I think that lets investors off the hook without doing their homework. Those who don't want to learn about investing can simply claim they have a low tolerance for risk.

The truth is that no one wants to lose money. Inexperienced investors see risk in very simple terms: If I invest $10,000, will I get my $10,000 back? If there is a chance that they might lose some of it, the risk is too great. For them, that's it for determining risk tolerance. And that limits those people to a handful of investments such as Treasury bills and money market funds.

But that's far too simplistic. Every one of us would like to put our money into something that is guaranteed and still grows at 15 to 20 percent a year. That's simply not possible. Instead, you must weigh all of the different types of risks you face with your money—including the risk that you won't have enough if you don't make some prudent investments. That's because money has to *grow* to beat the risk of inflation. So, if your risk tolerance is too low for your own financial good, you must do something to increase it. Perhaps learning more about investing might help. Or making a few small investments to get comfortable with the idea of putting money in stocks.

Risk tolerance is still a fuzzy concept even among investment professionals. But professionals are busily immersed in a hot new specialty area of economics called behavioral finance. I have spent the past several months doing research on behavioral finance for a book I'm working on for Bloomberg Press. And I think there are some nuggets of wisdom here for novice investors that might shed some light on risk tolerance. So bear with me for a brief rundown on some of the issues.

To understand behavioral finance, we have to take a step backward to what the economists call standard finance. Standard finance assumes that people act in a rational way to achieve what is in their own best interest. Now on the face of it, that seems to make sense. The problem is with how the economists define rational. Their idea of rationality assumes that we all know a great deal more about finance than we do. It also assumes that we ignore issues of fairness and many other emotions that motivate most people.

Let me give you just one example. Suppose you and John are asked by an economist to participate in an experiment. You are told that you are to split $100 between yourself and John in a manner that will be acceptable to John. If John accepts your split of the hundred bucks, you and John keep the money. If John turns down your offer, the economist keeps the $100. What do you offer John? Well, I read about this experiment, or "game" as the economists call it, when I first began researching behavioral finance. It looked like an easy problem to me. Are you ready with your answer? The correct answer is: You offer John one penny. If John is a rational man, he will take the penny, realizing that that is more than he otherwise would have had. And, of course, since you are a rational person, you are offering him only a penny. Why should you offer him any more than you have to if you are acting in your own best interest? Well, I was totally bowled over by this game. I suspect most people would just give John $50. Both you and John would be better off. And it would be fair. So this is what the economists consider rational.

Over the past several years, a group of economists

has begun to poke holes in standard finance. These behavioral economists argue that people are not rational with their money; that there are many anomalies in the way they invest. Well, anyone of us who is not a mathematician or an economist could have told them that some time ago. But their studies provide something of value. Because economists look at the irrational ways we invest from an objective point of view and group them into certain patterns, looking at behavioral finance can teach us something about our mistakes.

Much of the work in behavioral finance has to do with the irrational way investors view risk. For example, Dr. Amos Tversky, a pioneer in the field who died in 1996, along with Dr. Daniel Kahneman at Princeton University, described what they called "prospect theory." The two researchers found that investors feel much more pain when they lose $1 than they feel pleasure when they gain $1. (Under the old view, of course, a rational person would have been assumed to view the gain or loss of $1 equally.) Yet Tversky and Kahneman found that most of us are actually willing to take more risk to avoid a loss than we are willing take to achieve a gain.

Dr. Meir Statman at Santa Clara University has done considerable work on what he calls the "fear of regret." Investors feel sad and foolish when they make an error in judgment, Statman says. I can certainly attest to that. So can you if you've ever bought a stock or a mutual fund based on a tip from a friend and then watched it plunge. Likewise, when you sell a stock or a mutual fund, do you watch the price in the paper and pat yourself on the back if it goes down or kick yourself if it goes up, second-guessing your decision to sell?

Well, Dr. Statman argues that these emotional feelings affect the way you invest. He's right, too. For example, many investors buy a stock and then, if it goes down, refuse to sell it, even if they can see that it may well decline further. Why? It's embarrassing to admit their mistake. It's not just novices who do this. Much of the real damage is done by professional money managers who would rather buy a popular company that everyone else is buying than take a chance on an unpopular one, be wrong, and feel foolish. That's why it's so hard to find a mutual fund manager with conviction and the courage to take a stand. And why it's so easy to find index huggers—those managers who buy lots of the same stocks that everyone else buys. Statman also shows that sophisticated investors—executives, members of boards, securities analysts—believe that the stocks of "good companies," or those that produce quality products and services and employ superior managers, are better long-term investments than the stocks of "bad companies."

Why do we let our emotions intervene when we invest our money? I don't feel regret when I buy a rug or pay a doctor bill or fill the car up with gas. Do you? So why do we load all this passion and emotion into investing? Why do we expect all this romance from our investments? Why do we want to read about what our portfolio manager does on Sunday afternoons?

Now Dr. Statman, a charming man I had lunch with at the Sir Francis Drake Hotel in San Francisco one November Sunday in 1997, does not make any of these mistakes. He believes the only way to avoid them is to buy index funds. For most of us, Dr. Statman's solution is a good one. For all of us, his work and the work of other behavioral economists should help to pinpoint some of the investing mistakes that leave us poorer and sadder.

Most importantly at the moment, how should we be looking at risk? Investment professionals see time horizon as one of the biggest factors in determining risk tolerance. If you have 10 or 20 or 30 years to invest your money, you can afford to be a big risk taker. In fact, you can't afford *not* to take risk if what we mean by risk is volatility or fluctuation in value. To earn a decent return, you must learn to live with some volatility. Even if you don't invest at all, you still take on plenty of risk: the risk that your savings won't grow enough so that you can do the things you want to do in the future, like buy a house, pay for college for your kids, or have a comfortable retirement. Dr. Richard Thaler, a behavioral economist from the University of Chicago, describes the perfect investor as Rip Van Winkle. He buys stocks. He goes to sleep for 20 years. And he wakes up a rich man. Try to remember that when you invest. Don't watch your stocks or stock mutual funds every day. Don't be influenced to trade by articles you read on the "hot funds to buy now." Develop a plan, invest, and then play Rip Van Winkle.

Just because an investment is risky doesn't mean it's a good one, though. Some risky investments are just plain foolish. And some people who sell them are looking to make a quick buck at your expense. Lots of people jump at every opportunity to take a risk without even considering whether they stand a chance to do well with the investment.

I don't think people have a "risk tolerance" that they're born with and are destined to live with. Instead, you have a risk profile, which goes deeper than the willingness to take a calculated chance with your money. It includes the type of decisions you make about your job, your career, your family, and where you live. It might include a decision about how many children to have—or even whether to have a child, if you are financially strapped.

Although studies show that the willingness to take physical risks—like skydiving or driving race cars—has nothing to do with the willingness to take financial risk, other types of decisions probably do. Some people make seat-of-the-pants decisions about their careers and eagerly move forward, while others hang on to their jobs with all their might, even when the handwriting is on the wall. Some embrace all kinds of new experiences and refuse to second-guess themselves. Others painstakingly comb through everything that might go wrong if they were to decide to vacation at a different spot this year.

So when you think about your risk personality, don't focus only on whether you are willing to invest in India. Think also about how you decided whom to marry, what kind of house to buy, where you would vacation, and where you would shop.

Equally important—perhaps more important—in thinking about your risk profile are your investment knowledge and sophistication, your financial resources, and your disposable income. You should consider how much time you're willing to spend reading and learning about investments and keeping up with the investments you make. Do you enjoy it? Or would you be happier with something you could simply invest in and check on quarterly?

## THE RISK QUIZ

Here is a quiz designed to get you thinking about your attitude toward risk and the amount of risk you can afford to take:

1 **Your age is:**
   **a.** under 30
   **b.** 0 to 39
   **c.** 40 to 49
   **d.** 50 to 64
   **e.** 65 or over

2 **You and your family have saved for a once-in-a-lifetime vacation. Two weeks before departure, you lose your job. You:**
   **a.** cancel your vacation
   **b.** make plans for a modest vacation at the beach instead
   **c.** go as scheduled, reasoning that job hunting will go better after a good vacation and that your family has been counting on it
   **d.** extend your vacation and plan a real blowout; this

might be your last opportunity to go first-class

**3 You move into a new neighborhood. You:**

a. go door-to-door inviting neighbors to a barbecue on Saturday night

b. watch TV and wait for the phone to ring

c. join a church or temple and the PTA

d. answer an ad in the personals

**4 Your current income is:**

a. under $25,000

b. between $25,000 and $50,000

c. between $50,000 and $100,000

d. over $100,000

**5 You are financially responsible for:**

a. only yourself

b. older parents

c. both children and parents

d. yourself and working spouse, no kids

e. working spouse, plus kids you both support

**6 Your job:**

a. is iffy

b. is secure with good potential for income growth

c. doesn't matter because you expect a large inheritance

d. doesn't matter because you expect to go out on your own soon

**7 After you make an investment, you typically feel:**

a. thrilled

b. satisfied

c. confused

d. regretful

**8 You take a job at a fast-growing small company. The first year, you are offered these employment choices. You choose:**

a. a five-year employment contract

b. a $25,000 bonus

c. a 10 percent pay increase on your $100,000 salary

d. stock options (the opportunity to buy company stock at a set price) with a current value of $25,000 but the chance for appreciation

**9 This statement best describes you:**

 a. I don't see any point in saving
 b. I'd like to save something, but there's never anything left over
 c. I try to tuck away a little whenever I can
 d. I put away 5 percent or more of my salary regardless of other circumstances

**10 You invest $10,000 in a stock that drops 10 percent in value the following day. You:**

 a. put in another $10,000 while it's down
 b. sit tight, because you did the research
 c. sell and go back to certificates of deposit
 d. wait for the stock to regain the $1,000 loss and then sell when you have your money back

**11 How would you describe your investment knowledge? Choose one.**

 a. I am a knowledgeable investor, well able to explain concepts such as standard deviation, beta, and other risk measurements to friends
 b. I understand how mutual funds work, am familiar with the different types of funds, and feel confident discussing the best funds in different categories
 c. I understand investment basics and the major markets, such as stocks, bonds, and money markets, and could explain to a friend how they work
 d. I have only a vague idea about financial terminology
 e. I never get into financial discussions, because I don't know any of the concepts

**12 How would your spouse or best friend describe you as a risk taker?**

 a. foolhardy
 b. willing to take risks after research
 c. cautious
 d. risk averse
 e. afraid of your own shadow

**13 How would you describe yourself as a consumer of investment information?**

 a. I am a business-news junkie, spending a few hours a day

digesting investment information

**b.** I regularly read *The Wall Street Journal* and at least one specialized business publication, such as *Barron's* or an investment newsletter

**c.** I spend about 20 minutes a day on the financial pages

**d.** I watch the business news on television but don't understand much

**e.** I use the business section to walk the dog and avoid business news whenever possible

**14 How far away are your major financial goals?**

**a.** less than 2 years

**b.** 2 to 5 years

**c.** 5 to 10 years

**d.** more than 10 years

**15 When you are faced with a major financial decision, you:**

**a.** flip a coin

**b.** agonize

**c.** call each of your friends and ask what they would do

**d.** go with your gut

**e.** research the options

**16 How do you feel when you suffer a financial loss?**

**a.** I think I am a bad person

**b.** I feel guilty

**c.** I view it as a personal failure

**d.** I see it as an obstacle to be overcome

**e.** I almost never suffer losses, because I don't take risks that would lose me money

**17 Your employer has offered one year's severance pay to the first 100 employees in your division who accept the package. You would most likely:**

**a.** take it immediately

**b.** take it only if you had been researching business opportunities and felt you had a good option ready to go

**c.** freshen up your résumé and start looking around; you can't afford to leave now, but you're not going to wait for the other shoe to drop

**d.** ignore it; you intend to spend the rest of your career with this company

**18 When you buy a health- or property-insurance policy, you:**

   **a.** try to get the lowest possible deductible or none at all; after all, what is insurance for?

   **b.** raise the deductible to save the premium

   **c.** get catastrophic coverage only

   **d.** ignore the deductible and focus on the total lifetime coverage

**19 You are the winner on a television game show. You have these choices. What do you do?**

   **a.** take $10,000

   **b.** flip a coin; if you win, you get $35,000 in cash; if you lose, you get nothing

   **c.** take $25,000 in prizes; you do not know what they are

   **d.** spin a wheel and take the amount that you land on; it could be any of 15 possibilities, distributed equally from $1,000 to $50,000

**20 You put 10 percent of your portfolio in emerging markets because that's where you think the growth will come from over the next decade. Two months later, emerging markets have declined by 20 percent. You:**

   **a.** sell

   **b.** double your holdings

   **c.** do nothing

   **d.** wait until the end of the year to rebalance, adding to your stake if necessary to bring it back to 10 percent

**21 You are buying a home. Your strategy would probably be:**

   **a.** to buy something you can comfortably afford; you don't want to be house poor

   **b.** to stretch a little for the house you want

   **c.** to buy the most expensive house you can qualify for; you know your income will grow, and you don't want to feel squeezed in a couple of years

   **d.** to borrow money from friends and relatives and ask your employer to inflate your salary so you can qualify for a bigger mortgage

## WHAT IT MEANS

IF YOU SCORED 90 or above, you may be a bit too much of a gambler. Prudent risk taking is a necessary part of a good investment program. But be careful to avoid foolhardy risks. If, for example, you answered that you typically feel "thrilled" after making an investment, that is a danger signal.

Scores in the 75-to-89 range indicate that you have a healthy tolerance for risk—and probably the wherewithal to take selective investment risks. If you are currently very conservative in your investments, perhaps

### SCORING

|    | A. | B. | C. | D. | E. |
|----|----|----|----|----|----|
| 1  | 5  | 4  | 3  | 2  | 1  |
| 2  | 1  | 2  | 3  | 5  |    |
| 3  | 4  | 1  | 2  | 5  |    |
| 4  | 1  | 2  | 3  | 4  |    |
| 5  | 4  | 2  | 1  | 5  | 3  |
| 6  | 1  | 4  | 2  | 1  |    |
| 7  | 5  | 4  | 2  | 1  |    |
| 8  | 1  | 3  | 2  | 4  |    |
| 9  | 1  | 2  | 3  | 4  |    |
| 10 | 5  | 4  | 2  | 1  |    |
| 11 | 5  | 4  | 3  | 2  | 1  |
| 12 | 5  | 4  | 3  | 2  | 1  |
| 13 | 5  | 4  | 3  | 2  | 1  |
| 14 | 1  | 2  | 3  | 4  |    |
| 15 | 5  | 1  | 3  | 4  | 2  |
| 16 | 1  | 1  | 1  | 4  | 1  |
| 17 | 5  | 4  | 3  | 1  |    |
| 18 | 1  | 2  | 4  | 3  |    |
| 19 | 1  | 3  | 5  | 4  |    |
| 20 | 1  | 5  | 4  | 4  |    |
| 21 | 1  | 2  | 3  | 5  |    |

you need to learn more. Knowledge is a necessary ingredient of prudent risk taking.

Scores in the 55-to-74 range show a moderate risk tolerance. If you are in this category, you can find good, conservative equity funds that will not generate too much volatility. But increasing your risk tolerance by learning more—and saving more—should be a goal.

If you scored 54 or under, do something now to increase your risk tolerance. Your overall score indicates that you approach many of life's situations with caution. So you probably will never invest in emerging markets or small-company growth stocks. That's OK. But you should learn enough to feel comfortable putting money in the stock market for long-term investments. Start a regular savings program to provide a nest egg.

When you have accumulated a nest egg, set up an automatic investment program where $50 or $100 a month is transferred from your bank savings account to a conservative stock fund such as T. Rowe Price Equity-Income, Neuberger & Berman Guardian, or USAA Income Stock.

## THE RISK-REWARD
## CONTINUUM

MOST INVESTMENTS stretch along a risk-reward continuum from those that produce a steady, predictable income to those that offer the chance—but not the guarantee—of growth. Even if you don't have much experience as an investor, you've probably encountered an "income" investment and a "growth" investment. A bank passbook account is a conservative, guaranteed-income investment. If you take, say, $10,000 and put it in the bank, you are guaranteed that you will get your $10,000 back. And you are guaranteed "income" of perhaps 5 percent—or whatever the going interest rate is—for as long as it is in the bank.

Now consider a real estate investment. Let's say you take the same $10,000 and use it as a down payment on a $100,000 house. There is no guarantee that you will ever see your $10,000 again. But if the house appreciates to $120,000 in two years, you will have a $20,000 gain. Your $10,000 is now worth $30,000 (minus commissions). If you put the $10,000 in the bank, you would have income of about $1,150 in two years. If you put the $10,000 into a house, you might have earned nothing, or you might have earned $20,000, or even more.

Just what are the risks involved in making these choices? For many people, risk is simply the chance that a catastrophe of some kind or other will befall their investment and they will lose money. Even the slightest probability of that happening persuades them to keep everything in the bank, where it is guaranteed safe by the U.S. government. For these savers, investment decisions are simple: which bank pays the best rate? But investors need to know more about the different types of risks in order to make informed judgments. Here are some of the major types you can face as an investor:

**Inflation Risk** The risk that your money will not be worth as much in the future. Inflation is a general and continual increase in the prices of the things you need to buy. The cost of housing, clothing, medical care, and food all increase constantly. Guaranteed investments simply do not earn enough to keep pace with inflation.

**Opportunity Risk** The risk that you will tie up your money in a so-so investment and lose the chance to put it into something with real growth potential. Investors who buy long-term bonds or certificates of deposit face this risk. Say you put $10,000 into a 10-year certificate of deposit paying 6 percent. Next year interest rates go up to 9 percent. But you are stuck with your 6 percent CD. You've lost the opportunity to put your money where it will earn more. The risk with a long-term bond is greater still. You can get out of the CD by paying a surrender penalty. But if you buy a long-term bond and rates go up, the value of your bond goes down. So with bonds, your principal, too, is at risk.

**Reinvestment Risk** The risk that you will not be able to invest your earnings, dividends, or even your principal at the same earnings rate next month or next year. For example, if you invest $10,000 in a bond that matures in 10 years and pays 7 percent, you will earn 7 percent, or $700 a year, for 10 years. But what will you do with that $700? If interest rates drop to 5 percent, you will not be able to reinvest it at 7 percent. When your $10,000 bond matures in 10 years, you may not be able to reinvest your principal at the same rate, either.

Reinvestment risk was a big problem for retirees who bought long-term fixed investments in the early 1980s when interest rates were in the double digits. Rates fell throughout the '80s *(see graph at right)*. When those bonds came due, the money could not be invested at the same high rate. So retirees who had come to expect a high income from their investments watched that income slip away.

Reinvestment risk is a big factor for long-term investments. Clearly, the best time to buy one is when rates peak. For example, in 1982, you could have bought a long-term bank CD with an interest rate of 14 percent.

**Concentration Risk** With eggs (too many in one basket) as with money (too much in one stock), concentration means more risk. Portfolios containing many investments carry less risk than those with only a few, because the diversification reduces the effects of losses or gains on any particular investment.

Mutual funds provide a ready-made way to diversify your holdings over a wide range of investments and thus reduce concentration risk. Large mutual funds

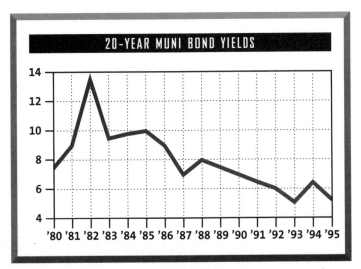

**20-YEAR MUNI BOND YIELDS**

may hold dozens or scores of different investments. A loss on one or two of them will do relatively little damage; conversely, a big gain on one or two is hardly noticed, either.

Consider this example of an investor holding a single stock bought for $10,000 and another who put $10,000 into a mutual fund owning that stock and 39 others in equal proportions. Say the stock drops from $40 a share to $8 after the company's major product is shown to cause cancer. The investor who bought the stock by itself now holds shares worth $2,000 and has lost 80 percent of his money. The mutual fund investor has a loss, too: only $200, or 2 percent of the amount invested.

But what if the company's product were a medical miracle and the stock, instead of falling, jumped by 80 percent? The first investor would now be sitting on an $18,000 nest egg. The second, who diversified the risk by choosing a mutual fund instead of direct stock ownership, would have a total of $10,200.

There are other ways of looking at concentration risk, beyond just the number of different investments you hold. Buying a dozen auto-industry stocks, for example, provides some diversification but still leaves your investments fairly concentrated in one sector of the economy. A big drop in auto sales will hurt your portfolio more than it would have if you were diversified across many economic sectors. The same can be said of geographic concentration. If you buy only stocks of hometown companies, you may find all your investments turning sour at once if the local economy goes into a tailspin. For bond investors, maturity concentration is another important consideration. A diversified portfolio of bonds with a range of maturities, short term to long term, is less risky than one holding bonds of a single maturity. Why? Because its total value will be more stable as interest rates move up and down over the economic cycle.

Mutual funds can help you diversify your investments to reduce risk. But remember, not all mutual funds are broadly diversified. Some are concentrated in a single industry, geographic region, or bond-maturity range. That means they carry a higher degree of risk. If you're just starting out as an investor, avoid them. On the other hand, these concentrated funds—or sector funds—may carry the opportunity of a greater return and may be appropriate as one of many holdings for an investor's portfolio.

**Interest Rate Risk** Changes in interest rates—and in expected future interest rates—can cause the prices of some investments to rise or fall suddenly. When interest rates climb, for example, bond prices fall in lockstep. The reverse is also true: falling rates mean higher prices for bonds.

The prices of all types of investments reflect expectations about the future course of interest rates and thus to some extent are subject to interest rate risk. But the average investor is most likely to encounter interest rate risk in the bond market. If you buy a long-term bond or bond mutual fund and interest rates rise, your investment will drop in value. Should rates fall, on the other hand, you can expect to enjoy a profit as the investment gains value.

These price fluctuations can be dramatic. For example, if long-term rates double, say from 7 percent to 14 percent, the value of your bond will be cut roughly in half. You can sell it, hope to recoup something through a capital-loss tax deduction, and invest in a higher-yielding security. Or you can hold on to it, collecting 7 percent on your investment at a time when the market rate is 14 percent.

How can you reduce your exposure to interest rate risk? Pick a short-term bond fund. They're hurt less by rising rates than long-term bond funds. What if you want to increase your exposure to interest rate risk because you think rates are going down? Buy shares in a zero-coupon bond fund. If you're right, and rates fall, you'll profit handsomely.

**Credit or Default Risk** Credit risk, quite simply, is the chance that a borrower won't repay an obligation. Bankers deal with it every day. You may not realize it, but as a small investor, so do you. Of the $4.5 trillion in U.S. mutual funds, more than 46 percent is invested in debt obligations, ranging in quality from U.S. T-bills all the way down to junk bonds that pay interest not in cash but in more junk bonds.

The greater the credit risk, the greater the interest rate a borrower or issuer of securities must pay. As a result, mutual funds that invest in lower-quality securities like junk bonds offer higher yields than those that invest only in top-quality obligations like Treasury bonds. In theory, this higher yield compensates investors who are willing to take on the higher risk of loss of principal if some issuers don't repay and their bonds become worthless.

Financial experts have long debated whether the prices of various securities accurately reflect their true credit risk. Some have argued, for example, that junk bonds are a great bargain. That's because, in their view, the high junk-bond yields have overcompensated buyers for a level of credit risk that has actually turned out to be low, with fewer-than-expected losses and defaults.

Other experts criticize the prices of high-grade corporate bonds, those issued by large corporations with the top credit ratings. Their prices are out of whack, too, the critics say, not because yields are too generous but because they're too low. For only slightly less yield, these critics say, you can get a government bond with no credit risk at all.

By investing in a corporate bond fund, you get the kind of diversification that reduces your exposure to the risk of one particular company defaulting on its obligations. You can reduce risk further by picking a fund that buys only the securities of big, highly rated corporations. Or you can increase your credit risk, and your potential return, by buying shares in a junk bond fund or other type of fund that invests in low-grade debt securities.

**Marketability Risk** This is the chance that there will be no ready market for your investment if you want to sell it in a hurry. One of the chief advantages of mutual funds is the marketability you enjoy as a mutual fund investor. Your shares can be redeemed at any time at their net asset value per share. If you sell, you can receive cash for them in a few days, or even the next day if you have the fund company wire the proceeds from the sale directly into your bank account.

Moreover, mutual funds provide you with a way to invest indirectly in securities that would be less marketable if you bought them directly. Two examples are stocks of very small companies and mortgage securities of the Government National Mortgage Association (Ginnie Mae). The market for some small companies' stock may be inactive. Shares may trade only occasionally, and a wide spread may exist between the price being offered by sellers and what a broker will pay to take the shares off your hands. Likewise, the Ginnie Mae market features stiff charges by brokers to small investors. Buying mutual funds that specialize in small stocks or Ginnie Maes lets you participate in these investments without the marketability risk posed by owning them directly.

Because mutual funds must stand ready to repurchase shares for cash, their managers must maintain adequate cash holdings and bank credit lines to handle redemptions by any fundholders who might be selling. Funds that invest heavily in less-marketable securities, such as certain types of stock known as letter stock or restricted stock, could face problems if they are hit with a rush of redemption orders.

**Currency Translation Risk** Opportunities have grown in recent years for small investors to buy securities outside the U.S. through international mutual funds. Many of these investments are denominated in currencies other than the dollar. That means the value of your investment will change as the dollar rises and falls relative to these other currencies. For example, a U.S. mutual fund that invests in Japanese securities will rise in value when the value of the dollar falls compared with the Japanese yen. Why? The securities denominated in the now higher-valued yen, when translated into their value in terms of the U.S. currency, buy more dollars than they did before. The reverse is also true. A rising dollar will hurt the value of investments denominated in foreign currencies.

That is one of the major risks of investing in international funds. If you buy a fund that invests in Japanese stocks, you face two major risks: market risk, or the risk that the Japanese market may decline, and currency translation risk, or the risk that a rising dollar will hurt the value of your investments in yen. The dollar began rising in the spring of 1995 and meandered upward for the following three years. The impact on international investments by U.S. investors has been severe. It blunted any gains in foreign markets achieved by U.S. investors. If they had losses, the rising dollar amplified them.

The chart below compares the risk levels of some mutual fund investments.

## SO INVESTING IS RISKY...

SO IS BUYING a house. So is working for a single employer. And so, too, is keeping all your money in U.S. dollars. If the dollar declines against other currencies, your money is worth less. Not investing is risky, too. If you are to reach your goals, you must learn to accept some risk in your investments. For the most part, that means you must invest in stocks. Getting comfortable with stock investing is worth the effort. It helps to understand how the stock market—and other investment markets—work.

In mutual funds, the risk-reward continuum starts at the low-risk, low-reward end with money market funds.

**Money Market Funds** The most basic mutual fund investment that provides income is a money market fund. Whatever you do with the rest of your portfolio, you will probably want to keep some of your money in a money market fund.

Money market mutual funds invest in short-term debt, or short-term "paper," issued by the U.S. Trea-

| LESS RISK/ LESS OPPORTUNITY FOR RETURN | MORE RISK/ MORE OPPORTUNITY FOR RETURN |
|---|---|
| Bond funds | Common stock funds |
| Stock index funds | Sector funds |
| Short-term bond funds | Long-term bond funds |
| Growth-and-income funds | Growth funds |
| T- bond funds | Zero-coupon T-bond funds |
| Multicountry int'l funds | One-country int'l funds |
| Corp. investment-grade bond funds | Corp. junk-bond funds |

sury, state and local governments, banks, and large corporations. So the money you invest in a money market fund is lent to government agencies or corporations. But the loans are for very short terms, ranging from just overnight to perhaps 90 days. The SEC mandates that the average maturity of a money market portfolio cannot be more than 120 days. It also requires that money market funds invest only in the top two credit-quality grades of debt: A-1 or A-2, as listed by Standard & Poor's Corp., or P-1 or P-2, by Moody's Investor Services.

It is because the credit standards are so high for the borrowers and because the loans are for such short terms that money market funds are safe. They can be converted into cash so quickly that they are often considered to be the equivalent of cash. (When investors say that they moved out of the stock market and into a "cash position," they generally mean that they've moved their money into a money market fund.)

Because the investments made by the money market fund manager are so stable, these funds offer a fixed share price instead of one that fluctuates from day to day. In a money market fund, each share is valued at $1. So if you invest $1,000 in a money market fund, you will own 1,000 shares. Because the share price always remains at $1, you know that a money market fund will preserve your principal.

The way you earn money on these funds is through the interest they pay. The interest rate is adjusted daily to reflect changing conditions in the money market. Often these fluctuations are so tiny as to be almost unnoticeable. Still, over time, money market interest rates can change a great deal. In the early 1980s, these funds paid more than 16 percent; by the mid '80s, they paid about 6 percent; by the late '80s, they were up to 11 percent; and in the early '90s, they were down to about 2 percent. In 1998, money market funds were paying about 5 percent.

These are the chief advantages of money market funds:

◆ They pay competitive short-term interest rates.
◆ They are extremely safe.
◆ They are liquid. That means you can get your money out quickly and easily. You can usually write checks on a money market fund, or you can have withdrawals wired from the fund into your bank.
◆ If you use a money market account that is part of a mutual fund family, you can move money from the stock or bond market into your money fund and vice versa.

**U.S. Government Securities Funds** All money market funds are considered safe, although they are not guaranteed the way a bank account or a bank certificate of deposit is. The safest money market funds are those that invest only in the debt of the U.S. government. There are two kinds of government-securities money market funds. One invests only in securities issued by the U.S. Treasury. If you measure safety by the certainty that you will get your money back, this is the safest mutual fund investment you can find. The other invests in debt issued by U.S. government agencies, such as the Federal National Mortgage Association (Fannie Mae) and Ginnie Mae. Remember that we are measuring safety here by the probability that you will get your money back. The difference in safety between the government and its agencies is tiny. The difference between the government funds and those that invest in both government and corporate debt is a bit larger. A corporation could default on its debt. But the chance of that happening on the very short-term loans in the money markets is still small.

Here, then, is a lesson in how risk affects return. Because the government funds—those that buy securities of the government and its agencies—are lower risks, they will pay lower returns than money funds that include corporate debt. The difference might be between $\frac{1}{10}$ and $\frac{2}{10}$ of one percentage point, or what financial people call 10 to 20 basis points. (A basis point is $\frac{1}{100}$ of 1 percent.) So, for example, on a day when the Schwab Money Market fund was paying 5.02 percent, the Schwab U.S. Treasury Money Market fund was paying 4.75 percent. To figure out what this means to an investor in dollar terms, consider that if you put $1,000 in the Schwab Money Market fund (which includes government and federal agency debt, as well as bank loans and other corporate borrowings) for a year, you would earn about $50.02 (actually it would be a little more, due to the effect of compounding). If you chose instead to put your money in the Schwab U.S. Treasury Money Market fund, it would earn about $47.50.

**Tax-Exempt Money Market Funds** Most money market funds produce income that is taxable, just like your salary and other earnings. But some money market funds offer tax-exempt income. These funds invest in short-term municipal bonds or other municipal paper. Municipal bonds are securities issued by state and local governments and their agencies. These securities are exempt from federal tax. Bonds issued by the state where you live are also free of state taxes, and sometimes local taxes as well, if your city has them. Of course, tax-exempt money market funds pay you less income. For example, on the day that the Schwab Money Market fund paid 5.02 percent, the Schwab Tax-Exempt fund paid 2.92.

## MOVING ALONG
## THE CONTINUUM

MONEY MARKET FUNDS are a key investment for most people most of the time. There may be times when you want to have most of your money in the money markets. For example, if you're about to buy a house or make some other major purchase, and you want to make certain to preserve your capital, money market funds are a good choice. But when you are investing for long-term goals, like retirement or college education for your children, you need some investments that provide opportunity for growth of principal. That means you need to look beyond the money markets to the stock market and sometimes the bond market.

**Bonds** As you just read, money market funds invest in the money markets. Because the securities they buy are very short term, your investment is extremely liquid. Longer-term debt securities are called notes or bonds. A bond is a debt, a loan by the investor to the issuing corporation or government agency. The issuer promises to repay the principal at a specific time that might be two years, 10 years, or 30 years away. In addition, the issuer promises to pay interest at a specified rate. These terms are set when the bond is issued.

Bonds, too, produce income. Some investors buy bonds because they need a steady income stream. If you invest in a bond mutual fund, you can arrange to have the income either reinvested in the fund or paid to you in regular checks.

What then distinguishes a bond fund from a money market fund? Because bond funds invest in longer-term securities, they are subject to both interest rate risk and credit risk. Unlike the share price of a money market fund, the net asset value of a share in a bond fund does not hold steady. It fluctuates as the value of the bonds held in the fund changes. For example, if interest rates go up, the resale value of all outstanding fixed-rate bonds will go down, and your principal will decline in value. Because you are taking a greater risk with your principal in a bond fund than in a money market fund, a bond fund should also pay you a higher return.

**Stock** Bonds are the debt of corporations or government agencies. Stock is equity, or a share of ownership, in the company. When you buy stock, you become a part owner. There are no set terms or provisions to a stock investment as there are with bonds and money market funds. The stocks of big, well-established companies like DuPont Co. and General Electric Co. are likely to pay dividends. Dividends are income. But you aren't guaranteed a specific income from a stock. And dividend income from stocks is generally much lower than interest income from bonds.

Small-company stocks, like those in the technology sector, rarely pay dividends at all. These companies plow their profits back into growth and expansion. In fact, remember our discussion about behavioral finance and the seemingly irrational ways that investors put values on securities? Behavioral economists like Meir Statman argue that only an irrational investor would place additional value on dividends. Rational investors understand that receiving a dollar in dividends is no different than receiving a dollar in capital gains. In fact, a dollar in dividends is worth less, because it is taxed as income. Capital gains are taxed at capital gains rates, which are generally lower than regular income rates.

Yet many investors do get upset when a company decreases its dividend. Statman believes that irrational investors put more value on dividends because they use a process he calls "mental accounting." Remember the old axiom about how you should spend income but never touch principal? Well, Statman says that some shareholders buy that rule. And they like dividends because they can spend them as income. As Statman points out, a rational investor would see that there is no difference between spending the money you receive as a dividend and selling enough stock to raise the same amount of money and spending that. It is a difference only in people's minds. But most large, established companies recognize that many investors put a high value on dividends and they pay them.

Many modern investors shun dividends, though. I think here of Eddie Yandle, my editor at *Microsoft*

*Investor*. He looks at companies that pay dividends as dinosaurs that have no better growth use for their money. That's not the kind of company he wants. So Eddie takes the argument full circle. He buys small growth stocks that pay no dividends.

Indeed, the chief reason investors choose stock investments is for growth. And Eddie would argue that a stock that doesn't pay a dividend is a higher growth stock. In general, if the economy expands and the stock market does well, a good stock mutual fund will provide growth of principal. If the stock market crashes, you will probably lose principal in a stock fund. Stock mutual funds carry a higher risk than either money market or bond funds. And they offer a higher potential reward.

Over time, stocks have provided a return superior to most other investments. But they are also more volatile. Think back to the research of Dr. Statman and his colleagues and it will be easy to see why. Investors buy and sell, often on whim. They pile into the market and pull out. They make irrational decisions. That's what makes stocks risky. Still, you should aim to put a portion of your assets into stocks to provide growth. And you should resolve to avoid second-guessing yourself, buying and selling with your emotions, making decisions based on regret or the fear of regret. The longer you have until you need the money, the more you should put into stocks.

There's something else you should consider when you look at the investment markets: the concept of yield versus total return. Yield is an expression of current investment income in the form of dividends or interest. When expressed as a percent, yield refers to the annual dividend per share divided by the price of a share. Total return combines the yield, or current income, with gains or losses in principal. For example, if you own a stock with a dividend of 5 percent and the stock's price goes up 5 percent, your total return is 10 percent. As Statman would be quick to point out, though, another stock with no dividend and a 10 percent gain in its price would actually be worth more to a rational investor. As an investor, you should focus on total return. With a money market fund, there is no gain or loss in principal, only current income. So the yield and total return are the same. But with stock and bond funds, the total return can be quite different from current yield.

Although knowledge of these three markets will allow you to understand how most types of mutual funds work, some specialized funds do not invest in them or invest only in very narrow segments. These include funds that invest in gold and precious metals, in real estate, in commodity futures, or in a narrow sector of the stock market such as high-tech companies.

These funds are more sophisticated than broadly diversified stock, bond, and money market funds. Some of them are ideal for investors with large portfolios who are looking for specialized investments. *(For more information, see Part 4 on strategies.)* But they are not for beginners, who should be working to set up a core portfolio.

**Risk Measurements** Professionals have developed a number of yardsticks to measure the risk of various investments, including mutual funds. None of them is perfect. They all measure risk based on past performance and cannot predict what might happen to an investment in the future. But they can be useful.

The most common measurement of risk—and perhaps the most useful to individual investors—is standard deviation, which shows how far the return of a mutual fund might be expected to deviate from its average return, based on its history. Think of a bell curve with the average—or mean—in the middle, and a wide band above and below the mean. A standard deviation is an equal number of returns above and below the average. Statistics tell us that we can expect the returns of a fund to fall within one standard deviation from the mean two-thirds of the time. And returns can be expected to fall within two standard deviations 95 percent of the time.

A high standard deviation means that the investment can be expected to have wide fluctuations in returns. When you measure the standard deviation, you must do it for a specific time period. By looking at a couple of examples, we can see the strengths—and the weaknesses—of standard deviation. In 1995, Twentieth Century Ultra had a three-year average annual return of 10.14, according to Martha Conlon at Morningstar. The standard deviation for the fund during the same period was 16.75. This means that over that three-year period, roughly two-thirds of the annual returns fell within a range of -6.61 to 26.89. So if we were to rely on standard deviation as our risk measure, we might say: This fund is too risky. The standard deviation is too high. Many investors would not stand for that kind of variability in returns.

But now look what happened when Conlon went back to look at the data for the three-year period ending at the end of 1997. Now Ultra had a three-year return of 24.50 with a standard deviation of 5.27. Using that standard deviation, you might predict that most of the returns would fall in a range between 19.23 and 29.8, certainly a much more acceptable figure. Conlon collected the same data for the Vanguard STAR fund, which is made up of a group of Vanguard funds. The diversification across the stock and bond markets should make STAR less risky than Ultra. And it does. For the first period, STAR had an average return of 9.41 percent with a standard deviation of 5.57. For the second period, the three-year average return of STAR was 21.89 and the standard deviation 1.97. So you learned something. Clearly, STAR offers a slightly lower return for considerably less risk. But the huge difference in standard deviation for Ultra between the two periods shows the shortcomings of using these risk measures as well.

Let's look, too, at the three tools of modern portfolio theory. The beta coefficient measures the fund's volatility relative to the market. Alpha attempts to measure the value added—or subtracted—by a portfolio manager by showing the performance of a fund relative to the risk it took. And r-squared attempts to show how much confidence you can put in a fund's beta and alpha by showing you how similar the fund is to the market. I say "attempts" because these measures are certainly not infallible. But you should understand what they are and decide how much credibility you want to place in them. We'll start at the bottom.

R-squared shows the percentage of movement in a particular security or mutual fund that is explained by the movement in an index, ranging from 0 to 100. So a stock or fund that moves in tandem with the S&P 500 would have an r-squared of 100, because 100 percent of its movement is explained by the movement of the S&P.

So it is that the Vanguard Index 500 has an r-squared of 100. All of its movement is attributed to changes in the index itself. But the T. Rowe Price Japan fund has an r-squared of just 2 to the S&P because this fund invests in Japan. A better fit for it is the Morgan Stanley Capital Index-Pacific. Here it has an r-squared of 73, according to Morningstar.

Beta measures the volatility of a fund by comparing its return to the return of a benchmark, which has a beta of 1.0. A fund with a beta of 1.0 tracks the movement of the index exactly. Any fund with a beta higher than 1 is more volatile than the market as a whole. For example, a fund with a beta of 1.25 is 25 percent more volatile than the S&P. You can expect it to rise 25 percent more in an up market and sink 25 percent more in a down market. If the index rises 10 percent, the fund would be expected to rise 12.5 percent (10 x

1.25) A fund with a beta of .75 is less volatile than the market. You can expect it to get a return 25 percent lower than the overall market when the market goes up and to lose 25 percent less when the market falls.

Beta is neither good nor bad. But it is meaningful only if the r-squared is high. For instance, the T. Rowe Price Japan fund has a beta of .23. But its r-squared of 2 shows that its movements don't correlate with the U.S. market. When measured against the Morgan Stanley Pacific index, it has a beta of .83. So far this is pretty straightforward even for a novice, right? Well, it seems so. Yet even at investment seminars and conferences for professional investors, it's not uncommon for someone to point proudly to the low beta of a particular investment, completely ignoring the fact that the investment is not correlated at all to the U.S. market. So understanding this little piece of information can make you more sophisticated than lots of investors, even many professionals.

Alpha is an attempt to measure the value a manager adds or subtracts. A positive alpha implies the manager delivered more return than could be expected given the risk that he took. A negative alpha implies that the portfolio was not compensated for the risk.

## GETTING GOING

UNDERSTANDING HOW THE markets work should help you feel comfortable with taking on more risk. Investors must learn to take informed risk if they are to earn good returns. Sometimes that means making mistakes in the learning process. I suspect most investors—even those we think of as the true greats, such as Warren Buffett, the "sage of Omaha," who sometimes buys entire companies—make mistakes. I've certainly made lots of them. And I'm sure I haven't made my last one. But the work of behavioral economists like Meir Statman can help us to avoid common mistakes and to strive to be unemotional, objective, and "rational" in our investments. Remember that successful investing requires a plan. It requires discipline. You must be methodical if you are to develop an investment portfolio. Instead of buying this fund or that because you saw it advertised in *The Wall Street Journal*, start with a list of asset classes. That sounds jargony. But all it really means is different types of investments, like large company stocks, small company stocks, foreign stocks, bonds, real estate, gold.

The point of having a portfolio is to diversify. Remember, the investment markets are cyclical. Some asset categories will do better in a given year, some will do worse. The next year they may change places. Professional investors endlessly attempt to qualify and quantify these movements in the market. But the mystery and unpredictability of the markets are what provide their rewards. If the stock market were predictable, it would provide money-market-type returns. So when you set up your portfolio, you must stretch it across different asset classes and then be prepared to sit tight. When one class outperforms, you will have that in your portfolio. You'll have the one that underperforms as well. But they will balance each other out. You must wring out the emotion from your investing and resist the urge to try to move your assets to the current top performer.

That's exactly what professional investors do. Take Harold Evensky, a financial planner and investment manager in Coral Gables, Florida, who also happens to be chairman of the board of governors for certified financial planners as well as an engineer educated at Cornell University. Evensky looks at a portfolio purely in terms of the potential return and the level of risk, which he measures by estimating a worst-case scenario for that particular group of assets. The latest trends, news about hot stocks, sizzling sectors of the economy, or predictions that the market will plunge never turn

Evensky's head.

We asked Evensky to set up model portfolios for investors with varying risk tolerances from very low to very high. He used these 10 asset classes:

1 Money market fund or short-term bonds with maturities of one to three years;

2 Short- to medium-term bonds with maturities of three to five years;

3 Medium-term bonds with maturities of five to 10 years;

4 A large-company stock index fund like the Vanguard Index 500;

5 A large-company fund that uses a value approach to investing;

6 A large-company fund that uses a growth approach;

7 A small-company value fund;

8 A small-company growth fund;

9 An international fund that invests in developed countries;

10 An international fund that invests in emerging markets.

If you have a large portfolio, you will have no trouble using these asset classes. If you have are just starting out or if you have a more limited portfolio, you might find you need to collapse some of these categories. For example, you might use these five:

1 A short-term bond or fixed income fund;

2 A medium-term bond fund;

3 A large-company fund;

4 A small-company fund;

5 An international fund.

Evensky set up 14 portfolios based on these asset classes, ranging from conservative to aggressive. The names are mine. For each portfolio, Evensky provides an estimated real rate of return, which is the return after inflation. He also provides a measure of estimated risk. He does this by indicating the risk in the short term as Low (L), medium (M), or High (H) and then risk in the long term with the same measures.

## STOCKS-BE-DAMNED (PORTFOLIOS 1-3)

**PORTFOLIO 1:** Seventy-two percent of this portfolio is in fixed income. It has low risk in both the short term and long term. Here's what it looks like:

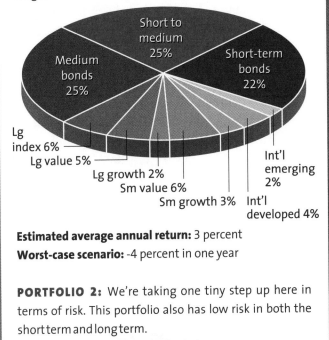

**Estimated average annual return:** 3 percent

**Worst-case scenario:** -4 percent in one year

**PORTFOLIO 2:** We're taking one tiny step up here in terms of risk. This portfolio also has low risk in both the short term and long term.

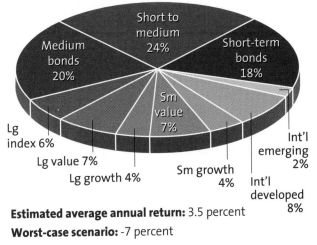

**Estimated average annual return:** 3.5 percent

**Worst-case scenario:** -7 percent

Finally, he gives what he considers a worst-case-scenario loss figure for each portfolio. This number, which is a percentage, is meant to indicate what Evensky thinks that portfolio might possibly be down in a 12-month period. He figures that in nine out of 10 years, this is the worst you could expect from this collection of assets. That doesn't mean it's the most the portfolio could ever lose in a day or a week. It's the worst loss over a 12-month period. So suppose the stock market crashes on January 2, 1999. Fast forward to January 2, 2000. With portfolio No. 1, his most conservative portfolio, Evensky estimates that the worst case is that your entire portfolio might be down 4 percent. In contrast, with portfolio 14, you might be down 35 percent a year after the crash.

With this in mind, let's take a look at his portfolios (pages 219, and 221–226).

## STOCKS-BE-DAMNED (CONT'D)

**PORTFOLIO 3** carries medium risk in the short term and low risk in the long term.

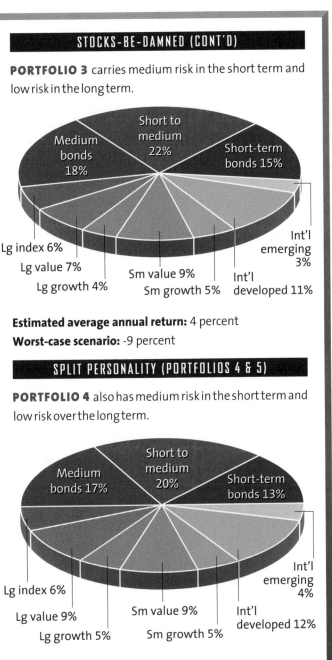

**Estimated average annual return:** 4 percent
**Worst-case scenario:** -9 percent

## SPLIT PERSONALITY (PORTFOLIOS 4 & 5)

**PORTFOLIO 4** also has medium risk in the short term and low risk over the long term.

**Estimated average annual return:** 4.3 percent
**Worst-case scenario:** -10 percent

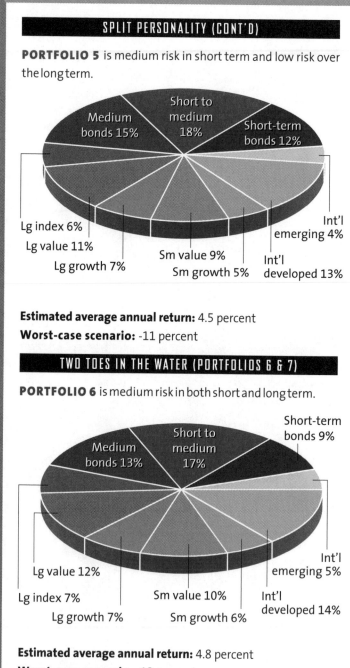

## SPLIT PERSONALITY (CONT'D)

**PORTFOLIO 5** is medium risk in short term and low risk over the long term.

Medium bonds 15%
Short to medium 18%
Short-term bonds 12%
Lg index 6%
Lg value 11%
Lg growth 7%
Sm value 9%
Sm growth 5%
Int'l developed 13%
Int'l emerging 4%

**Estimated average annual return:** 4.5 percent
**Worst-case scenario:** -11 percent

## TWO TOES IN THE WATER (PORTFOLIOS 6 & 7)

**PORTFOLIO 6** is medium risk in both short and long term.

Medium bonds 13%
Short to medium 17%
Short-term bonds 9%
Lg value 12%
Lg index 7%
Lg growth 7%
Sm value 10%
Sm growth 6%
Int'l developed 14%
Int'l emerging 5%

**Estimated average annual return:** 4.8 percent
**Worst-case scenario:** -13 percent

**PORTFOLIO 7** is high risk in the short term and medium risk in the long term.

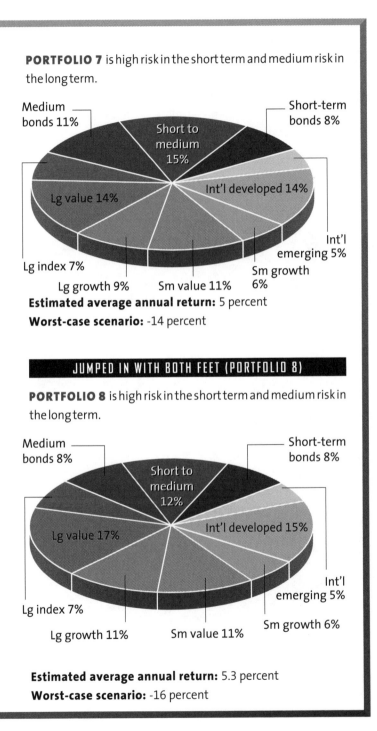

Medium bonds 11%
Short-term bonds 8%
Short to medium 15%
Int'l developed 14%
Lg value 14%
Int'l emerging 5%
Lg index 7%
Sm growth 6%
Lg growth 9%      Sm value 11%

**Estimated average annual return:** 5 percent
**Worst-case scenario:** -14 percent

## JUMPED IN WITH BOTH FEET (PORTFOLIO 8)

**PORTFOLIO 8** is high risk in the short term and medium risk in the long term.

Medium bonds 8%
Short-term bonds 8%
Short to medium 12%
Int'l developed 15%
Lg value 17%
Int'l emerging 5%
Lg index 7%
Sm growth 6%
Lg growth 11%      Sm value 11%

**Estimated average annual return:** 5.3 percent
**Worst-case scenario:** -16 percent

## "EXTREME INVESTING" (PORTFOLIOS 9-14)

Portfolios 9 through 14 are all high risk in both short and long term. In fact, on his fancy computer-generated model portfolios, Evensky prints out these six portfolios in red lest anyone miss the potential risks.

### PORTFOLIO 9

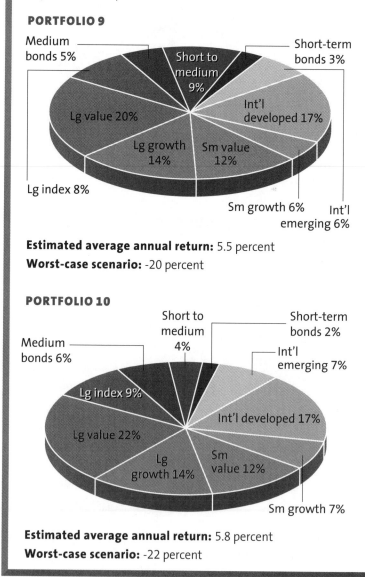

Medium bonds 5%
Short-term bonds 3%
Short to medium 9%
Int'l developed 17%
Lg value 20%
Lg growth 14%
Sm value 12%
Lg index 8%
Sm growth 6%
Int'l emerging 6%

**Estimated average annual return:** 5.5 percent
**Worst-case scenario:** -20 percent

### PORTFOLIO 10

Short to medium 4%
Short-term bonds 2%
Medium bonds 6%
Int'l emerging 7%
Lg index 9%
Int'l developed 17%
Lg value 22%
Lg growth 14%
Sm value 12%
Sm growth 7%

**Estimated average annual return:** 5.8 percent
**Worst-case scenario:** -22 percent

## PORTFOLIO 11

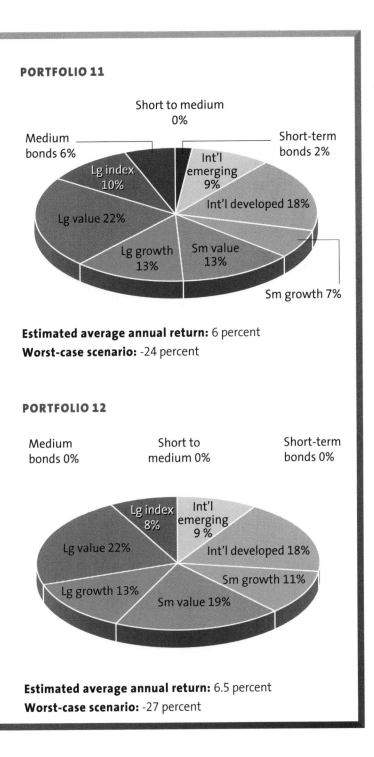

Short to medium 0%

Medium bonds 6%

Short-term bonds 2%

Int'l emerging 9%

Lg index 10%

Int'l developed 18%

Lg value 22%

Lg growth 13%

Sm value 13%

Sm growth 7%

**Estimated average annual return:** 6 percent
**Worst-case scenario:** -24 percent

## PORTFOLIO 12

Medium bonds 0%

Short to medium 0%

Short-term bonds 0%

Lg index 8%

Int'l emerging 9 %

Lg value 22%

Int'l developed 18%

Sm growth 11%

Lg growth 13%

Sm value 19%

**Estimated average annual return:** 6.5 percent
**Worst-case scenario:** -27 percent

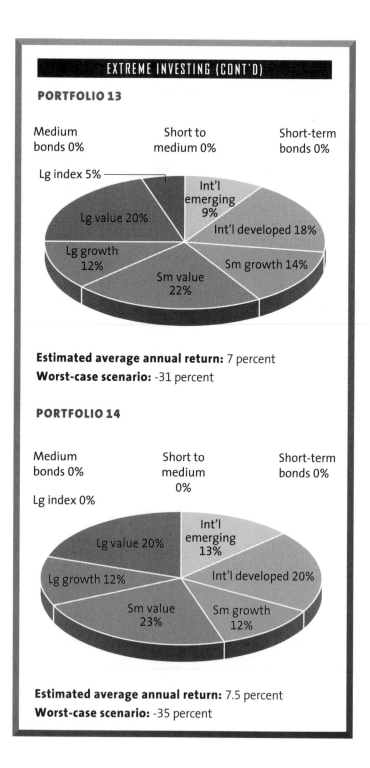

## EXTREME INVESTING (CONT'D)

### PORTFOLIO 13

Medium bonds 0%       Short to medium 0%       Short-term bonds 0%

Lg index 5%

Int'l emerging 9%

Int'l developed 18%

Lg value 20%

Lg growth 12%

Sm growth 14%

Sm value 22%

**Estimated average annual return:** 7 percent
**Worst-case scenario:** -31 percent

### PORTFOLIO 14

Medium bonds 0%       Short to medium 0%       Short-term bonds 0%

Lg index 0%

Int'l emerging 13%

Int'l developed 20%

Lg value 20%

Lg growth 12%

Sm growth 12%

Sm value 23%

**Estimated average annual return:** 7.5 percent
**Worst-case scenario:** -35 percent

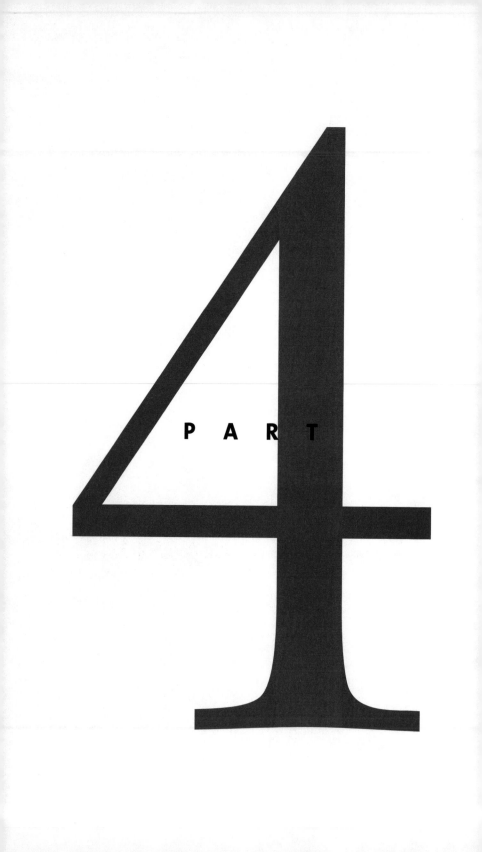

PART

4

# Common
# Sense
# STRATEGIES

UCCESSFUL INVESTING requires a plan and the discipline to see it through. Novice investors believe the magic is in the plan; that they must find the right fund or the right stock if they are to succeed. But more experienced investors understand that the specifics of the plan are less important than the discipline.

This is something Judy Shine learned 15 years ago. Shine, who was in her 20s, was a top sales rep in Manhattan for Xerox Corp. Because she had a lump-sum bonus to invest and didn't want to make a mistake, she went to a financial planner for help. "Back then there was one portfolio," says Shine, who today is a financial planner herself with a practice in Denver. "It consisted of Magellan, Windsor, Twentieth Century Select, and Vanguard Intermediate Bond Fund. You split it up four ways and that was it." Today, of course, planners use complex modeling to set up different portfolios for each client. But the early days taught Shine a valuable lesson: "Any plan works as long as you stick with it." She did. And when she turned 40 recently, she had reason again to look back and tip her hat to Pat Feeney, the financial planner who set up her portfolio. Thanks to Feeney and the bull market, Shine has a great deal of flexibility and freedom in setting up the life she wants for herself.

Shine was a winner because she stuck with her four funds. Losing investors are easy to spot. They rush into the market when it looks like everyone else is making money and then run for the exits when it sinks. They are always searching for hot tips and watching to see what others are buying. They buy a stock or mutual fund. But they quickly get discouraged and sell if it doesn't begin to move up in price. These are the obvious mistakes.

But some errors are much more subtle. In 1997, I began writing an on-line investing column for *Microsoft's Investor* and corresponding on-line with readers in the newsgroups. It's been great fun to see how people approach investing and other financial planning issues, to watch how they work them through, and to think about how we all might do better. A common question in the newsgroup is something like this: "My husband and I just got married and we received $8,000 in cash as wedding gifts. Where should we invest it?" Now here is a young couple with the right idea. Rather than taking an expensive vacation or blowing the cash on home furnishings, they want to get started on a nest egg. But before they can decide where to invest, they need to set goals. They need a plan. Do they want the money in three years to buy a house? Can they put it away for five years? For 10 years? All investing decisions rely on doing this up-front work.

Thinking about your goals can be the best—and the most difficult—part of financial planning. It allows you to dream dreams and to spin out all your fantasies, then winnow them down to the most important ones and try to put a time frame on them. It is this part of financial planning that most Americans never do. What's the old saw about life is what happens when you're busy making other plans? It doesn't have to be that way, though. You can realize your dreams if you're willing to do the work. It requires a great deal of thought—about who you are, what you want, what you enjoy, where you're going. This is the very toughest part of financial planning because it requires facing up to who you are and what you dream about. Top financial planners, like Stan Breitbard in Los Angeles, say they have lost clients because they've asked them to face these questions.

For example, Stan, who teaches financial planning to MBA students at Berkeley, asked these students to draw up a five-year financial plan for themselves. The students fell into three groups. The first concentrated on simple bookkeeping tasks: paying off bills, developing a filing system, getting organized. The second group focused on saving and investing and some intermediate-term goals. But Stan said only the third group really understood what he meant by financial planning—dreaming dreams and thinking about where you will go in life and how you will get there. It is this critical part of planning that you must do before you choose an investment strategy.

One thing I've learned from visitors to our *Investor* Web site is that Gen-Xers as a group take personal finance and career issues very seriously, certainly much more so than my generation—the baby boomers—did at their age. Perhaps more seriously than the baby boomers do now. In fact, we've gotten several questions from Gen-Xers worried about their boomer parents who are still frittering their money away as retirement looms.

So perhaps it is the boomers (and *their* parents) who are still the novices and who need the advice on setting up an investment strategy. As Shine found out, a strategy can be simple. Not every successful investor uses the same strategy. But every successful investor has one. A strategy can be as simple as researching a single fund to start an investment program, buying it, and holding it. Or it might be a contrarian strategy that involves buying the worst performers of the previous year. It might combine a bit of each: buying some core funds to hold and then dabbling a bit around the edges. But successful investing is never haphazard. It requires a plan. Here are some strategies to think about.

## BUY AND HOLD

THIS IS WHERE all investing should start. Buy and hold is by far the simplest and, for most investors, the best strategy. Jim and Priscilla Humphry are real people who followed this traditional investment advice and were well served by it.

Jim Humphry, who was trained as a librarian, started tucking away $100 a month in 1960. He initially picked the First Investors Fund for Income, a bond fund. Jim soon realized that bonds, which provide income, are not a good choice for a long-term investment. He wanted growth for his retirement money. To compound the problem, bonds did poorly in the '60s, with an average annual return of less than 2 percent. The fund went nowhere. "We were looking for growth, and it didn't grow," Jim says. Still, he gave it a chance, sticking with it for nearly a decade.

Then he realized that what he needed was an investment in stocks. By this time it was the early 1970s, a terrible time for the stock market. Large-company stocks returned an average of only 5.9 percent a year during the decade. But Jim had done his research and knew that, over time, stocks outperform all other investments. He picked a number of stocks and stock mutual funds and followed the same strategy: buy and hold for the long term.

By investing in a handful of good stock funds and sticking with them, he accumulated enough money to put his two daughters through college, buy them cars, pay for their weddings, and help each make a down payment on a first home.

Here is one example of how his money grew. In 1971, Jim bought 100 shares of the Smith Barney Shearson Appreciation fund for $12.50 a share, a total investment of $1,250. He has not touched that fund. At the end of 1994, he had 900 shares, worth $9,774 at $10.86 a share, thanks largely to reinvestment of dividends and capital gains. That works out to a gain of $8,524, or 682 percent, an average of 9.35 percent a year. Jim's success was hardly due to the fact that the Smith Barney fund was the top performer over that 20-plus–year period. It was not. But like many established stock funds, it was a fine performer. By sticking with it, Jim avoided the costs associated with buying and selling.

And he avoided another mistake many investors make: selling after a bad year only to miss out on a subsequent great year. For example, in 1984, the fund gained a paltry 1.77 percent, underperforming the market as a whole. Had Jim bailed out, he would have missed the 33.96 percent gain the following year. Similarly, the fund lost 0.27 percent in 1990, but racked up a 26.94 percent gain in 1991.

When the Humphrys retired, they were able to live the life many of us just dream about: trips to Honolulu, Australia, Tasmania, Thailand, Nepal, and India. It was not because they earned a great deal of money in their working years but because they did their research, picked some good funds, and stuck with them. Their success proves that it is not so much what you buy as your persistence and diligence that pay off. There is no magic to getting rich. It is simply a matter of setting money aside on a regular basis.

## THE ACTIVE VERSUS PASSIVE DEBATE

WHAT ARE THE BEST funds for a buy-and-hold strategy? Index funds are a natural choice. And this is an obvious place to probe a bit into the active versus passive management debate, one of the hot buttons for professional investors over the past five years. *(For the basics, see page 28.)*

An index fund invests in all the stocks that make up a particular market index like the Standard & Poor's 500 Stock Index or the Lehman Brothers Bond Market Index or, sometimes, in a sampling of stocks or bonds in these indexes. Once invested, the fund is "passive," which means it simply holds the stocks, trading only to invest new money, to handle redemptions, or to recognize occasional changes in the index. An index fund does not need a manager to select stocks. And it need not pay a manager to do that. Likewise, there are few trading costs. A good index fund moves up and down with the market. The Vanguard Index 500 charges just one-fifth of 1 percent in expenses. That compares to 1.43 percent for the average actively managed stock fund.

Passive management grew out of the work in efficient market theory by a number of economists in the 1960s. John C. Bogle, chairman of the Vanguard Group, explains efficient market theory this way in his book *Bogle on Mutual Funds*, (Irwin, 1994):

◆ **All market investors together own the entire stock market.** Passive investors as a group will match the gross return of the overall market because they are invested in all the stocks. So active investors, as a group, can do no better. They, too, must simply match the market.

◆ **Because the fees and transaction costs incurred by the passive investors are much lower than those paid by active investors and both groups get the same gross returns, then it follows that passive investors will get the higher *net* returns.** Indeed, a Nobel laureate economist, Paul Samuelson, found that active managers must beat the market by 2 percentage points just to come out *even* after paying expenses.

Yes, investors argue, but active managers as a group include some good managers and some bad managers. The key is to select the good ones—the ones that beat the average. Bogle concedes that there are excellent managers who outperform the average and mentions Warren Buffett, Peter Lynch, and John Neff. But, he adds, "such extraordinary managers not only are few in number but are difficult to identify in advance."

Bogle cites academic studies that show that only two in five stock mutual funds outperform the market over time and only one in five does so once sales charges are taken into account. The performance of active managers is inconsistent—usually the same ones do not outperform from year to year.

Wells Fargo was an early developer of index funds for institutional investors like pension funds, which immediately saw the merits of passive management. The first institutional index fund was opened in 1971, and billions of dollars poured into these funds throughout the 1970s. The first retail index fund, the Vanguard 500, was set up by Bogle in 1976, and its early success was much more limited. The indexing story lacked romance and passion—two things that lure individual investors. Indeed, Bogle told me years ago that he "used up the shoe leather in three pairs of shoes" trying to get someone to agree to help him raise money for his first index fund, which was considered "un-American" on Wall Street in the 1970s.

But American investors grew wiser, particularly as they began investing in earnest in 401(k) plans in the 1980s. By the early 1990s, money was pouring into the fund. In 1995 and 1996, as the fund was beating most of the active managers on the Street, the Vanguard 500 grew to number two in size behind Fidelity Magellan, putting it in the unlikely position of being the hot fund of the year. So in 20 years, Bogle had gone from "un-American" to "hot" and "trendy."

Bogle must have received a great deal of satisfaction from seeing his idea so widely accepted. But Bogle, a maverick and a visionary, would *never* want to field the hot fund or be called trendy. I'm sure he wasn't pleased to see investors pick the Vanguard 500 simply because they were following the crowd. Indeed, much of this money was coming into the fund for the wrong reason. Many of the new shareholders were not selecting the index fund for the mathematical reasons outlined by Bogle. They saw that the index 500 was outperforming in the bull markets of 1995 and 1996, and they wanted in on the action.

This doesn't dampen the mathematicians' argument for indexing, of course. Many economists, like Meir Statman, a behavioral economist at Santa Clara University, endorse indexing, too. Statman believes that the markets are efficient and that investors are largely irrational. Professional or novice, investors make decisions for the wrong reasons, Statman says. For example, Statman believes that many investors are driven by fear of regret. An irrational investor may leap into an investment merely because he fears being left behind; a rational investor would never do that, Statman says. So Statman urges us to buy index funds and save ourselves from ourselves and from bad—or irrational—money managers. So does Jonathan Clements, author of *The Wall Street Journal's* "Getting Going" column and of a 1998 personal finance book: *25 Myths You've Got to Avoid.* Myth number five is "you can beat the market," and Clements dubs it "the big lie." Clements, too, urges us to buy index funds.

Ah, but hope springs eternal. Most of us understand and accept the argument for indexing. At least we buy it with our rational selves. But many of us still stray into actively managed funds. Meir Statman does not. But I do. And so do investors who have a lot more experience than I do—investors like Don Phillips, president of Morningstar Mutual Funds. Don is certainly an advocate of indexing. He buys the argument. But he doesn't buy the funds. Before he joined Morningstar and became the maven of mutual funds, Don dreamed of getting his Ph.D. in literature and teaching. He'd been an investor since he was a kid. And he always expected to invest on the side. But literature was his first love. Like many of us, though, Don flipped his two interests upside down. Once he got involved with mutual funds at Morningstar, he became passionate about investing and decided to read great novels on the side. But he looks for the same drama, adventure, and mystery in funds that he found in literature. He wants a manager who feels as passionate as he does. Some of the managers that Don has felt passionate about are Shelby Davis, who until recently managed Selected American Shares and New York Venture, Marty Whitman at Third Avenue Value, Jim Gipson at Clipper Fund, and Don Yacktman at Yacktman Fund.

Perhaps Ross Levin, a financial planner from Minneapolis, said it best when he introduced a panel on active versus passive management at a financial planning conference in Palm Beach, Florida, in 1997. Levin said he uses active funds because he enjoys doing the research to find the funds. Active managers are more interesting to him and more interesting to his clients. "Active managers keep my clients interested and keep them in the investment game," Levin said.

I watch this debate in the on-line newsgroups, too. One investor will bemoan a stupid mistake he's made by buying for the wrong reasons or selling on panic. Sometimes that's me. Then a more rational investor will say, "Shame on you. Don't you know that index funds are the smartest way to avoid mistakes?" The index argument is always well reasoned and cogent. Yet I suspect many investors will continue to wander into actively managed funds.

Consider Professor Burton G. Malkiel, author of *A Random Walk Down Wall Street*, friend of Bogle, and a great advocate of indexing. In his book, he takes up the efficient market argument and says that most active managers fall behind the market index. Yet Malkiel uses active funds himself. Investing is fun, he says. "A successful investor is generally a well-rounded individual who puts a natural curiosity and an intellectual interest to work to earn more money."

So which way will you go, active or passive? There is

a good argument to be made for making index funds the core of your portfolio. Index funds are an ideal buy-and-hold investment because there is no fund manager to monitor. It is more difficult to find actively managed funds to buy and hold. Many fund companies, most notably Fidelity, rotate managers regularly. I don't think you should buy and hold Fidelity funds. Michael Price's Mutual Series funds were once good buy-and-hold candidates because Price was such a consistent manager. But when Price sold out to the Franklin/Templeton group and began to ease himself out of the management of those funds, they came off the list. Similarly, when manager Shelby Davis left Selected American Shares and his son took over management, that fund, too, was off the slam-dunk list. So index funds go at the top of the buy-and-hold, no-fuss list. Add active funds carefully. And watch for portfolio manager changes.

When you are setting up your buy-and-hold portfolio:

**DO** use index funds

**DON'T** bail out after a bad year

**DO** set up a portfolio of three to five low cost funds

**DON'T** include sector funds or funds that invest on the fringes.

## ROTATION

MANY INVESTORS NEED not move beyond buy and hold. But for those who are a bit more adventuresome, there are ways to improve returns over the buy-and-hold strategy. One of the best ones is a contrarian strategy. Again, you must be disciplined.

Studies show that different types of assets—such as bonds, gold, large-company stocks, and small-company stocks—move in cycles. Most investors put their money in at the very top of the cycle, just as performance for that asset has peaked, because that's when the investment gets the most attention. Remember the dazzling performance of emerging markets funds in

1993? That brought in a lot of investors just in time for those funds' whipping in 1994.

A much better strategy is to put your money into the asset that has had the worst recent performance. But you must do it systematically. You can't simply choose the worst fund of the year before. Instead, you must set up in advance the group you will work with and then plot your strategy.

For example, when Jon Fossel was chairman of the Oppenheimer Group of funds in New York, he did a study of the performance of three asset classes over the previous 50 to 60 years: long-term bonds, small-company stocks, and utility stocks. He looked at each asset type's average annual return over the period. Then he looked at how it did in its worst 10 years. Finally, he looked at the two years following each of the 10 worst years. In every case, the asset performed much better following a bad year than it did in an average year.

Consider small-company stocks, which he looked at from 1934 to 1993. Small-company stocks, which are a top-performing but volatile asset class, had an average annual return of 15.1 percent during that 60-year period. In their 10 worst years, the average decline was 22 percent. Following those bad years, small-company stocks returned an average of 21.3 percent for the next two years. So Fossel argues that an investor can improve returns by disciplined investing in the group that has recently turned in the worst performance. Here's what he found for long-term bonds in the period from 1934–93:

| | |
|---|---|
| Avg. long-term annual return | **+5.0%** |
| Avg. decline in 10 worst years | **-4.3%** |
| Avg. annual 2-year recovery | **+7.4%** |

In 1994, long-term bonds lost 12 percent, which, according to Fossel's theory, would make 1995 a good year for investing in bonds. That turned out to be the case. As interest rates dropped, the long bond gained more than 30 percent, and taxable bond funds gained an average of 15.62 percent for the year. The pattern was similar for utility stocks during the period 1945–93:

| | |
|---|---|
| Avg. long-term annual return | **+10.4%** |
| Avg. decline in 10 worst years | **-7.2%** |
| Avg. annual 2-year recovery | **+16.8%** |
| 1994 decline | **-15.3%** |

In 1995, utility funds gained an average of 27.34, according to Lipper Analytical Services, which produces statistics on the mutual fund industry.

Fossel uses the strategy himself. When he joined Oppenheimer in 1987, he rolled over a retirement nest egg of $31,000 from his former employer and invested in the two Oppenheimer funds that had been the worst performers in 1987. He also directed all his 1988 401(k) contributions into the same two funds.

He did tinker just a bit with the list before picking his funds, though. First, he used only stock funds. Like most investment pros, Fossel believes that stocks provide the best long-term performance. The second thing he did was remove "sector" funds, those that invest in only one industry or type of security. That eliminated Oppenheimer's gold fund and Global Biotech fund from his list and left him with nine diversified stock funds.

The first year the strategy worked "spectacularly," Fossel says. He continued it for each of the seven years he served as Oppenheimer chairman, moving all his retirement money into the two bottom performers. The result? The average cumulative return of Oppenheimer's equity funds over the seven years 1987 to 1994 was 118.1 percent, a tad better than the market as a whole. But Fossel's portfolio, which hit a quarter of a million dollars before he left Oppenheimer in 1996,

thanks partly to regular 401(k) contributions, enjoyed
a return of 227.7 percent over those years. Had he
instead selected the two top-performing funds of the
previous year—a strategy that many investors use—his
cumulative return would have been 73.2 percent. "It's
really pretty simple," Fossel says. "You're buying low
and selling high. But the end result is staggering."

Fossel's experience is hardly luck or happenstance.
Although the execution is simple, the "upside-down"
strategy is based on a more complex theory. Each
diversified stock fund uses a different investment strategy. For example, one might invest in small-company
stocks, another in international stocks, and yet another
in stocks that pay high dividends. Some managers look
for "growth" companies, those that are expected to
grow rapidly. Others search for "value" companies,
whose share prices have been beaten down based on
some measure of their intrinsic value.

These different investment styles work well in different investment climates. "What happens is that
there is an equilibrium price in the market," says A.
Michael Lipper, president of Lipper Analytical Services. "Markets almost always get overexcited or
overdepressed, and then that works itself out and
prices return to the equilibrium."

That makes Fossel's strategy of choosing funds that
are out of favor vastly superior to choosing the current
top performers, Lipper says, although he notes that
Fossel had an advantage as head of the company that
runs the funds. "What Jon can feel certain of is that the
funds on the bottom are reasonably well managed," he
says. "He's not buying turkeys. He's buying funds that
are out of favor."

Fossel acknowledges that the strategy would not
work if an investor used a group of funds that included
some true dogs. Over the seven years, Fossel used every
one of the funds at least once. However, he argues that
the application goes far beyond his own fund group.

"I thought maybe it was just Oppenheimer, so I tested it with another fund group with the same result," he says. "Then I tested it going back to 1985 to give me 10 years of data, and it was the same thing."

If you want to use Fossel's strategy of upside-down investing:

**DO** define your universe of funds before you start.

**DON'T** be sidetracked by hot performers that are not on your list.

**DO** set in stone a date once a year when you will "rotate."

**DO** consider using the two worst-performing options in your 401(k) plan for the new contributions you make the following year.

**DO** choose a good no-load fund group, like the Scudder Funds in Boston or T. Rowe Price in Baltimore, and set up an automatic-investment program in which you deposit money each year into the two worst-performing funds of the year before. "T. Rowe Price would be a good choice because of the variety and type of funds offered," says Don Phillips, president of Morningstar Mutual Funds.

**DO** assemble your own list of funds using a publication such as Morningstar Mutual Funds to select solid funds with various investment styles.

Jonathan Burton wrote an article on "good and cheap funds," for the May 1998 issue of *Bloomberg Personal Finance* magazine, that provided some options to consider for your list. You'll want to do your own research. But his article provided a good starting point. Here are some of them that I particularly liked:

◆ **Large-company growth.** White Oak Growth Stock, Harbor Capital Appreciation, Vanguard Index Growth

◆ **Large-company value.** Oakmark, Dodge & Cox Stock, Vanguard/Windsor II.

◆ **Mid-cap growth.** T. Rowe Price Mid-Cap, Brandywine Blue

◆ **Mid-cap value.** Strong Schafer Value, Neuberger & Berman Partners, MAS Value, Mutual Shares

◆ **Small-cap growth.** Baron Asset, Manager's Special Equity.

◆ **Small-cap value.** Barr Rosenberg US Small Cap, UAM FMA Small Company

◆ **Foreign.** Harbor International, Hotchkis & Wiley International

**DO** choose one fund from each category so that you will have seven mutual funds.

**DON'T** hesitate to add emerging markets if you've got the risk tolerance for it. One of the best candidates here is Templeton Emerging Markets, a closed-end fund run by Mark Mobius. Hang on to your hat, though.

**DO** set an annual date when you will pick the bottom two—or even three—performers.

Fossel's strategy of moving everything to the bottom two performers is a very aggressive one. If the idea appeals to you but you don't want to bet the bank, you might direct only your new contributions into the bottom performers. Or you might want to implement the strategy for only a portion of your portfolio rather than the whole thing.

It is important, though, to be certain that your funds are all solid performers in their categories and that they all have distinct—and different—styles. For example, you will notice that the funds on our list do not include any that are designed to do well in all market climates. Those are ideal for one-fund portfolios or for a core holding. What you want here are funds with different strengths and weaknesses. "You pick one fund differently than you pick a plate of 10," says Morningstar's Don Phillips. "What you want is a group of funds that are designed so that one zigs when another zags."

## STRIKING A COMPROMISE

THE HUMPHRYS BUY and hold. Fossel rotates. Now consider what Steven Norwitz, a vice president at T. Rowe Price, does to juice up his portfolio. Norwitz has been observing the fund industry and talking with managers at T. Rowe for more than 20 years. So he's very close to what's going on. He knows he should buy and hold and that excessive trading is a mistake. But he also knows that Fossel's contrarian strategy has merit. So Norwitz combines these strategies.

Norwitz splits his portfolio 70 percent into equities and 30 percent into income. For the core of his equity portfolio—70 percent—Norwitz uses T. Rowe's Dividend Growth fund and T. Rowe's Blue Chip fund, both large-company U.S. funds. The other 30 percent goes half into international and half into small cap. In each of these cases, he has a core holding. But he tries to get some juice at the margins. For example, the bulk of his international money goes into the stalwart T. Rowe International. But in 1998, with the Asian markets in turmoil, he added to his holdings in New Asia and also dollar-cost-averaged into Emerging Market Stock.

He is even more aggressive with the income portion of his portfolio. Like most sophisticated investors, Norwitz knows that it's wise to allocate a portion of his assets to bonds. But, like his peers, he also knows that it's tough to get decent returns on the bond portion. His main allocation—20 percent—goes to Spectrum Income, a fund that includes several other T. Rowe Price bond funds and one stock fund. Because the fund is diversified, the manager can include emerging market bonds, junk bonds, and an equity income fund and still keep the risk profile low. "We bill this fund as the only bond fund investors need," Norwitz says. And T. Rowe finds that most investors use it that way.

Spectrum Income is permitted to put 2 to 3 percent of its portfolio into emerging market bonds. For himself, though, Norwitz was looking for a little more kick. So he put 10 percent of his overall portfolio into emerging market bonds. "This is one of the few asset classes that has beat the S&P index over the past few years," Norwitz says.

Once he's set up his portfolio, Norwitz says, he "tries not to second-guess myself." "Where I'm playing is in putting new money in on the fringes," he says. "I don't change my allocations or sell any of my core holdings." If one of his fringe funds—like New Asia—spurted up in price, Norwitz says he wouldn't sell. But he would move his new money to something else that is out of favor, much as Fossel does. "I don't play around with it too much," Norwitz says. "But it would be boring not to make any decisions at all. To make decisions, you have to stay abreast of what's going on. When you make decisions with your own money, it keeps you focused."

## BETTING ON BONDS

ONE THEME THROUGHOUT this guide is that investors with a long time horizon should avoid bond funds, keeping the majority of their assets in different types of stock funds, perhaps a portion in income funds like Spectrum Income or Vanguard/Wellesley Income and a small portion in cash, or in short-term bond funds, like the very solid choices offered by the Vanguard Group.

But adventuresome investors might occasionally find a time when it pays to make a bet on bonds. That is when the price of bonds is out of whack relative to stocks or when interest rates seem poised to decline. Investing in bonds at such a time amounts to a bet that they will appreciate relative to stock, providing investors with a capital gain. This is not a long-term buy-and-hold investment. It is a short-term bet that prices will realign themselves. That makes it an aggressive strategy for use by seasoned investors—or investment advisers.

One way professional investors try to gauge what is happening in bonds is to look at the yield curve. Because we're focusing on strategies now, let's take a look at how experts like Craig Henderson, a municipal bond manager in Chicago, look at the bond market. A math wizard who could have applied his talents to many different pursuits, Craig chose to use them to analyze the bond market. You already know that in the bond market, changes in interest rates—and in expected future interest rates—cause the prices of bonds to rise or fall. When interest rates climb, bond prices fall. The reverse is also true: falling rates mean higher prices for bonds.

Well, it doesn't require a math whiz to figure that out. If Craig is going to manage bonds for his clients, though, he doesn't want to be in the position of *informing* them that rates have changed and that their bonds are worth less, right? No. He must try to anticipate interest rate changes and figure out how to manage his bonds to take advantage of them. One of the tools he uses to do that is the yield curve.

The yield curve should interest the rest of us, too, because it shows us where we can get the most bang for our buck with our income investments, which can include everything from passbook accounts to 30-year bonds. And, for those who want to bet on bonds, it can provide some information on where rates might be headed.

If you've been paying attention, you already know that short-term securities are far less risky than long-term securities because they are less exposed to interest rate risk. So it follows that long-term securities should pay the investor more for shouldering additional risk, right? More reward for more risk. Let's look at bank certificates of deposit as an example. If you are willing to lock up your money for five years, you will get a higher interest rate than if you lock it up for just three months. That's because the longer the maturity or term of the CD, the more interest rate risk you face. With a CD, though, your principal and interest are guaranteed by the federal government up to $100,000. When you buy a bond, you might lose principal if interest rates go up and you want to sell. That's why you need to know whether you will be paid enough in terms of higher yield for taking on the additional risk of a longer-term bond. The yield curve helps you decide.

The yardstick for the income market—and the yield curve—is Treasury securities, so it helps to have a passing knowledge of these instruments. Earnings on U.S. Treasury securities are exempt from state and local taxes. But they are taxable at the federal level. At the short end of the yield curve are Treasury bills, with maturities of under one year. Three-month, six-month, and one-year Treasury bills are offered at auction by the U.S. Treasury. The yields are followed closely because many indexes—like those for mortgages—are tied to them. Treasury notes occupy the mid-range of the yield curve. They are called medium-term—or intermediates—with maturities of one to 10 years. Treasury bonds are long-term debt instruments with maturities of 10 years to 30 years.

Treasury securities make a handy yardstick, with these denominations ranging from 90 days to 30 years. And that's what the yield curve is: A comparison of rates at the short end of the curve with those at the long end and everything in between. Once you've looked at the yield curve for Treasuries, you can build on that, comparing the Treasury yield to the yield on municipal bonds, like Henderson does. Or to junk bonds. Or to bonds in emerging markets. When you measure the yield of Treasury bonds against the yield of, say, emerging market bonds, the difference is called the *spread*. Bond gurus watch that spread carefully to see when it provides opportunities.

But let's go back to the yield curve. One of the questions you ask as an investor is whether you are being paid enough to "go long," or to buy long-term bonds. In other words, are you compensated enough in terms of extra yield for the extra risk you are taking? In early 1998, the answer is a definite no. The yield curve in early 1998 is very flat. That means that long-term bonds pay only a tiny bit more than intermediate-term bonds and those pay only a hair more than short-term bonds. So the pros are keeping their money at the short end of the curve. You should be, too. To get some examples, I called Steve Norwitz at T. Rowe Price & Associates, the Baltimore-based mutual fund company. Norwitz is one of those rare people who can put arcane topics like yield curves into layman's language.

In late winter of 1998, Norwitz told me that the current yield on T. Rowe's intermediate Treasuries fund was 5.45 percent. The yield on the long Treasury fund was 5.62 percent. So for taking on the additional interest rate risk of going to long bonds, an investor would get paid only 17 basis points, or $^{17}\!/_{100}$ths of 1 percent.

But what about those investors who want to bet on bonds? What the flat yield curve tells them is that the pros think interest rates are still going to drop. If interest rates drop, your bond appreciates. "So the only reason you would go to the long end of the curve now is if you think rates are heading down," Norwitz said.

Now let's see how Henderson plays the yield curve. He trades munis, which are issued by state governments or municipalities and are typically referred to as "tax-free" bonds because they are free of federal tax and also free of state and local taxes if you buy one in your own state. So the rates Henderson looks at are those in the muni market. He sees three basic patterns to the yield curve. Here they are:

**1 Upward slope.** A typical yield curve slopes upward with the short end paying less than the intermediates and the intermediates less than the long-term bonds. With a gentle slope in the muni market, you might see the short end at 5, the 10-year muni at 6, and the 30-year at 6¾. In that scenario, "I'll go out five to seven years," Henderson says. "I don't get paid enough on the short end and I don't want the risk on the long end."

If the curve slopes up very steeply—say 2½ percent

on the short end and 7 on intermediates—Henderson might use what pros call a barbell strategy, concentrating his money in two-year bonds and 10-year bonds, like a barbell. If it slopes upward and then flattens out, he may use what is called a ladder strategy, which means he buys a rung of the ladder in each maturity. Perhaps he starts with a rung of three-year bonds, then a rung of four-year bonds, a five-year rung, and so forth.

**2 Flat.** A flat yield curve like the one at the beginning of 1998 offers pretty much the same yields at each maturity. For instance, perhaps one-year munis pay 5½; 10-year pay 5½; and the 30-year bond pays 5.60. With a flat curve, Henderson looks at where he gets the highest yield for the lowest risk. It's bound to be close to the short end.

**3 Inverted.** An inverted curve, where the short end pays more than the long end, is rare. For example, munis might pay 7 percent on the short end, 5 percent in the middle, and 5¾ at 30 years. The U.S. had an inverted yield curve in 1982. Even though you're dying to snap up those 7-percent short-term bonds, the best strategy with an inverted yield curve is to buy long. "This is really tough," Henderson says, "because it goes against all your instincts. But what an inverted yield curve is saying is that short rates are going down."

Now that you've survived this long-winded discussion about the yield curve, let's get back to the point: strategies. How can you use the yield curve to figure out when to bet on bonds? And what do you do about it? Well, that's a whole book unto itself. If you're really interested, you should read one. But here is a brief introduction. If you believe interest rates are heading down and you want to speculate or bet on bonds, remember that the longer the term, the more the bond will respond to a change in interest rates. So a 30-year bond is a better choice than a five-year bond. Best—and most volatile—of all is a zero-coupon bond.

Zero-coupon Treasury bonds have been around since 1981. Unlike regular Treasury bonds, which provide semiannual interest payments or coupons, zeros pay no coupon or interest. Instead, they are offered at a deep discount and appreciate to face value at maturity. They were initially pitched as a way to target a particular time when an investor would need money for, say, college tuition. So you could pay for your child's college tuition at a discount by buying zeros. But speculators use zeros to make bets on interest rates. Because there is no interest payment to cushion it, a zero is much more volatile than a coupon bond. If interest rates fall, it will appreciate much more than a regular bond.

If you, the investor, believe that interest rates will fall and that bonds will appreciate over the next several months—and you are willing to put your money on it—you should pick the longest-term zero-coupon bond to get the most bang for your buck. The longer the maturity, the more the price will swing. If interest rates do fall as you suspect, you will be able to sell your bonds for a nice gain.

The Benham Group of mutual funds in San Francisco was the first to see the potential of zeros for mutual funds. In 1985, Jim Benham set up five funds with maturities of 1990, 1995, 2000, 2005, and 2015. Today the maturities are 2000, 2005, 2010, 2015, 2020, and 2025. Clearly, these are not diversified funds. All the bonds mature on the same date. There are only two reasons to buy these funds. First, because you know you will need money for a specific financial need on a specific date and you like the idea of knowing exactly how much you will have. Second, because you believe interest rates are about to decline, and you want to make a bet on them. These funds provide a low-cost way for investors to participate in the zero-coupon market.

Of course, investors look at much more than just

the yield curve before deciding to bet on bonds. They also look at the relative attractiveness of various assets to decide where to put more money on the margins. From that perspective, bonds looked good at the end of 1994, which was the first losing calendar year for bonds since 1969. "Bond prices had declined sharply during the year, but U.S. stock prices had been flat on balance," according to a study by Sanford C. Bernstein & Co., the Wall Street research and investment firm. Because the lower the price of an asset, the better its value, "an important by-product of 1994 market movements was a change in the relative value of bonds and stocks," the report said. The loss in bonds in 1994 created an anomaly in prices that made bonds look like a "substitute stock," Bernstein concluded. The investment firm put 8 to 10 percent of its all-stock portfolios into 10-year Treasury bonds at the beginning of 1995. This strategy is similar to Fossel's contrarian method of investing in the worst-performing stock fund. If you were going to make a bet on bonds, January 1995 seemed one good time to do it. And it was. The average bond fund gained more than 15 percent in 1995; long-term bonds were up more than 30 percent.

So let's take a look at how betting on bonds worked in 1995, which provides a nice example of the momentum you pick up by going long when interest rates drop. It was a good year for the bond market. As interest rates headed down, bonds, as measured by the Vanguard Total Bond Index mutual fund, gained 18.2 percent. Take a look at the Benham funds:

| | |
|---|---|
| Vanguard Total Bond Index | **+18.2** |
| Benham Target 1995 | **+6.8** |
| Benham Target 2000 | **+20.7** |
| Benham Target 2005 | **+32.6** |
| Benham Target 2010 | **+42.1** |
| Benham Target 2015 | **+52.7** |
| Benham Target 2020 | **+61.3** |

You certainly would have been well rewarded for your bet in 1995. The stock market, as measured by the Vanguard Index 500, was up 37.5 percent for the year, a little more than the 10-year maturity zero-coupon fund. The 25-year maturity fund was up 61.3 percent. Since then, Benham has merged with the Twentieth Century funds in Kansas City and the merged group is called American Century. The funds are called American Century-Benham Target Maturity Year.

In 1997, the bond market provided a less spectacular return. But whatever return there was was still amplified by zero-coupon bonds.

| | |
|---|---|
| Vanguard Total Bond Index | **+9.44** |
| AmCentury Ben Target 2000 | **+7.05** |
| Target 2005 | **+11.63** |
| Target 2010 | **+16.75** |
| Target 2015 | **+22.92** |
| Target 2020 | **+28.62** |
| Target 2025 | **+30.11** |

Had you been a student of the yield curve back in 1982, when it was inverted with short rates at 20 percent, long rates at 15 percent, and intermediate at 14¾, you might have observed that that, too, looked like a good time to bet on bonds. Henderson advised a client to put $1 million in zero coupon bonds with a 10-year maturity. His million grew to $2½ million in three years. Going out to a longer maturity would have paid even more.

Before we get too greedy, though, let's look at the downside. The long-term Benham funds are market-timing tools. That's helpful to you if you want to time the market and bet on bonds. It's a drag if you're a long-term investor who is using the money for, say, college savings. In July 1997, the Benham Target 2020 fund lost one-third of its assets as market timers pulled out, expecting a rise in interest rates. They were correct. Bond rates went up in August and the fund suffered a big loss, according to Morningstar analyst Todd Porter. But the long-term investors suffered in more ways than one. The fund manager was forced to sell bonds to raise cash for redemptions, incurring capital gains. So those who held onto the fund were handed a tax bill along with their losses. As Porter points out, the Benham funds make a good vehicle for bond speculators. But long-term investors would be better served by buying individual zero-coupon bonds.

## USING SPECIALTY FUNDS

THERE IS LOTS of information available about how to find the best all-weather funds to use in every person's portfolio. But there's much less information available about how to add funds around the core. There's good reason for that. Most investors should stop once they've put together a portfolio of core holdings. But for investors with substantial assets, high risk tolerance, and the desire for a little spice, special funds have a place. Sometimes even volatile funds have a place.

Having said that, I must say they are hard to find. I spent a great deal of time thinking about this section of the book. It seems that as the number of funds has mushroomed, they have become more and more lookalike. No one wants to be different. Most funds are too big; they include too many stocks (hundreds of them); they cost too much; and they hug the index. Those do not add spice to your portfolio.

Nor do you want what I call gimmicky funds *(see page 94)*. This is one category that will always be with us. When the stock market crashes, investors don't want to hear about stocks, so we get asset allocation funds. In 1998, after a new tax law allowed mutual fund managers to trade heavily and sell stock short on a larger scale—that is, to borrow stock and sell it betting that the price will come down—we got the "market neutral" funds *(see page 158)*. Gimmicks amount to marketing ploys that make a good story. But they do not make good investments.

What, then, can add some spice? I called Don Phillips at Morningstar for some ideas. One of Phillips's old favorites is the Third Avenue Value Fund, managed by Martin Whitman. Whitman's strategy sounds like the stuff investment nightmares are made of. Consider this: he invests in both U.S. and foreign securities, including junk bonds. "A substantial portion of assets may be invested in securities having relatively inactive markets," according to Morningstar. That means he may have trouble getting out if prices tumble. He also uses risky techniques. For example, he is permitted to leverage the portfolio with up to 50 percent of assets. That means if there is $2 billion in the fund, he could borrow $1 billion. And Whitman loves depressed industries. He's always looking for bargains.

So what is there to like about this fund? Whitman's record. The fund, introduced in 1990, had racked up a 22.53 percent annualized return by year-end 1997 compared to a 20.58 return for the S&P 500 in the same period. And this was a time when the S&P was hard to beat. In other words, Whitman is very good at doing some very risky things. Funds like his—and others run by talented, unconventional managers—can spice up a portfolio.

Phillips is optimistic about the trend toward focused funds, too. How many great ideas can one fund manager have? Concentration can be powerful. And it can be volatile. "Some of the best managers are starting new funds that concentrate in just 15 or 20 issues," Phillips says. For instance, he mentions Ken Heebner with CGM Select, Don Yacktman at Yacktman Select, and the folks at Harris Associates with Oakmark Select. "These aren't particularly good first investments," Phillips says. "But they are good seventh or eighth investments because you're getting a portfolio that doesn't look much like the rest of the market."

## GOLD

I ONCE PUT gold funds into the spicy category. Gold is certainly not a good long-term investment. It pays no dividends and earns no interest; gains come only as the price goes up. Still, when you saw that some gold funds rose more than 80 percent in 1987 and 90 percent in 1993—two years that were poor to middling for the stock market—and that they gained 20 percent in the first month of 1996, it did make you want to put on your thinking cap.

But I don't know that you'll get anywhere with gold. In 1996, I worked out a strategy, with a great deal of help from Don Phillips, on how to use the volatility of gold to pump up your portfolio. Our idea was that you put a set amount of money in gold—say $5,000—and at the end of each year, you rebalance, bringing your gold stake back to $5,000. That would allow you to nearly double your money in years that were good for gold and cut your losses in the years that gold took a drubbing. Morningstar dutifully tested the strategy over a 10-year period—from 1986 to 1995. The investor who used the gold rebalancing strategy came out ahead of the one who invested in stocks.

Still, in the two years since we did the study, I've lost my enthusiasm for gold. Totally. I'm certainly not a contrarian here. As *Money* magazine said in its March 1998 issue, "Few investments have ever experienced the total meltdown that gold has suffered lately." In early 1998, gold was trading at $278 an ounce, its lowest point in 18 years. Gold mutual funds did even worse than the Asian funds in 1997, down an average of 42.5 percent.

You could argue that that makes gold a good contrarian play. *Money* did. But I'm not going to. I've long been an investor in SoGen International, and I believe that manager Jean-Marie Eveillard is one of the few

successful gold investors around. Many financial planners buy that fund—and his newer fund SoGen
Gold—for Eveillard's gold savvy. But even Eveillard is
ready to throw in the towel, announcing that he will
liquidate the second fund if gold hasn't recovered to
the $320 to $350 range by the end of the year. So I
think that's it for gold as a recommended investment.
Gold was a different vehicle 25 years ago when there
were controls on currencies and currencies were not
convertible. Then investors moved in and out of gold,
seeing it as a safe harbor, particularly when they didn't
like the outlook for the dollar.

But in the mid 1970s when the controls on currency
were lifted, investors began to trade in and out of currencies. One investor recently posted a message in an
on-line newsgroup criticizing me for my negative comments on gold. "Asian investors would not have been
very well served by your notions on gold during the
final quarter of 1997," he wrote. "They would have
been much better off if they had invested in gold than
in their own devalued currencies." While I was mulling
this over, another investor came to my rescue. "Asian
investors would have been much better off if they had
invested in the U.S. dollar rather than gold," he said.

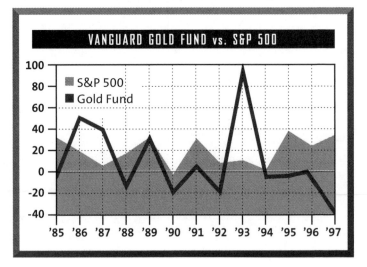

That's certainly true. So I vote for forgetting about gold as a specialty investment.

## SECTOR INVESTING

MOST INVESTORS SHOULD not own sector funds. They are volatile, unpredictable, and, worse yet, they defy the clean logic you must use to pick a mutual fund. When you buy a sector fund, you do not look for one with a good long-term record. Sector funds are not buy-and-hold investments. Buying them means making a bet on a particular industry in the short term. Short term could mean anywhere from six months to two or three years. And sector investors must be committed to doing research on the industry they choose before they invest and then doing a lot of reading to keep abreast of changes in that industry.

That said, there is a big difference between investing in gold and in sector funds. Gold is just a bad investment under any circumstances. But that's not the case with various industry sectors. They are a concentrated, undiversified investment. But there is an argument to be made for seasoned investors to consider them. Often, one particular industry leads a market advance, with stocks in that group gaining twice the market average. Sometimes one sector has fallen out of favor—and stocks in that industry have been beaten down far below their value. Sector funds allow you to make a bet on industries like biotech, financial services, or retail without taking the risk of buying a particular stock.

Sector funds have been around for years. But sector investing came of age in 1981 when Fidelity introduced the first batch of its Select funds. Since then, the number of sector funds has ballooned to a recent total of *498*, according to Morningstar. Fidelity Investments still has the most, at *63*. The Invesco Group in Denver has several. There are also some independent sector funds, like Seligman Communications & Information.

If you look at mutual fund performance over any particular quarter—or year—chances are good that a sector fund will head the list of top performers. And another sector fund will probably bring up the rear. That's why sector investing is not appropriate for most investors. It's too dicey. The tendency of a novice investor is to buy when a sector is hot. That's when you hear a lot about it. And that's when buying it is a big mistake. Buying the top-performing sector can set you up for a fall if that industry has run its course in the current cycle. "The worst mistake is to show up when the party is ending and have to pay the bill," says Albert J. Fredman, a professor at California State University in Fullerton.

What then is a reasonable way to invest in sectors? Some investors simply pick the sector on the bottom, reasoning that what goes around comes around. Remember Jon Fossel? This approach at first glance seems to resemble his "upside-down" investing. It's different, though. Applying Fossel's strategy to sectors is flawed because the dozens of industry sector funds available do not move in any rational pattern.

If you want to invest in sectors, you must be an active and knowledgeable investor who is willing to do some research. You might start with the sectors whose performance placed them at the bottom of the heap and find out why. For example, Fredman points out that a value investor might choose a sector fund that invests in an industry with a below-average price-earnings ratio. A growth investor might look for a hot industry on the move. A chart developed by Sam Stovall at Standard & Poor's Corp. (*right*) shows how different sectors might rotate in and out of favor during an economic cycle. This is a start. But if you want to invest in sectors, you must do more research.

Some investors identify the sectors that they believe will outperform over the next decade. There is one logical candidate here and everyone knows what it is:

## THE ECONOMIC CYCLE

One model that uses phases of the economy
to predict the best sectors for investment.

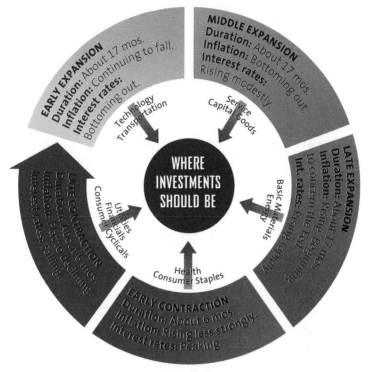

technology. Unfortunately, though, there's not a great
fund candidate to play that sector. An article in the
March 1998 issue of *Money* magazine recommended
the T. Rowe Price Science and Technology fund. But
that fund blew up in 1997 and it still doesn't look like
a slam-dunk to me. The idea, though, of looking for
strong sectors is an appealing one.

There's a good argument to be made for health
care given the aging of the population. My favorite is
Vanguard Specialized Health Care. It's more conservative than many of the others, with big positions in
established drug companies rather than hot biotech
firms. But I've used the fund for years to tuck away college money for my kids. On their birthdays and at

Christmas time, I put a gift into this fund and have been extremely pleased with the results. That said, you must remember that sector funds can be very volatile. The health-care sector had fabulous results in 1990 and 1991. Then the Clintons were elected and started talking about their health-care reform package. In the tank: Most of the health-care funds had big, double-digit losses in 1992. Clearly, the risk is much higher when you invest in one sector of the market.

One final thought on sectors. As I was doing the research for this book, I came across a very intriguing fund called White Oak Growth Fund. This fund, which made its debut in 1992, is managed by James D. Oelschlager, a former pension fund manager. There are three things I loved about this fund in addition to its record, which is spectacular. First, Oelschlager targeted just three sectors of the economy that he expects to outperform: technology, health care, and financials. Second, he concentrates in just 25 stocks in those industries. Third, expenses are in line—under 1 percent a year. This is what a mutual fund should be! Oelschlager is no index hugger. He has convictions. And he puts them on the line. This is a fund to watch. It will be interesting to see, for example, if Oelschlager moves out of financials and into another industry if he thinks that sector has run its course. Stay tuned.

## KEEP IT SIMPLE

BUT SECTOR INVESTING may not be for you. You don't need any of these complex strategies if they intimidate you or give you a headache. Remember that the idea of mutual funds is to simplify investing. The simplest strategy—and the one that is always successful—is buy and hold. Remember, too, what you've learned about mutual funds in this guide. You can put together a portfolio with just one fund if you are a beginner. Even if you have a great deal of money, a dozen funds should be enough to get adequate diversification.

Within these boundaries, pick out a handful of good funds representing different investment styles that will do well in all types of market environments. And then buy them and keep them. Good luck.

PART 5

# Resources

OW YOU'RE READY to begin — or modify—your investment program. The first question you must answer is whether you will choose the funds yourself or use an investment adviser. If you've already decided to choose your own funds, skip to page 277 where you will find a list of resources.

If you think you might need help with choosing your funds, read on to learn about how financial planners work and how you might find the right one for you. I gained some insight into financial planning a couple of years ago when I wrote a book for financial planners—a "best practices" guide that described what the very best planners were doing in different aspects of their business— marketing, working with clients, resolving conflicts of interest, and so forth. To do the research, I put together a group of 55 planners and arranged conference calls with them on a variety of topics.

The two things that stick out in my mind as being of interest to investors trying to decide whether to hire a planner are these. First, a good planner does far more than just pick mutual funds for you. A planner looks at your life and your finances objectively and helps you figure out how to best use your resources to realize your dreams. He helps you set up an investment plan and then helps you stick with it through thick and thin.

The best planners are part psychologist. They are always watching and listening to see if you are in tune with your life. Are your relationships happy? Do you enjoy your work? Is your family provided for? Do your kids have a career strategy mapped out? A financial planner with an inquiring mind is a great sounding board on how to weigh a new job offer; whether to have another child;

what to do if your spouse wants a divorce. I've certainly gained some insights into my life from the conversations I've had with planners. Some of them had to do with nuts-and-bolts things like investing and buying disability insurance. But many times, the conversations were about intangible things that made me think about life in a new way.

I think here about a conversation I had with Ross Levin, a planner in Minneapolis, one day during the 1997 holiday season. We were talking about some financial planning topic like how to invest for income. "Let me peer into your soul, Mary," Ross said, as a prelude to asking me about which books I was reading and delving into my general philosophy of life. Snooping, actually. Solely as a result of what had started out as a casual conversation with Ross, I read eight to 10 pretty heavy books that changed my inner life in a perceptible—and really positive—way. That conversation with Ross made my life better.

So the first reason to use a planner is as a helpmate to both identify and realize your dreams.

The second thing I learned in working on the planning book is much more basic and more related to investment success. The biggest mistake most investors make is to invest with their emotions—to jump in and out of investments based on news stories or tips from friends. Professional planners do not do that. They invest and then they sit tight. If the *only* service a planner provides is to hold your hand through market swings and to keep you focused on the long term, that would be enough to earn his fee.

So with those two ideas in mind, you can probably decide whether you need a planner or whether you will fend for yourself. Your decision need not be set in stone. Perhaps you will start out investing for yourself but find yourself in a situation one day where you need help.

Whichever road you choose, be consistent. Develop a plan or a strategy and then carry it out with your investments. Be patient.

If you decide to use a planner, here are some tips on how to find one:

**Look for a certified financial planner, or a planner with a CFP designation, issued by the CFP Board of Standards, Inc., in Denver (888-237-6275).** The CFP board has been working hard for several years to upgrade the CFP designation to make it more like the certified public accountant designation. It's not there yet, but the CFP has become the must-have designation for serious planners. For names of CFPs in your area, call 800-282-PLAN.

When I wrote this in my book, *Best Practices for Financial Advisors* (Bloomberg Press, 1997), I received a letter from Stuart Kessler, a very fine planner in New York who is also chairman of the American Institution for Certified Public Accountants. Stu wanted to make an argument for the personal financial specialist or PFS designation offered by the AICPA to accountants who qualify as specialists in financial planning. Stu is right. The PFS designation shows considerable knowledge of financial planning. If you find a planner you really like with a PFS but no CFP, it's OK. But I still believe that CFP is the must-have designation. For the name of a certified public accountant with a specialty in personal financial planning, call 800-TO-AICPA.

**Ask your candidate if he is registered as an investment adviser with the Securities and Exchange Commission or with the state.** Advisers who manage more than $25 million in client assets are required to register with the SEC; those who manage less must register with the states where they do business.

The Investment Advisers Act of 1940 requires that anyone in the business of giving advice in exchange for compensation must register as an investment adviser with the SEC. A 1997 change in that act requires only those that manage more than $25 million to register with the SEC; others are regulated by the states.

Most financial advisers argue that the law was not drafted to apply to financial advisers. But the good ones comply with it anyway because they know that's the right thing to do. When you interview candidates, you want to know whether they're complying with the law, not their opinion of the law.

**Ask for details on the costs and risks of doing business with the candidates you interview.** The planners who worked with me on my book went overboard in disclosing both. Be suspicious of anyone who balks at disclosing fees.

One thing I learned when I researched the book was that most consumers don't really understand how planners get paid. They realize that some earn sales commissions and some work for fees. In fact, there are several different methods of compensating planners. Here are the basic ways planners get paid:

♦ **Assets under management.** Like many other planners, Harold Evensky charges an annual management fee based on a client's assets. Fees are 1 percent of assets up to $1 million, 80 basis points to $3 million, and negotiable over $4 million. (Evensky's minimum is $1 million. Other members of his firm manage smaller accounts based on model portfolios developed by Evensky.)

The firm charges a fee of $1,000 to $2,000 for developing an investment policy for a client. The client is free to take the policy statement elsewhere or to implement it himself, if he likes, rather than hiring the firm to manage his assets with no-load mutual funds.

♦ **Flat fees.** Some planners charge an annual retainer for all planning work. For example, when he first meets with a client, Bob Willard, a planner in Colorado Springs, Colorado, sets an annual fee that is based loosely on assets under management, but also includes such factors as whether the client is equipped to trade electronically; whether the account is with Charles Schwab & Co. (which makes it easier for him because he can download it on his computer) rather than with a full-service broker; and a range of other considerations.

For Willard's clients, the fee stays roughly the same. He argues that managing a client's affairs actually gets easier as he gets things in order. Further, a good client brings him other good business. Andy Hudick in Roanoke, Virginia, uses a similar system, setting a fee for the first year that covers the time it will take to develop a comprehensive financial plan. It is a dollar amount rather than a percentage. At the beginning of the second year, he sets a lower fee because the bulk of the work is already done.

◆ **Commissions.** Commissions have gotten a black eye over the past few years, as most of the top planners have moved to fees. Fee planners argue that those who use commissions have an inherent conflict of interest because they are paid by the company that makes the product rather than by the client.

There's a large dose of truth to that. Still, I found some commission-based planners who put the client first. One of them is Cynthia Meyers in Sacramento, California, who believes that commissions are more fair for the client than fees. "I'm suspicious about the trend to assets under management," Meyers says. "I think it's more expensive for the client. And I think it can result in the planner putting his interest before the client's."

◆ **Fees plus commissions.** Like Evensky, Ross Levin in Minneapolis charges an asset-management fee of 1 percent. But he is not a pure fee planner, chiefly because insurance plays an important role in Levin's practice and he is not happy with any of the no-load disability and life-insurance policies available. So when a client needs an insurance product, Levin's firm collects a commission.

♦ **Fee offset.** Some planners who are in Levin's position elect instead to charge a fee and to offset that fee with commissions when they are forced to use a product that is structured with a commission.

♦ **Strictly by the hour.** Sharon Rich does not sell products. She does not manage assets. She collects an hourly fee of $120 for the time she spends with clients. Period. Like many purists, Rich is a member of the National Association of Personal Financial Advisors, or NAPFA, which does not permit members to accept commission income.

♦ **Fee by formula.** Bert Whitehead's average client is a middle-American family with a household income of $100,000 that needs the full gamut of planning, from budgeting, cash flow, insurance analysis, and college saving to retirement planning. A client might want to know what type of mortgage to get or whether to buy or lease a car, for instance. Whitehead says he tried asset-based fees but came to believe they represented a conflict of interest. For example, if a client needed to make a decision about paying off a half-a-million-dollar mortgage, the paydown could reduce his annual fee by $5,000 because the client would be taking the assets from the money he managed for a fee and paying off the loan. Likewise, if a client wanted advice on whether to leave his 401(k) money with the company or roll it into an IRA, the decision would affect the amount of assets under management—and thus Whitehead's fee.

Now his fees are based on a formula that takes into account income and total net worth with "a factor built in for complexity." A typical first-year fee is $6,000. The renewal fee, which includes preparation of tax returns, is based on total net income and assets. "Our renewal range is $500 to $3,000, with an average of $1,500," Whitehead says.

◆ **Hourly fees plus asset-based fees.** Bob Wacker combines the compensation systems of Sharon Rich and Harold Evensky by doing some hourly fee planning and some investment-management work. Wacker charges a one-time fee that might be as low as $2,400 for a comprehensive financial plan. He will also do an investment review and make investment recommendations for as little as $750. "That would be a case where we're not going to be monitoring it on an ongoing basis," Wacker says. "That makes it affordable for someone with $20,000 to $30,000."

He has no asset minimums for managing money, but his minimum annual money-management fee is $1,200, considerably lower than that of most fee planners. Wacker aims to keep the total cost to clients under 150 basis points—including his own fees and the fees they must pay to the mutual fund company. Wacker, too, is a NAPFA member.

◆ **Fee cap.** Like Sharon Rich, Mike Chasnoff in Cincinnati is a fee-only planner and a member of NAPFA. But in addition to hourly fees and asset-based fees, Chasnoff estimates how much time he will spend on a financial plan and then tells the client the maximum he will charge. For clients who prefer a retainer, Chasnoff estimates how many hours he will spend and then caps his fee at that upper end of the range. "But we have a little special arrangement that says our total retainer expense cannot exceed one-half of 1 percent of the assets in their investment portfolio," he says. Minimum assets under management: $400,000.

**Ask the candidates you interview whether they will act as a fiduciary.** This is a hot topic in financial planning circles. Accepting a fiduciary role means that the planner puts your interests above his own. Period. That's what you would want him to do, of course. But from the planner's perspective, that's pretty scary. It means he could be sued, for instance, if your investments lose money. Even if he did everything properly, that's no protection against a lawsuit. And nobody welcomes a lawsuit.

Still, planners at the top of the profession accept the label without comment. Many of them—like pioneer planner Jack Blankinship in Del Mar, California—include it in their marketing brochures.

But another contingent of planners is still attempting to sneak out from under the label because it carries too much liability for their taste. "Too many people still want to duck it," says James Wilson, who fought to have the word "fiduciary" included when he helped write practice standards for the International Board of Certified Financial Planners in 1992.

To Wilson, a fiduciary relationship means that you have a client rather than a customer. "You owe the duty of a merchant to a customer," Wilson says. "You have a duty not to defraud. But you have no duty to protect. With the client, you owe a duty to protect." Webster's definition of a client is "one under the protection of another." When you look for someone to help you with your finances, you want someone who is willing to accept the fiduciary role; someone you can trust completely to put your interests first.

**Ask about conflicts of interest.** Everyone doing business has numerous conflicts of interest. "The relationship you have with a client is really serving two interests," says Violet Woodhouse, a lawyer and financial planner in Newport Beach, California, "and so there is an inherent conflict." Adds Myra Salzer, a planner in Boulder, Colorado, "You're not ever going to be able to completely avoid conflicts of interest. Dealing with them with integrity and openness is what you must do to be effective."

That integrity and openness is what you should look

for in the planner you select. You want a planner who lays out the conflicts and tells you that he will do his very best to always put your interests first.

Of course, compensation represents the largest area of potential conflict. Many Wall Street firms pay brokers more to sell in-house products. Or they offer bigger trailing—or annual—commissions for keeping customers in these funds. Some sales people are offended by the suggestion that you should know what they earn. But a top planner never is.

Here are some other pressure zones for planners that you might wish to explore:

◆ **How will you handle my 401(k) assets?** If a planner charges fees based on assets under management, how will he handle assets in your 401(k) plan? Will he give you advice on it? Will they be included in the assets for the purpose of determining the fee?

◆ **What about buyout offers?** If your employer offers you a buyout with the choice of taking a lump sum or an annuity, which is income for life, the planner earns more if you take the lump sum and add it to the pot of assets he manages.

◆ **How will you evaluate paying down debt?** The same conflict exists with paying down debt. If you take money from the assets under management to pay off credit card bills, a car loan, or home mortgage, that reduces the planner's fee if it is based on assets under management. How will he handle this conflict? Ron Rogé, a planner in Centereach, New York, advises his clients to pay off the mortgage before starting an investment program, even though it means his fee will be lower.

◆ **How will you decide how much time to give me?** Planners say they sometimes wonder just how much time it takes to do a top-notch job for a client. "I can always spend more time with a client," says Myra Salzer. "So the conflict for me is: How much should I do?" You should be particularly interested if you are a small client. Ask how the planner allocates time among clients. Because

planners who charge based on assets under management earn more depending on how wealthy the client
is, how will he decide how much time to give you?

**Ask how the planner will choose investments that are
right for you.** We've all heard the horror stories about
people who were fleeced by unscrupulous salespeople.
These situations result from greed on the part of both
parties—the salesperson who wants to make a profit
and the investors who want to make a killing.

You are responsible for having realistic expectations. If you expect a planner to double your money
in two years, you're going to get someone who makes
false promises. Given that your expectations are in
line, you want to know how the planner will determine
what is suitable for you.

Top planners typically work with a small core of
investments, chiefly mutual funds, that they put
together in portfolios depending on your needs and
risk tolerance. They must assess your resources and
goals and then write a prescription to help you reach
them. If you are not prepared to take the necessary
risk, they must badger and cajole you to do what you
must to reach your goal. That's how a top planner
works. Top planners *never* make foolish promises like:
"You'll earn 50 percent [or even 30 percent or 20 per-
cent] in this investment."

What is a reasonable return? Most planners will tell
you what your portfolio will earn after inflation. And
7 percent is high. That represents a high-risk, all-stock
portfolio. So keep that in mind.

**Find out how the planner researches the investments he
will recommend to you.** This is called due diligence. A
planner must research the investments he will recommend to establish that they are sound ones. That's his
responsibility. Of course, he will read the offering
prospectus and publicly available information on the

investments he uses. What else does he do? For example, Lou Stanasolovich, a planner in Pittsburgh, interviews more than 50 fund managers a year looking for new investments for his clients. You want to get some sense of what a planner does to perform due diligence.

In the last analysis, though, you want a planner with whom you can have a personal relationship; someone you trust and whose values you share. Do not focus on investment performance when you look for a planner. The top planners spend a great deal of time educating themselves on investments and asset allocation. The return that you get from a well-constructed portfolio will not vary that much from one good planner to another.

What does vary is the relationship. That's the chief thing you should be looking for. In fact, the planners who worked with me on my book all agreed that when clients first came to interview them, they invariably focused on investment performance. But once they had become established clients, they rarely asked about investment performance. It was the relationship they valued. "How do you tell somebody that it is a relationship they really want, when they think what they want is for you to beat the S&P 500?" asked Roy Diliberto, a planner in Philadelphia.

## FOR DO-IT-YOURSELFERS

MORNINGSTAR, THE CHICAGO rating service, is the best source of information on mutual funds for consumers (800-876-5005). The company's flagship product, which is called *Morningstar Mutual Funds*, is a loose-leaf binder that includes one page on each of the 1,500 funds covered. This service now costs $395 a year, which is a steep price for individual investors. It also provides more information than most of them need. In 1995 Morningstar introduced a shorter version that includes 700 no-load and low-load funds. This product, at $145 a year, is a much better choice for investors who plan to pick their own funds.

Both publications carry the same analysis. You will be able to see whether the fund you are interested in carries a load and how much it is, how big the fund is in terms of assets under management, and the net asset value. I particularly like the year-by-year performance numbers going back 10 years, which are compared with a market index such as the S&P 500 for large-company stocks or the Russell 2000 for small-company stocks. This shows me how the fund compares with a benchmark. It also shows volatility. For example, if a fund is up 55 percent one year and down 25 percent another, I might avoid it.

There's also a performance graph which indicates changes in portfolio managers with an arrow. The fund's long-term record is not so important if there's been a recent manager change.

I look at the style box, a nine-square grid that shows whether the fund buys small, medium, or large companies and whether it is growth- or value-oriented. I look at the style history, too, to see if the manager has been consistent or if he skips from one style to another. The 200-word prose analyses are terrific and accessible even to beginners.

In 1997, Morningstar made a major change in the organization of its data—one that is most helpful to fund investors. Like many mutual fund information services, Morningstar had categorized funds according to the investment objectives used by the industry. So, for example, funds were listed as "growth and income," or "aggressive growth." But Morningstar recognized that these labels were increasingly meaningless to those who used the funds. The new categories are not. They break funds up in much the same way as the style grid just described. So you can see, for instance, that a fund is a small-company value fund or a large-cap growth fund. That is much more helpful in building a portfolio than the old, vague categories.

Although I urge you not to make too much of the star rankings, which award a fund zero to five stars, it certainly makes sense to look at them. The star system is based largely on the fund's recent past performance, so looking only for five-star funds is not a sure-fire way to pick a winner. The better the recent performance, the better the rating. As a result, they are backward looking, measuring something that has already happened. Yet what matters in investing is what happens tomorrow, not what happened last quarter or last year. So the ratings tend to highlight the hot fund categories and downplay laggard groups whose performance may be about to turn around.

There are good reasons to consider funds with lower rankings. For example, a good manager's style may have been out of favor and be due for a comeback. Or the entire fund category—like international funds—may have been out of favor for a while. And that might make it a good choice for investment. Still, the ratings are clearly useful in comparing funds within a category. If you are comparing two small-company growth funds, for example, it could be very enlightening to see that one had five stars and the other just one star.

I sometimes buy funds that are not yet rated by Morningstar, which waits until they are at least three years old. An analysis may be included on a new fund, but it will indicate that it is "not rated." Morningstar sends updates to the volume every two weeks, with commentaries by editors and studies the company has done. These are usually excellent. *Morningstar Mutual Funds* is available in many libraries.

Really serious investors swear by *Morningstar Principia Plus,* a CD-ROM that includes all the mutual funds available and allows investors to sort funds, set up portfolios, compare one fund to another, and so forth. The CD-ROM costs $295. If you want monthly updates, it runs $795; with quarterly updates, it costs $495.

Look in the library, too, for the *Value Line Mutual Fund Survey*. Value Line is the traditional source of research on individual stocks, and the mutual fund service was introduced to compete with Morningstar's service. Value Line now has a number of products including the print survey, which costs $295 a year, and a software product for $395 that "will even bake bread," says Steve Savage, who is in charge of Value Line's mutual fund service. Value Line also introduced a no-load version—with 4,000 funds—especially for do-it-yourself investors. A two-month trial subscription goes for $29. For $95, you get quarterly updates. If you want monthly updates, it costs $149. Subscribers to Value Line's *No-Load Advisor* for $58 get subscriber services on Value Line's Web site at www.valueline.com.

## BOOKS

**A Commonsense Guide to Your 401(k)** (Bloomberg Press, 1997, $19.95). OK, I wrote this book, so I'm not objective. But it's meant to be a helpful guide for 401(k) retirement plan participants.

**A Random Walk Down Wall Street: Including a Life-Cycle Guide to Personal Investing**, by Burton G. Malkiel (W.W. Norton & Co., 1996, $15.95), lays out the argument for the efficient market and makes the case for indexing.

**Against the Gods**, by Peter Bernstein (John Wiley & Sons, Inc., 1996, $27.95), is a fascinating account of the role of risk in our society.

**Bogle on Mutual Funds: New Perspectives for the Intelligent Investor**, by John C. Bogle, chairman of the Vanguard Group (Irwin, 1994, $14.95), earns high praise from such investors as Warren Buffett, the sage of Omaha. Bogle is Mr. Mutual Fund. Everything he has to say on funds is worth listening to.

**Buffett: The Making of an American Capitalist**, by Roger Lowenstein (Doubleday, 1996, $14.95). Buffett's genius is a genius of character. In an age without fixed standards,

Buffett's notion of investment value harks back to more principled times. Lowenstein does a masterful job of portraying Buffett the investor.

**The Intelligent Investor**, by Benjamin Graham (Harper Collins, 1997, $30), is a classic that belongs on every investor's bookshelf.

**One Up on Wall Street**, by Peter Lynch (Penguin USA, 1990, $12.95), doesn't really tell you the secrets of Lynch's stock picking. But it's good reading and good fun.

**Investing in Small-Cap Stocks**, by Christopher Graja and Elizabeth Ungar, Ph.D., my colleagues at Bloomberg, is a thoughtful piece of work that is still fun to read. Most investing books require a commitment of several dozen hours to grapple with the principles. Not so with those from Bloomberg Press. This book is basic enough for the novice yet chock full of ideas that can help an intermediate investor learn more (1996, $19.95).

**25 Myths You've Got to Avoid If You Want to Manage Your Money Right**, by Jonathan Clements (Simon & Schuster, 1998, $23). The author of *The Wall Street Journal*'s "Getting Going" column, which runs every Tuesday, is both savvy and entertaining. A veteran observer of the fund industry, Clements wrote a solid guide to funds in 1993, *Funding Your Future: The Only Guide to Mutual Funds You'll Ever Need* (Warner Books).

## OTHER PUBLICATIONS

CLEARLY YOU SHOULD read the daily business pages of your local newspaper even though you need not check on the price of your mutual funds each day. Don't pay attention, though, to stories about whether the stock market is getting too high and is due for a correction. Instead you will want to keep abreast of general business news. Look, too, for items about new funds, funds that are due to open or close, and manager changes. **THE WALL STREET JOURNAL** provides good basic information on mutual fund investing.

Most magazines today include some information on investing and personal finance, but the quality varies widely. Ignore all stories with headlines like "The Five Funds You Must Buy Now." Look for publications that are willing to take responsibility for the advice they give you. I don't put *Money* in that category, although Jason Zweig's column is always worth reading and there are big changes in the works at *Money* now. But I would put **SMART MONEY** there. I don't like *Smart Money*'s insistence on picking the five hot funds. But I do admire the way the publication revisits its picks from the year before and takes responsibility for them, no matter how painful it sometimes is.

One of the problems is that nobody wants to write about the mundane stuff even though that's what investors need most. I'm proud of the work that's been done in **BLOOMBERG PERSONAL FINANCE**, though. *Bloomberg Personal Finance* has done big articles on the importance of expenses, for example. Nothing new here; Jack Bogle has been talking about it for years. But it's one of the most important factors consumers should be focusing on. *Bloomberg Personal Finance* also did a cover story under the headline: "Are You a Performance Pig?" The cover shot showed a pig with a looking glass (actually the understudy for the porker in the movie *Babe*), and the article asked people if their greed was getting in the way of finding good financial planning advice. Many magazines seem to encourage greed and unrealistic expectations. This forced you to take a look at yourself in a new way. Lots of *Bloomberg Personal Finance* stories—like those by Chris Graja—are fresh and informative.

I like the straightforward, no-nonsense advice in **KIPLINGER'S PERSONAL FINANCE** magazine. And hardcore investors will want to subscribe to **BARRON'S**, the weekly journal that comes out on Saturday with news and commentary on the markets. **THE AMERICAN ASSOCIATION OF INDIVIDUAL INVESTORS** (AAII), based in Chicago, provides excellent information for investors in its monthly journal, as well as free investment seminars for members. Some of the best investment minds in the country agree to speak at these seminars because they believe in helping to educate individual investors. For example, Jeff Vinik, then the manager of Fidelity Magellan fund, took a Saturday off in early 1995 to go to Chicago and speak to the AAII chapter there. To join, send $49 to AAII, 625 North Michigan Avenue, Chicago, IL 60611.

## NEWSLETTERS

NEWSLETTERS GIVE ADVICE rather than just information. An investment newsletter might tell you which funds to buy and which to sell. It might tell you to get out of the stock market and into the bond market or into cash or a money market fund. Some newsletter editors also serve as money managers, and they will manage your money for you, moving it from one fund to another. If you want to take a look at some of the newsletter options, check in *Barron's* for ads that offer trial subscriptions. My advice, though, is to learn about investing yourself and make your own decisions.

Investors who wish to subscribe to only one newsletter should choose the monthly **MORNINGSTAR INVESTOR**, available for $79 a year. Look here for information on funds that plan to close or reopen, portfolio manager changes, and discussions of different investing styles. The centerpiece of this newsletter is the Morningstar 500, a list of 500 funds the rating agency believes have special merit.

**THE NO-LOAD FUND INVESTOR**, written by Sheldon Jacobs, a longtime observer of the mutual fund industry, is also well worth the $99 subscription price for investors who want no-load funds. Jacobs includes news of new funds, recommendations, and suggested portfolios for investors depending on their goals. Write to *The No-Load Fund Investor,* P.O. Box 318, Irvington-on-Hudson, NY 10533 (914-693-7420).

If you are *really* committed to learning about investing, consider the **OUTSTANDING INVESTOR DIGEST**, a quirky, thick newsletter that is published erratically, costs a lot, and can run to 64 pages of small, gray type. I subscribed in December 1996 at a cost of $295, reduced from $495 because I agreed to an automatic credit card renewal.

I received my first 64-page issue in January 1997, including lengthy interviews with investors like Michael Price of the Mutual Series funds and Ron Baron of Baron Asset. I have to admit it was daunting. But I read every word of how these experts pick stocks, what they look for in companies, when they sell. I figured I had to hurry and finish before the next issue came.

On June 4, I realized I hadn't yet received it. I called to see if I'd missed it. No. The December issue was the latest. The second one showed up on August 8. And the third on December 29, 1997. Which was a relief in a way. I certainly couldn't get through one a month. The subscription covers 10 issues, however long it takes to get them out. The editor, Henry Emerson, is a somewhat eccentric, humble guy, which I discovered when I called to request an interview. Emerson declined, claiming that his readers came first and he couldn't spare the time from his work.

I learned about *OID* from Don Phillips, president of Morningstar Mutual Funds, who told me it is one of the two publications that he reads immediately when he receives it. The other is **INSIDE INFORMATION**, a newsletter for financial planners published by Robert N. Veres from Kennesaw, Georgia (770-424-8755, $95). Like other subscribers, Phillips reads *OID* to learn more about investing. It is for the hard core. And it's among the best.

## WHAT'S ON-LINE?

FINALLY, THE INTERNET is beginning to live up to its promise. You can organize your finances, budget, manage your money, shop for a mortgage, monitor your portfolio, and find lots of investing information. Be careful, though. People love to gripe about journalistic bias in newspapers and magazines. But most newspapers and magazines do attempt to separate advertising from editorial information and to make the latter objective. That's not the case for much of the stuff on the Web. That's partly because companies are still struggling with how to make money on the Web. The result is that there is often no line whatsoever between editorial material and advertising.

Of course, there are many exceptions. Here are some Web sites worth checking.

**www.bloomberg.com** links you to Bloomberg on-line, where you will find some of the resources of Bloomberg Financial Markets, which are used by professionals in the financial world. The site also provides financial and world news updated continuously, and data on all types of bonds. Subscribers to *Bloomberg Personal Finance* magazine can tap into material that is not available to others.

**www.brill.com** is a guide to mutual fund resources on the Web.

**www.indexinvestor.com** is an Internet newsletter that provides information on investing using indexes as well as recommended asset class allocations for an indexed portfolio.

**www.investor.com** is the site of *Microsoft Investor,* an on-line magazine with weekly features and columns on the markets. In 1998, *Investor* is being merged with *Money Insider,* which discusses personal finance basics including taxes, retirement, insurance, savings, estate planning, home buying. I write a weekly column on investing on this site. The columns are also linked to

Money 98, Microsoft's competitor to Quicken.

**www.investorsquare.com**, the site of *Investor Square,* provides 9,500 mutual funds that you can screen by various categories.

**www.mfea.com** is the site of the Mutual Fund Investor's Center, which is the trade group for funds that are sold direct through the mail or over the phone. You can find fund manager interviews, lists of top-performing funds, retirement and college calculators, and links to fund companies that are members of this group such as Janus, T. Rowe Price, Vanguard Group.

**www.morningstar.net** offers information from Morningstar Mutual Funds.

**www.mfcafe.com** has great information on the mutual fund industry, including new funds, tax law changes, in-depth info.

**www.oid.com** is the Web site of *Outstanding Investor Digest,* introduced in 1998. I expect to see good things develop from *OID* editor Henry Emerson, who is passionate about investing.

**www.rothira.com** is a great site for those wishing to analyze the new Roth IRA and compare it to traditional IRAs or 401(k) retirement plans. Gregory Kolojeski, the tax attorney who runs Brentmark Software, put together this site and he's passionate about the topic.

**www.nasdaq.com** provides price quotes by Nasdaq on the over-the-counter market.

**www.quicken.com** In 1998, business journalist Tony Cook, formerly of *Money* magazine, took over as editor of this site. Look for interesting changes here.

**www.russell.com** offers asset allocation and market performance information from the Frank Russell Company, which compiles the Russell 2000 index.

**Charles Schwab Online (www.schwab.com)** provides information about Schwab's own funds, as well as One-Source (no transaction fee) funds and fund tools.

The two largest fund companies, of course, are on-line: Fidelity Investments offers information at

**www.fid-inv.com**. Vanguard's site (**www.vanguard. com**) allows you to download prospectuses for funds. Vanguard also has a presence, including a bulletin board, in the Personal Finance section of America Online.

**www.icefi.com** is the site of the Internet Closed-End Fund Investor.

**www.numeric.com** is the Web address of Numeric Investors, John Bogle Jr.'s shop. Bogle, a "quant" or quantitative manager who uses computer models to pick stocks, is a rising star in the fund industry and one of the most highly respected managers among the financial adviser crowd. Don Phillips picked him as keynote speaker at Morningstar's 1998 mutual fund convention because, Don said, "he's asking all the right questions about mutual funds." He's giving the right answers, too. Check out his site.

Among the features on *The No-Load Fund Investor* (**www.sheldonjacobs.com**) site is the Wealth Builder recommended portfolio, which is updated continually with Sheldon Jacobs's recommended no-load mutual funds.

I asked Cebra Graves, who is in charge of Morningstar's Web site, which sites he checks regularly. His answers:

**ici.org**, the Web site of the Investment Company Institute, the fund industry trade group, intrigues him because it shows what the industry is thinking about and what kind of information the ICI is sending to member fund companies.

**fundspot.com/hotspot.htm** is a site run by "just one guy," Graves says. "But one thing he does is a hot list that links to stories he likes."

**mfcafe.com**, the site of Mutual Fund Cafe, is "another insider site," Graves says. "They're trying to speak to the industry more than to shareholders. So I like to see what the industry is thinking about." For example, Graves says he found good articles here about the profile prospectus, which was approved in March 1998. "They had a short, bulleted list of what the SEC is requiring in the prospectus," he said. "It was an easy-to-use description for a fund-company executive." The site also shows market share pie charts with fund flows into different sectors of the market and different fund companies.

**www.brill.com**, the site of Mutual Funds Interactive, provides "great conversations."

William Bernstein runs an on-line financial journal that shows how to get to the efficient frontier using asset allocation information at **mail.coos.or.us/(ciba)wbern**. "This is a little high-end," Graves says. "You have to know something about asset allocation to begin with."

A layman's asset allocation Web site, with "a nice explanation of modern portfolio theory," can be found at **www.fee-only-advisor.com/book/index.htm**. This site is done by Frank Armstrong, who writes a monthly column for Morningstar.

**www.investor.com** is great for tracking and screening portfolios, Graves says. He loves vanguard.com for investor information, and he gives a nod to bigcharts.com, a charting site, even though "I don't like technical analysis."

# INDEX

NOTE: Page numbers for entries occurring in figures are followed by an $f$; those for entries occurring in tables, by a $t$.

**Yacktman, Donald**, 131, 239, 256
**Yacktman funds**
  Focus fund, 114, 141
  Select fund, 256
  Yacktman fund, 131, 239
**Yield.** *See* Return
**Yield curves**, 248–52

**Zero coupon Treasury bonds**, 251–54
**Zweig, Jason**, 282

## ABOUT BLOOMBERG

**Bloomberg L.P.**, founded in 1981, is a global information services, news, and media company. Headquartered in New York, the company has nine sales offices, two data centers, and 80 news bureaus worldwide.

Bloomberg Financial Markets, serving customers in 100 countries around the world, holds a unique position within the financial services industry by providing an unparalleled combination of news, information, and analytic tools in a single package known as the BLOOMBERG® service. Corporations, banks, money management firms, financial exchanges, insurance companies, and many other entities and organizations rely on Bloomberg as their primary source of information.

BLOOMBERG NEWS℠, founded in 1990, offers worldwide coverage of economies, companies, industries, governments, financial markets, politics, and sports. The news service is the main content provider for Bloomberg's broadcast media, which include BLOOMBERG TELEVISION®—the 24-hour cable television network available in ten languages worldwide—and BLOOMBERG NEWS RADIO™—an international radio network anchored by flagship station BLOOMBERG NEWS RADIO AM 1130℠ in New York.

In addition to the BLOOMBERG PRESS® line of books, Bloomberg publishes *BLOOMBERG® MAGAZINE* and *BLOOMBERG PERSONAL FINANCE*™.

To learn more about Bloomberg, call a sales representative at:

| | | | |
|---|---|---|---|
| Frankfurt: | 49-69-920-410 | San Francisco: | 1-415-912-2960 |
| Hong Kong: | 852-977-6000 | São Paulo: | 5511-3048-4500 |
| London: | 44-171-330-7500 | Singapore: | 65-438-8585 |
| New York: | 1-212-318-2000 | Sydney: | 61-29-777-8686 |
| Princeton: | 1-609-279-3000 | Tokyo: | 81-3-3201-8900 |

## ABOUT THE AUTHOR

**Mary Rowland** is a distinguished columnist and author specializing in personal finance and financial planning issues. Her work has appeared in *The New York Times* and in *Bloomberg Personal Finance, Dow Jones Investment Advisor, Modern Maturity,* and many other major magazines. For 20 years she has looked at financial planning from both sides, interviewing financial advisers and portfolio managers for professional journals and writing for consumers on such issues as selecting a financial planner. She is the author of *A Commonsense Guide to Your 401(k)* and *Best Practices for Financial Advisors,* and speaks frequently at industry conferences and investment seminars. She lives in New York's Hudson Valley with her husband and two children.